2.95

Under the editorship of

DAYTON D. McKEAN

University of Colorado

OTHER TITLES IN THE SERIES

Government and

Politics in

Malaysia

R. S. MILNE
THE UNIVERSITY OF BRITISH COLUMBIA

HOUGHTON MIFFLIN COMPANY · BOSTON

54823

CONTENTS

PREFACE

Malaysia's government and politics have not yet been comprehensively described in any single book. The period of colonial rule has been well covered and there have been good chronological accounts of particular periods since Independence (1957). Racial questions and the civil service in Malaya have been treated at some length; so have the formation of Malaysia (1963), the separation of Singapore (1965) and Indonesian Confrontation (1963–1966). Other aspects have hardly been touched: Parliament; the Cabinet; federal-state relations including Sabah and Sarawak; local government. Certainly no single book has attempted to cover, even in outline, all these topics, in informal as well as formal aspects. The present volume tries to fill this gap, although in a modest way. It aims to provide information and to analyze and interpret it, but does not seek to advance any grand conceptual scheme. However, some comparative references to countries other than Malaysia are included. It should be added that the book in fact deals with Singapore as well as Malaysia; the fortunes of the two are in practice inextricably linked.

Bibliographical references, where they exist, are given at the end of each chapter. Among newspapers in English published in the area, *The Straits Times* (Kuala Lumpur), *Sarawak Tribune* (Kuching) and *Sabah Times* (Jesselton), will be found most useful.

It is not possible to thank the hundreds of people who have helped me in writing this book, particularly through interviews—politicians, civil servants, journalists, academics. I am, however, particularly indebted to Mrs. Wang Chen Hsiu Chin and Miss Manijeh Namazie of the Library of the University of Singapore for finding references, and to my friend and former colleague, Professor K. J. Ratnam, for reading the manuscript.

My thanks are also due to Dr. Dayton D. McKean, editorial adviser to Houghton Mifflin Company, and to Mr. Richard N. Clark and his associates of the Houghton Mifflin editorial staff.

The manuscript was typed, with her never-failing accuracy, by Mrs. Lilian Wong, to whom I am most grateful.

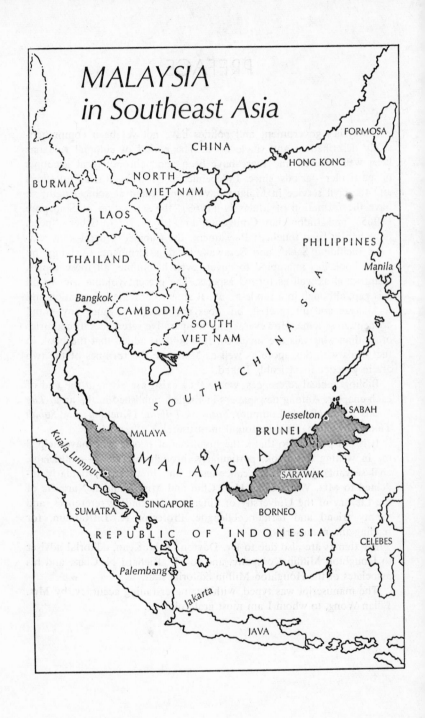

MALAYSIA
in Southeast Asia

CHINA

FORMOSA

HONG KONG

BURMA

NORTH
VIET NAM

LAOS

THAILAND

Bangkok

CAMBODIA

SOUTH
VIET NAM

PHILIPPINES

Manila

S O U T H   C H I N A   S E A

Kuala Lumpur

MALAYA

Jesselton

SABAH

BRUNEI

M A L A Y S I A

SARAWAK

SUMATRA

SINGAPORE

BORNEO

R E P U B L I C   O F   I N D O N E S I A

CELEBES

Palembang

Jakarta

JAVA

1

Introduction

Malaysia[1] consists of the peninsula which forms the most southerly portion of the land mass of Southeast Asia and of the northern quarter of the island of Borneo. It extends south nearly as far as the equator. At its tip, joined by a short narrow causeway, is the sophisticated island city of Singapore with 1¾ million people, situated at a strategic and commercial crossroads of air and sea routes. When Malaysia was formed in 1963 Singapore was included, but it ceased to be part of Malaysia in August, 1965. To the north is Thailand, formerly called Siam. To the west and south lie Sumatra, the Riau Islands, and the rest of the island of Borneo, all parts of Indonesia. To the east of Borneo are Palawan and other smaller islands, belonging to the Philippines.

The Malay peninsula has an east and a west coastal plain, with a central mountain range in between. The Borneo area consists of an alluvial, often swampy, coastal plain, hilly country further inland, and mountain ranges in the interior, in which majestic Mount Kinabalu rises to 13,500 feet. The climate is tropical; it is humid, with a range of temperature (except in a few hilly areas) from 75 degrees to 90

[1] To prevent confusion, *Malay* should be distinguished from *Malayan* and *Malaysian*. A Malay is a person of the Malay race, distinguished by use of the Malay language and belonging to the Muslim religion. A Malayan is a person who lives in Malaya; he may racially be a Malay, a Chinese, an Indian, a Eurasian, or something else. Similarly, nowadays, a Malaysian is a person of whatever racial origins, who lives in Malaysia. All these three words — Malay, Malayan, and Malaysian — may also be used as adjectives in corresponding senses. Before the formation of Malaysia, *Malaysian* was sometimes used to include persons racially akin to the Malays, who were Muslims and spoke a similar language, but who originated from a territory other than Malaya, for instance from Indonesia. But nowadays it would be ambiguous to continue to use "Malaysian" in this sense.

1

degrees. The average rainfall is about 100 inches a year. There is no completely dry season, except in Northwest Malaya and in Borneo, but the rainfall is heaviest in the two yearly monsoon seasons, which occur at different times in different parts of Malaysia.

Part of the attraction of Malaysia lies in the scenery, the contrast between dense rain forest in the interior and the rice fields of northwest Malaya or the silvery beaches with waving palms of Malaya's east coast. But much of the appeal arises from the close juxtaposition of races and cultures. Where else, in such a short compass, can so many colorful varieties of women's dress be seen — the Malay *sarong kebaya,* the Chinese *cheongsam* and the Indian *sari,* to say nothing of the exciting costumes of the women of Borneo? Where else, in a single country, are there public festivals, and in many cases public holidays, for the Prophet Muhammad's birthday, *Hari Raya Puasa* (the end of the Muslim fasting month), the Chinese New Year, Wesak Day (the Buddha's birthday) and *Deepavali,* the Hindu festival of lights, when homes are decorated with oil lamps or candles? To the Malay *ronggeng* and *joget* (dances) have been added Chinese *wayangs* (operas) and funerals, with music, as well as a wide range of picturesque weddings and religious observances.

This melting pot of races and cultures has not yet produced any artistic flowering. To begin with, there is no great architectural heritage remotely corresponding to Cambodia's Angkor Wat. Malaya has only Kuala Lumpur's "Moorish Victorian" railway station. Some recent architecture in the modern style, however, is impressive, notably the Parliament Buildings in Kuala Lumpur. Malay craftsmen turn out artistic pewter in Selangor, and silverware in Kelantan. But in literature and painting there is, as yet, little of note. It is curious that so fascinating a part of the world has given rise to so little good fiction. The writings of Joseph Conrad on the area generally and some short stories of Somerset Maugham are exceptions. But since the Second World War writers have tended to concentrate on the theme of the Communist rising, 1948–1960, and have written it almost to death. Of these novels, perhaps the best is Han Suyin's *And the Rain My Drink.* Other books which are worth reading for background are a hilarious trilogy by Anthony Burgess and Katharine Sim's perceptive *Malacca Boy.*[2]

Malaysia is a new country, which was formed only in 1963 by a federation of Malaya,[3] Sarawak, North Borneo (Sabah), and Singa-

[2] Han Suyin, *And the Rain My Drink* (London: Jonathan Cape, 1956); Anthony Burgess, *Malayan Trilogy* (*Time for a Tiger; The Enemy in the Blanket; Beds in the East*) (London: Pan Books, 1964); Katharine Sim, *Malacca Boy* (London: Hodder and Stoughton, 1957).

[3] Consisting of eleven states: Johore, Kedah, Kelantan, Malacca, Negri Sembilan, Pahang, Penang, Perak, Perlis, Selangor, Trengganu.

pore. Even Malaya, the chief component in terms of population, did not become an independent nation until 1957. Before 1963 Sarawak and Sabah were still British colonies; Singapore was independent in its internal affairs, but its defense and foreign policy were still controlled by the British. Malaysia is also a small country with an area of about 129,000 square miles, rather more than twice the size of Florida. After Singapore left in 1965 Malaysia's population was only slightly over nine million. To a large extent its problems are the same as those of the other countries of Southeast Asia: Indonesia, the Philippines, Thailand, Viet Nam, Laos, Cambodia, and Burma. Like all of these, except Thailand, it was at one time under European rule, although independence was won without the bitterness of the struggles which took place in Indonesia or former French Indochina. It has all the usual economic problems of underdevelopment, being dependent on the production and export of a number of crops, notably rubber, for which long-term prices are falling.[4] Added to these are the pressures of rapid population growth, resulting from a yearly increase of about 3 per cent. Less tangible, but nevertheless real, are the psychological stresses and strains imposed by modernization. Malaysia faces the familiar problem of how to reconcile traditional ways with Western ideas of "progress." How fast must modernization be pressed, if it sets up conflicts over values? Again, like all of these countries, it has had to face the threat of Communist subversion. From 1948 to 1960 Malaya was in a state of "emergency," provoked by Communist guerrillas, and, particularly since Malaysia, Communists have been active in carrying out subversion in Sarawak.

In spite of these similarities to neighboring countries, Malaysia has a distinct individuality of its own. It is not just a "typical" slice of Southeast Asia: it is unique. There are four main ways in which it differs substantially from its neighbors — in its racial composition, in its economy, in its Constitution, in the nature of its democratic government and party system.

More than anything else, the racial composition of Malaysia is the key to understanding the whole picture. It dictates the pattern of the economy, has helped to shape the Constitution, and has influenced the democratic process and the party system.

Table 1 indicates how complex the racial patchwork is.

Even this table has been simplified. The "Malays" in Malaya in fact include persons of Indonesian origin who have been largely absorbed into the Malay community and about 45,000 aborigines. "Sabah and Sarawak indigenous (non-Malay)" covers several distinct tribal groupings, who speak different dialects. To amplify the table,

---

[4] Gunnar Myrdal, *Economic Theory and Underdeveloped Regions* (London: Duckworth, 1957).

Table 1[5]

Population of Malaysia (in thousands) in 1960

	Malays	Chinese	Indians and Pakistanis	Sabah & Sarawak indigenous (non-Malay)	Others	Total
Malaya	3,461	2,552	773	—	123	6,909
Sarawak	129	229	2	378	6	744
Sabah (North Borneo)	25	105	3	283	39	455
Total	3,615	2,886	778	661	168	8,108

it should be said that the Chinese tend to be concentrated in the towns, and also that Malaya has an area which is less developed than the rest, the picturesque northeast coast, where the population is overwhelmingly Malay.

The table shows clearly that, even with the simplified classification adopted, no single racial group has a clear majority. The Chinese have about 36 per cent of the total, the Malays about 45 per cent. On paper, it would seem that a system of checks and balances could exist, by which, if any single community attempted to dominate the rest, it could be checked by the superior strength of the other groups combining against it. In practice, the problem is not as simple as this. The Malays and the other indigenous peoples feel that they have a special claim to be prominent, if not dominant, in the government of the country, just because they are indigenous, and therefore the original "sons of the soil." This claim was recognized by the British when they were the colonial power, and, as will appear later, the structure of government is based on this assumption.

Everything political or economic in Malaysia is dominated, and must be dominated, by considerations of "racial arithmetic." There are two schools of thought on whether the results of such calculations should be made public or not. But, whether made public or kept private, the calculations have to be made. The best way of illustrating the dimensions of the racial problem is perhaps to recall that the

[5] Source, T. E. Smith, *The Background to Malaysia* (London: Oxford University Press, 1963), p. 3. In addition to the comments in the text note that, for Sabah, "Others" includes natives of Malaya, Sarawak, Singapore, the Philippines, Indonesia, India and Ceylon.

More recent official figures do not give as complete a breakdown. But by 1964 the population of the three territories in the table had risen to over nine million. Singapore's population is three-quarters Chinese.

Philippines and Indonesia have both shown extreme concern about the Chinese in their respective countries. In particular they have been worried about how the Chinese are to be integrated into the life of the country and also about, in their view, the excessive degree of control which the Chinese have exercised over retail trade.[6] Yet in both these countries the proportion of Chinese in the population is under 5 per cent. In Malaysia it is about 36 per cent! With this proportion of Chinese, it is quite unrealistic to adopt merely restrictive measures, such as expulsion, or to prohibit the Chinese from engaging in retail trade. Yet the alternative of assimilating the Chinese, which has been attempted with some success in Thailand, is not so easy in Malaysia. Ethnically the Chinese and the Thais are closer than the Chinese and the Malays. And the fact that practically all Malays are Muslims makes assimilation difficult. The racial mosaic is made more intricate by the existence of "Indians and Pakistanis" and the large variety of groups which are indigenous to the Borneo territories.

Consequently there is a racial pattern which defies any simple solution. It is paralleled by a complex language pattern. The élite of all races speak English, and this is also at present an official language of government along with Malay. But communication among other groups is difficult, except, for example, in the market place, where "bazaar Malay" is common. In addition to Malay, Chinese is spoken in the form of Mandarin or any one of half a dozen South Chinese dialects. Most Indians speak Tamil, but may use other languages, mostly from South India. In Sarawak the most common native language is Iban, and in Sabah, Kadazan, but many others are spoken in each territory. From 1967 on, Malay will be the only official language, except in the two Borneo territories, unless Parliament decides otherwise. In the long run this will make for greater ease of communication, although there may be difficulties during the transitional period. The language question also extends into the schools, and the problem of education, particularly Chinese education, has been the cause of much controversy. It would be unrealistic to try to impose the same pattern for language and educational policy all over Malaysia. It is clear that policies on language and education ought to take account of the existence of a high proportion of indigenous non-Malays in the two Borneo territories, constituting over 50 per cent of their population. Wisely, it has been decided that, at least for some time, language and education policies in the two Borneo states shall differ from the pattern in Malaya.

[6] See, on the Philippines, Remigio E. Agpalo, *The Political Process and the Nationalization of the Retail Trade in the Philippines* (Quezon City: University of the Philippines, 1962).

The divisions in the population just mentioned are intensified by religious differences. Malays are nearly 100 per cent Muslims, but hardly any Chinese are Muslims; some are Christians, others are Buddhists, Confucianists, or Taoists or a combination of these. In other races the dividing line is less marked. An appreciable number of the "Indians and Pakistanis" are Muslims, and many of the indigenous peoples of Borneo are Muslims. But religion adds an extra dimension of possible trouble. In 1964, when Singapore was part of Malaysia, the riots there had a racial side, and they were also encouraged by Indonesian saboteurs and by demonstrators and looters who were "straightforward" criminals. But it is significant that the first riot actually "exploded" during a religious procession.

On a longer perspective, language and education are bound up with the sensitive topic of nationalism.[7] National feeling developed later in Malaysia than in most parts of Southeast Asia. This was partly the result of the type of rule exercised by the British, which worked mainly through the existing Malay Rulers and so softened the reactions against colonialism. But is was chiefly due to the mixed racial composition of the population. What common focus for nationalism could attract the loyalties of a Malay farmer and also of a Chinese trader and an Indian laborer on a rubber estate, whose families might have been only two generations in Malaya? One of the few readily available instruments for creating a common focus is the use of Malay as a national language. Its role in this connection is described in the last chapter of this book.

Racial differences express themselves clearly, too clearly, in the economic sphere. Some of the accepted stereotypes are exaggerated, or out-of-date. But it is worth while looking at two of them. It has been said of the Chinese that, of all communities, theirs is "the most obtrusive, the most tenacious, the most feared, a people whose virtues of thrift, self-help, industry have become almost vices. . . ."[8] A contrasting picture was painted of the Malay, half a century ago. "Nature has done so much for him that he is never really cold and never starves. He must have rice, but the smallest exertion will give it to him. . . . Whatever the cause, the Malay of the Peninsula was, and is, unquestionably opposed to steady continuous work. And yet, if you can only give him an interest in the job, he will perform prodigies; he will strive, and endure, and be cheerful and courageous

---

[7] See William L. Holland (ed.), *Asian Nationalism and the West* (New York: Macmillan, 1953); Rupert Emerson, *From Empire to Nation* (Cambridge: Harvard University Press, 1962).

[8] Richard Weston, "A Tragedy of Errors," *Eastern World*, X, No. 10 (1956), 35.

with the best."[9] The underlying reasons for the contrast are not difficult to see. The Chinese, mostly from southern China, who left their homeland to work in Southeast Asia, including the various areas which now make up Malaysia, were not a random selection. Those who made the journey and survived were exceptionally hardy and determined, rather like the early pioneers to the North American continent. Their attitudes were, and had to be, fiercely competitive. This was in striking contrast to the Malays, who were eminently non-competitive, because there was no point in being anything else. Given the numbers and the energy of the Chinese, it was natural that, under British rule, they should dominate industry and trade, always excepting the large share owned by foreigners, mostly the British. The Chinese, therefore, have tended to concentrate in the towns; the Malays, on the other hand, have formed a larger proportion of those who lived in rural areas.

Both before and after independence, attempts were made to improve the economic position of the Malays. Schemes were started for training them in business and making it easier for them to obtain capital. Especially since independence there has been a big drive for rural development and land settlement. The 1957 Constitution of Malaya, which came into force when Malaya gained independence, gave protection to Malays in certain types of occupation. These provisions have been continued after the formation of Malaysia in 1963. At the same time arrangements have been made to speed up the economic advancement of the indigenous people in the Borneo territories who were even more in need of such help than the Malays in Malaya. But these are essentially long-term schemes.

The economy of Malaysia is not typical for Southeast Asia. Its national income per head is the highest in Southeast Asia, apart from Singapore and Brunei, and in South and East Asia it is second only to Japan. And there are differences in the level of income between the various parts of Malaysia. In United States dollars the annual incomes per head (1961) were roughly: Malaya, $270; North Borneo $230; Sarawak, $180. (The corresponding figure for Singapore was $430.) But even the Sarawak figure is higher than that for the rest of Southeast Asia. These amounts may seem very low by North American standards, for many items which are expensive here, especially housing and clothing, are much cheaper in that part of the world. Furthermore, hardly anyone actually dies of hunger in Southeast Asia as compared, say, with India, although many suffer from faulty nutrition. Except in parts of Java there is no desperate shortage of land. Con-

[9] Sir Frank Swettenham, *British Malaya* (London: John Lane, 1920), pp. 136 and 139.

sequently, remembering that the conditions of economic life are less hard in Southeast Asia than in many other developing areas, to say that Malaysia's national income per head is the highest in Southeast Asia indicates a rather high standard of living compared with levels in most of the rest of the world.

Nevertheless, the basis for Malaysia's relative prosperity is far from secure. Unless she can export large quantities of rubber and tin, her economy will suffer. Malaysia is today the biggest producer of "natural" rubber; indeed, rubber accounts for about a quarter of the value of the gross domestic product, that is, all the goods and services produced inside Malaysia. Furthermore, half of the total export earnings come from rubber. But in the face of increasing competition from synthetic rubber produced in the industrialized countries, the price for "natural" rubber is falling, with a subsequent reduction of income from this source. Where tin is concerned, not only are her resources becoming exhausted, she also faces depressed prices for her tin whenever there are sales from the United States' strategic stockpile.

Malaya's economic plans have attempted to safeguard its economic future in two main ways. There has been an attempt at agricultural diversification by persuading farmers not to concentrate too much on rubber, but also to plant such crops as oil palm and pineapple. The main effort, however, has taken the form of attempting to industrialize. Factories have been set up to produce such goods as paints, matches, cigarettes, soap, chemicals, and automobile tires. Special incentives have been offered to approved "pioneer industries." Since Malaysia has been formed, Malaya's economic plans have been extended to include Sarawak and Sabah. In the short run, Malaysia's economic situation is better than that of her neighbors. But, because of the unpromising future of rubber and tin, which are mainly responsible for this superiority, she must make wise preparations for the future in order to avoid the stagnation, or even decline, of her economy.

Constitutionally, Malaysia is remarkable. Although in form a federation, like the United States or Australia, she breaks many of the "rules" which are generally believed to constitute the essence of federalism. Two states in the Federation of Malaysia, Sarawak and Sabah, have different powers from the rest; so had Singapore, when she was a member state of Malaysia. A United States parallel would be that, when Hawaii and Alaska were admitted as states, they would have come in on special terms, and would have been permitted to exercise some state functions not possessed by the existing forty-eight states. The justification for this apparently odd arrangement will be discussed later. Here it is enough to say, broadly, that it was adopted in order to allow for differences in culture and level of development between Sabah and Sarawak as compared with the states of Malaya.

Apart from the Philippines and Singapore, Malaysia is the only country in Southeast Asia which holds democratic elections. But there is a significant difference from the Philippines as regards the party system. The Philippines has *national* parties, which operate throughout the country. In Malaysia the party system is to a large extent still regional. In Sabah and Sarawak the fact that political development came late, compared with Malaya, is no doubt partly responsible. But even inside Malaya parties are much more dependent on the support of particular regions than in the Philippines. Originally, after the formation of Malaysia in 1963, the political scene was also complicated by the efforts of the People's Action Party, the government party in Singapore, to extend its activities into Malaya. As shown later, these efforts led to such an increase in political and communal tensions that the only peaceful solution was for Singapore to leave Malaysia.

It is impossible to ignore the influence of external forces. In a small country like Malaysia, the inhabitants are influenced by the example of what similar racial groups are doing overseas. This is obviously true of the Chinese and the Indians in Malaya, most of whose families have been settled there for only one or two generations. But it is also true of the Malays, who are linked to Indonesia by language and religion, and in some cases even through close relatives who live there. Also, beginning in 1963 Indonesia carried out a policy of "Confrontation" towards Malaysia, which took the form of armed attacks and sabotage on Malaysian territory. The occasion for this policy was the formation of Malaysia. But the policy also promoted two objects, to divert attention from inefficiency and economic muddle inside Indonesia and to advance long-term territorial ambitions of an *Indonesia Raya* (Greater Indonesia). Whatever the reasons, the effects on Malaysia were appreciable. It gave encouragement to subversives in Malaysia, particularly to Chinese Communists in Sarawak. It opened up possibilities of an increase in racial tensions, if Indonesia could succeed in playing one section of the population of Malaysia against another. By making increased expenditure on defense necessary, it slowed down economic advance. Because Malaysia was too weak to defend herself in the face of an enemy with ten times her population, it underlined her military dependence on Britain, Australia, and New Zealand, fellow-members of the British Commonwealth of Nations, and so seemed to support Indonesian taunts that she was really still a "colony."

In the face of such overwhelming odds, it may be wondered how Malaysia has managed to survive. Doubts about her viability increased temporarily after the separation of Singapore in August, 1965, although prospects improved when it was announced in June, 1966, that Confrontation would end. Her fight for existence and her struggle to find appropriate constitutional and political institutions, as well as a national identity, form the subject of this book.

SUGGESTED READINGS

Federation of Malaya Official Year Book. Kuala Lumpur: Government Press.

Ginsburg, Norton Sydney and Chester F. Roberts. *Malaya.* Seattle: University of Washington Press, 1958. Human Relations Area Files. Not always accurate.

Gullick, John Michael. *Malaya.* London: Ernest Benn, 1963. Comprehensive; especially good on history.

Hanna, Willard Anderson. *Reports on Malaya, Singapore and Malaysia.* New York: American Universities Field Staff, 1956– First-hand highly readable reporting.

Miller, Harry. *The Story of Malaysia.* London: Faber and Faber, 1965. History vividly told.

Parmer, J. Norman. "Malaysia," pp. 281–371, in *Government and Politics of Southeast Asia,* 2nd ed., George McTurnan Kahin, ed. Ithaca: Cornell University Press, 1964. Good on economics and labor.

Purcell, Victor. *Malaysia.* New York: Walker and Company, 1965. A well-illustrated general introduction.

Pye, Lucian W. "The Politics of Southeast Asia" in *The Politics of Developing Areas,* Gabriel A. Almond and James S. Coleman, eds. Princeton: Princeton University Press, 1960. Analytical.

Wang Gungwu. *Malaysia, a Survey.* New York: Praeger, 1964. Covers a wide range, including political, economic and social aspects.

2

Malaya until 1945

By the beginning of the Christian era the early inhabitants of the Malay Peninsula had contacts with traders from India and China. However, much of the early history of Malaya is based only on speculation.[1] Among the earliest kingdoms mentioned was Langkasuka, in northeast Malaya, which dated from about the second century A.D. For some time Langkasuka may have been subject to the empire of Fou-nan, which had its capital in Cambodia. After the decline of Fou-nan, about the end of the seventh century, the kingdoms on the west coast of Malaya, among which were Langkasuka and Kedah, became vassals of Sri Vijaya, an empire influenced both by Hinduism and Buddhism, based on Palembang in Sumatra. In the thirteenth and fourteenth centuries the power of Sri Vijaya waned, and the Javanese-centered empire, Majapahit, dominated Sumatra and possibly parts of Malaya. According to tradition, about 1400 A.D. a refugee prince of Palembang, after a brief stay in Temasek, the site of present-day Singapore, reached Malacca, where he set himself up as Ruler. To protect himself from Siam he secured recognition from China. He also embraced Islam, which had begun to spread in Sumatra and northern Malaya about a hundred years earlier, taking the name of Megat Iskandar Shah. During the rest of the century the kingdom of Malacca expanded territorially inside the Malay Peninsula at the expense of neighboring states in spite of the opposition of Siam; it fell heir to the commerce of the former Sri Vijaya kingdom, and traded with Sumatra and Java, India, Arabia, Persia, and China. Trade was followed by religion, and Malacca became an Islamic missionary center.

[1] D. G. E. Hall, *A History of South-East Asia* (London: Macmillan, 1964), chs. 2, 3, 4, and 10; Sir Richard O. Winstedt, *A History of Malaya,* rev. ed. (Singapore: Marican, 1962), chs. 1 and 2.

Portuguese, Dutch, and British

Whether or not, and in what manner, Malacca would have succumbed to local attacks and pressures after the fashion of Sri Vijaya and Majapahit can only be speculated upon. At the height of her ascendancy Malacca fell a victim to the Portuguese attempt to open up a trade route to the Far East. In pursuit of this aim Vasco da Gama had reached India in 1498. The great Albuquerque sent a fleet from Portugal which reached Malacca in 1509, and the port was captured by Albuquerque himself two years later. The Malacca dynasty fled south and eventually established a new capital in Johore. The Portuguese never kept a large garrison in Malacca, and they were subject to frequent attacks, mainly from Johore and from the Muslim kingdom of Acheh in northern Sumatra. Their lines of communication were overextended, and their fleet was beaten by the Dutch in the Straits of Malacca in 1606. The Dutch motive in penetrating so far east was also trade. Although they reaped no immediate advantage from their sea victory, they established themselves in Batavia, Java, in 1619. By this time Malacca's own importance as a trading center had declined. When the Dutch finally captured it in 1641, the motive was not to make a direct profit from its use, but rather to incorporate it in a system of trading bases and to *deny* it to the Portuguese.

During the next century or so Dutch attention was concentrated on establishing and enforcing monopolies, for example in tin, in the states surrounding Malacca, and in repelling the attacks of the Bugis warriors, who originally had come from the Celebes. Early in the eighteenth century the Bugis gained virtual control of the Malay Johore kingdom, which was based on the Riau Islands, off Singapore. The Bugis raids reached as far north as Kedah and seriously disrupted the trading activities of the Dutch. By 1785, the Dutch, by force of arms, had succeeded in imposing a Resident at the Court of Riau, temporarily removing the Bugis.

After the Dutch capture of Malacca the northern Malay states, Kedah, Kelantan and Trengganu, fell under Siamese suzerainty, sometimes effectively, sometimes only nominally. The sending, from time to time, of the "golden flowers" (*bunga emas*) to Siam could be interpreted either as a free-will offering or as tribute. Towards the end of the eighteenth century the British came upon the scene, partly in search of trade like most Westerners; more specifically, they were looking for settlements to further their trade with China and bases from which to prevent French domination of the Indian Ocean. The Sultan of Kedah, anxious for assistance against the Siamese, leased the island of Penang to Captain Francis Light, acting for the British East India

Company, in 1786. The Company agreed to pay an annual sum for Penang, and for the adjacent area of Province Wellesley. But Kedah failed to obtain any military guarantee, and the Siamese conquered it with great slaughter in 1821 and ruled it directly until 1842.

Malacca was added to Penang when the British took it over in 1795, as a result of the Dutch war against the French, who had occupied Holland the year before. It was later returned to the Dutch, but by the Anglo-Dutch treaty of 1824 was exchanged for the Island of Bencoolen in Sumatra. This marked the end of Dutch claims to Malaya. The British sphere of influence had by now been extended to include Singapore. In 1819 this barely inhabited island had been chosen for greatness by Sir Stamford Raffles, an official of the East India Company, who had had a meteoric rise in the Company's service and had already been Lieutenant-Governor of Java during the British occupation a few years before. The foundation of Singapore was "legalized" by the agreement of the eldest son of the deceased Sultan of Riau, who had been passed over by the Bugis in favor of a younger brother. As a fair exchange, the British recognized him as Sultan. It was the intention of Raffles that Singapore should become a free port, and its rapid growth in population and trade in the next few years fully justified his expectations. Of the three "Straits Settlements" — Singapore, Penang, and Malacca, combined in 1826 and governed from India — Singapore had by far the fastest rate of growth, Malacca the slowest. In 1832 Singapore became the capital of the Straits Settlements in place of Penang.

In 1826 the British, in a treaty with Siam, implicitly acknowledged that the states of Kedah (which then included the territory of the future state of Perlis), Kelantan, and Trengganu were in the Siamese sphere of influence. The rest of the peninsula was in the British sphere, but at this time the British had no reason to follow an expansionist policy. Expansion would have cost money, and the simple economy of the Malays did not then yield enough beyond subsistence to justify the expense. British activity was limited, essentially, to preventing further penetration by Siam and to suppressing piracy.

Indigenous Government

The way in which the west coast states were ruled up to this time has been admirably described by J. M. Gullick. The superstructure of government which hedged the Ruler was elaborate in comparison with his rather limited powers.[2] In spite of the pomp and circumstance of the Rulers and their role in symbolizing and preserving the unity

[2] J. M. Gullick, *Indigenous Political Systems of Western Malaya* (London: Athlone Press, 1958), p. 49.

of the state, the chiefs "under" them were in practice largely independent. A chief "did pretty much as he pleased so long as he professed allegiance to the ruler, did not interfere with him or his relatives, and gave to him some small portion of the taxes squeezed from Malay *raiyats* (peasants) and Chinese miners and traders."[3] The basis of the chief's power was a band of fighting men and, usually, a strategic position on a river, from which, like a medieval European baron on the Rhine, he could levy toll on passing boats. In more than one sense the system in each state was highly mobile. Succession to the office of Ruler was not in fact governed by fixed rules, so there was considerable opportunity for the circulation of élites. Mobility was also spatial, as is illustrated by the journeyings of the Sultans of Riau-Johore after they had to leave Malacca. Those who were followers of Rulers and chiefs were also relatively mobile. There was no general shortage of land, and, apart from limits imposed by the existence of slaves and debt-bondmen,[4] those who felt themselves unduly oppressed could always move on. The situation was in marked contrast to societies where water was scarce and the power of government was enforced by its control over irrigation.[5] In western Malaya elements of despotism were tempered by elements of anarchy.

British Expansion — Indirect Rule

Originally the British were not much concerned with the Malayan hinterland, so long as disorder did not impinge on their interests. Their attention was directed outwards, towards the trade which was carried on via the Straits Settlements. But in the middle of the nineteenth century the situation changed, and so did British policy. An important reason for this was an increase in the scale of tin mining in Perak and Selangor. The miners were largely Chinese, whose addition to the immigrants already in the Straits Settlements eventually contributed to producing a multi-racial society — and its problems. The immediate effect, however, was to open up new possible sources of revenue for Malay Rulers and chiefs, if they could gain control of the areas where tin was mined. A new financial edge was given to the previous intermittent disputes between Malay Rulers and chiefs. Alliances were formed between Malay and Chinese groups, and there was heavy fighting between them. British firms in the Straits Settlements were commercially interested in preventing the trade in tin from being dis-

[3] Sir Frank Swettenham, *The Real Malaya* (London: John Lane, 1907), p. 258.

[4] Gullick, pp. 104–105.

[5] Karl Wittfogel, *Oriental Despotism* (New Haven: Yale University Press, 1957).

rupted by the more intensive fighting. They therefore pressed the Colonial Office, which since 1867 had controlled the Straits Settlements, to agree to intervention. "The idea of the Straits Settlements merchants was that the Colonial Office should authorize a policy which could lead only to military and naval expense. The profits would go to Straits investors (who paid practically nothing in taxation), and the cost would fall on the British taxpayer."[6] Earlier requests for intervention had been resisted. But the new Governor of the Straits Settlements, Sir Andrew Clarke, appointed in 1873, had been given instructions to recommend how peace and order might be restored and to report whether it might be desirable to appoint a British resident adviser in any of the states.[7] The state which claimed the early attention of the new Governor was Perak. In spite of a structure of government which included fantastically elaborate provisions to determine the succession on the death of a Sultan,[8] in 1873 there were three claimants to the throne. One of these sought British help to advance his cause, stating his willingness to accept a British adviser. A meeting of the Perak chiefs chose, with some guidance from the British, this particular claimant as Sultan. At the same time provision was made for a British Resident (and Assistant Resident), "whose advice must be asked and acted upon [on] all questions other than those touching Malay Religion and Custom."[9] The system of Residents was afterwards applied to the states of Selangor, Pahang, and Negri Sembilan. It was apparently assumed, originally, that a single white man could solve all difficulties by tactful advice.[10] The position of the Resident in each state was awkward, and his task indeed delicate. Technically, he was an adviser rather than a ruler; in practice he was expected to be more than this. But after the death by violence of the impetuous Resident of Perak, and a single example of the use of armed force by the British to avenge it, the system worked quite smoothly. The Rulers were reconciled to it, partly by the tact of the Residents, but also by regular payments in exchange for former revenues they had given up and by the institution of State Councils, which nominally advised them, although actually advising the Resident.

The four states, as contrasted with the Straits Settlements, were examples of indirect rule. Indeed Sir Frank Swettenham[11] claimed that

---

[6] C. Northcote Parkinson, *British Intervention in Malaya, 1867–1877* (Singapore: University of Malaya Press, 1960), p. 62.

[7] Parkinson, p. 112.

[8] Sir Frank Swettenham, *British Malaya,* rev. ed. (London: Allen and Unwin, 1948), pp. 120 ff.

[9] Parkinson, pp. 136–137.

[10] Swettenham, *British Malaya,* p. 214.

[11] *Footprints in Malaya* (London: Hutchinson, 1942), p. 101.

the British concept of indirect rule originated in Malaya and not, as is often supposed, in Africa. The advantages of indirect rule, for the ruling colonial power, include cheapness, and, for the ruled, a softening of the impact of colonialism.[12] However, this second "benefit" is ambiguous; the protective cushion of indirect rule might also act as a drag on development by depriving the society of the full benefits of Westernization.

Federated and Unfederated States — "Decentralization"

When the system of indirect rule had been established in four states, there was a tendency for each Resident to go his own way in administration,[13] and some coordination became necessary. Consequently the states were formed into a "Federation" in 1895. This was not a "federation" in the accepted sense of a system of government in which powers are divided between a federal government and state governments. The Rulers of the four states agreed to accept a British Resident-General and to follow his advice; the only sphere in which they were not obliged to follow it was on questions touching Malay religion and custom.[14] The four Residents were made responsible to the Resident-General, who was in turn responsible to the Governor of the Straits Settlements, who would in the future also be High Commissioner for the Federated Malay States. Every important government department in the four states was put under a single administrative head, responsible to the Resident-General for securing uniformity in the four states.[15] In 1909 a Federal Council was created, consisting of the Rulers, the Resident-General, the four British Residents, and four "unofficial" members nominated by the Governor, who presided over the Council in his capacity as High Commissioner of the Federated Malay States. In 1911 the position of Resident-General was abolished and his duties given to a "Chief Secretary." These changes may have resulted from a desire to reassure the Rulers who feared that administration was becoming too centralized. But in practice they had an opposite effect, and the legislative powers of the states were diminished. Starting with Perak, in 1877, the states had set up State Councils, and legislative authority lay in the Ruler in State Council, of which the Resident was a member. But the new Federal Council could

[12] Rupert Emerson, *Malaysia, a Study in Direct and Indirect Rule* (New York: Macmillan, 1937), pp. 7 ff.

[13] Swettenham, *British Malaya*, p. 251.

[14] S. W. Jones, *Public Administration in Malaya* (London: Royal Institute of International Affairs, 1953), p. 19.

[15] Swettenham, *British Malaya*, p. 273.

pass laws intended to have force throughout the Federation or in more than one state, and laws passed by a State Council would not be valid if they were repugnant to the provisions of the law passed by the Federal Council.[16] Nor did the Rulers find that their own powers were appreciably increased by their sitting on the Federal Council, where their status prevented them from freely taking part in debate. In 1927 they ceased to be members of the Council and instead a Durbar of Rulers was set up, consisting of the four Rulers, the High Commissioner, and the Federal Secretary. This body was the forerunner of the Conference of Rulers in the present Constitution.

After Britain's *entente cordiale* with France in 1904 she was free to make advances in northern Malaya without fear of French countermoves in or against Siam. In 1909 the four northern states were transferred to British rule, and in time all the Rulers accepted British advisers. In 1914, the Sultan of Johore, who in many ways was more British than the British and prided himself on his friendship with Queen Victoria, accepted a British "General Adviser." The five states — Kedah, Perlis, Kelantan, Trengganu, and Johore — were not included in the Federation, and were therefore referred to as the "Unfederated States."

There were further constitutional changes before the Second World War, but they did not destroy the division into Straits Settlements, Federated Malay States, and Unfederated Malay States. Apparently the British wished to bring the Unfederated Malay States into the Federation; they did not, however, attempt to do so by force but rather by trying to make conditions inside the Federation more attractive to the states outside. This was one of the motives behind the policy of "decentralization" pursued in the 1920's and 1930's by Governors Sir Lawrence Guillemard and Sir Cecil Clementi.[17] The decentralization policy had limited results. Some administrative departments were handed over to the states from the Federation, state budgets rose, and state administrations were strengthened. In 1935 the Chief Secretary was replaced by a Federal Secretary who was lower in status.[18] There was opposition to decentralization from European and Chinese unofficial members on the Federal Council, who feared that the state governments would be freed from effective control by the Federation and that financial stability and favorable conditions for trade would be damaged.

[16] In the intervening period, 1895–1909, there was no Federation organ of government with legislative functions. The technique used was for a federal official to draft a law which was passed by each State Council in practically identical form (Jones, p. 34).

[17] Jones, pp. 88–89.

[18] Emerson, pp. 154–173 and 324–344.

Also, it was by no means clear exactly what authorities or persons would gain from a decrease in the power of the Chief Secretary. Might "decentralization" not lead to an increase in the power of the High Commissioner and to greater weight being given to interests in Singapore? In this sense, might it not even lead, paradoxically, to more *centralization?* Even if state powers were in fact increased, which *persons* would benefit? Would it be the Residents or the members of the State Councils? And would there not have to be an increase in non-Malay representation on the State Councils? In Emerson's view the constitutional structure of the states had survived partly because they were only backwaters. If the states were given greater powers, the old structures might be too weak to carry them and would have to be remodelled.[19] The Unfederated States were not tempted by decentralization and remained outside the Federation. The whole tripartite structure continued to be held together, constitutionally, by the Governor of the Straits Settlements, who, in his capacity as High Commissioner, was the superior of the Federal Secretary, who was responsible for the Federated Malay States, and to whom the advisers in the Unfederated States reported directly. The Governor was himself responsible to the Colonial Office in Britain.

Although constitutional changes took place, there were few signs of an approach to democratic elections before the Second World War. In the Straits Settlements, where Western democratic ideas were most familiar, there was a Crown Colony type of government, with a Governor, an Executive Council with advisory functions and a Legislative Council. On both of these councils there were "unofficial" members, that is, persons who were not employed by the government, but they were appointed, not elected. Two of the unofficials on the legislative council were elected by the Singapore and Penang Chambers of Commerce. Although these two councils and the Federal Council in the Federated Malay States were, in constitutional theory, purely advisory, in practice the Governor paid considerable attention to the wishes of the unofficial members who represented important local interests.[20]

Economic Development —
Chinese and Indian Immigration

Economic development outside the Straits Settlements had originally been based on tin. But, in the first decade of the twentieth century, rubber, which had previously been planted only experimentally in Malaya,

[19] Emerson, p. 342.
[20] Lennox A. Mills, "Malaysia," in *The New World of Southeast Asia,* L. A. Mills, ed. (Minneapolis: University of Minnesota Press, 1949), p. 180.

boomed with the invention of the pneumatic tire for automobiles. From this time on, the economy became heavily dependent on both rubber and tin. The severe drop in the prices of these commodities during the world depression of the 1930's hit Malaya hard, and led her to participate in restrictionist schemes. Development was aided by an improvement in communications, both externally (through the opening of the Suez Canal in 1869, which cut the sea journey from England by more than half) and internally through the building of roads and railways. Differences in development did not quite correspond to the division into Federated and Unfederated States. Pahang, which was relatively underdeveloped, was in the Federated Malay States. And there were considerable differences within the Unfederated States. Johore was the most developed, Kelantan and Trengganu, with a largely Malay population and poor communications with the rest of Malaya, the least developed.

Economic development in Malaya was carried on almost entirely by non-Malays, mostly Europeans and Chinese. After 1900 European enterprise became dominant, and Chinese enterprise, which had been prominent in tin, suffered a relative, although not an absolute, decline.[21] It is significant that when Swettenham asked the question how far the prosperity of the Federated Malay States was attributable to different groups, he considered the contributions of Chinese entrepreneurs, European entrepreneurs, and British government officials, but did not even think it worth while to mention the Malays.[22] It followed, therefore, that immigration was greatest in the areas which were most economically developed, namely the west coast apart from the extreme north. But there is no simple way of describing in a few words the character of the immigration.[23] Among the Chinese the earlier immigrants to the Straits Settlements (the "Straits Chinese") acquired roots, and some intermarried with Malays. Later the Chinese were transients; their aim, like the corresponding aim of British traders, was to make money and retire to their homeland. Some were brought to Malaya under appalling conditions and worked under a system of indenture which, in order to pay the cost of their passage and board, left them as badly off, temporarily, as slaves. Others were successful in becoming traders. Although in China they had been farmers or artisans, they were enter-

[21] G. C. Allen and A. C. Donnithorne, *Western Enterprise in Indonesia and Malaya* (London: Allen and Unwin, 1957), p. 42.

[22] Swettenham, *British Malaya*, p. 301.

[23] Victor Purcell, *The Chinese in Malaya* (London: Oxford University Press, 1948) and *The Chinese in Modern Malaya* (Singapore: Eastern Universities Press, 1960).

prising and adventurous, and their understanding of money, and the manipulation of men in relation to money, laid the foundation of business success.[24] In this transient population the ratio of males to females was high. There were also fluctuations according to the prosperity of the economy — for instance, the number of immigrants dropped during the depression of the early 1930's. But later in the 1930's, when fighting between the Chinese and Japanese in China became intense, the immigrants remained instead of returning to China. Also, partly because of government restrictions on male immigration introduced shortly before the war, the proportion of women among the Chinese rose.

Partly because of the transient nature of the Chinese population and partly because the British, in their colonial policy, still practiced laissez faire, little was done by the government for the Chinese in the early stages of their immigration except to try to provide the minimum conditions of law and order. Any analysis of British prewar policy in Malaya which criticizes the government for not welding the Chinese into a Malayan nation is making illegitimate use of hindsight. In the Straits Settlements, government of the Chinese was originally indirect. Rule was by Chinese custom administered by a Chinese headman ("Captain" or "Kapitan"). The headman was often also an important figure in a Chinese secret society.[25] In the absence of an appreciable degree of government control, the secret societies played a major role in organizing and ordering the life of the Chinese. Their power was probably greater than that of, say, Tammany Hall in the United States. Closer control was attempted in 1877 when a Chinese protectorate was established. This was intended to deal with the secret societies, whose criminal functions were often more prominent than their benevolent functions. It was also meant to control Chinese labor and immigration, the traffic in women for the purpose of prostitution and the suppression of a form of domestic servitude, known as *mui tsai* ("younger sisters"). This list of the protectorate's activities is rather a statement of intentions than a record of achievements. For instance, the passing of a law on secret societies in 1889 did not render them powerless. But the general tendency was to try to replace indirect rule of the Chinese by direct rule. However, the British, viewing the Chinese as transients, did not accord them equal treatment with the Malays. There were government schools and also mission schools (where the teaching was in English) that Chinese could attend, and from 1920 onward some Chinese schools were given government grants-in-aid. But, although

[24] M. Freedman, "The Growth of a Plural Society in Malaya," *Pacific Affairs*, XXXIII, No. 2 (1960), 162.

[25] L. F. Comber, *Chinese Secret Societies in Malaya* (Locust Valley, New York: Augustin, 1959).

free education was provided for some children in Malay, it was not provided in Chinese.

In several senses the Chinese immigrants and their descendants were not homogeneous. Some of the earlier arrivals, the "Straits Chinese," were relatively well assimilated to the Malay population, but other Chinese were not. Some young Chinese educated in Malaya had been educated in English; others had not. Unlike other Southeast Asian countries, where Chinese formed only two or three per cent of the population, in Malaya the number of Chinese was too great for them to be overwhelmingly concentrated in a narrow group of occupations, such as retail trade. Finally, although geography dictated that the great majority of the immigrants came from South China, they were split among several major dialect groups[26] and a number of minor ones. The different dialect groups tended to specialize in different occupations.

The "Indians" in Malaya were not homogeneous, either. Most of them were South Indians, largely Tamils, but even among the Tamils some had not come direct from India but had arrived via Ceylon. There was a sizable Sikh community, and also a number of Muslims. Many of the Indians were "imported," rather as if they were a commodity,[27] to work on the rubber estates, and were "exported" again when the economic demand for them fell. However, control of Indian immigration and working conditions was strict, if paternalistic, partly because of the Indian government's concern that the immigrants should have some protection.

Japanese Invasion and Occupation

The transition from prewar to postwar politics in Malaya was accomplished, painfully, through a Japanese invasion. The construction of the Singapore naval base, begun in the 1920's, depended on the risky assumption that the British navy would not have to fight two enemies at once, one in the West, the other in the Far East.[28] The gamble failed. After the fall of France the Japanese occupied French Indochina, within easy range (400 miles) for striking at North Malaya by air. On December 7, 1941, almost simultaneously with the bombing of Pearl Harbor, the Japanese landed troops at Singora in southern Thailand. In ten weeks the whole of Malaya and the island fortress of Singapore, undefended on the northern, or landward, side, had been

[26] Hokkien, Cantonese, Hakka, Teochiu, Hainanese (Hainan).

[27] T. H. Silcock and Ungku Aziz, "Nationalism in Malaya," in *Asian Nationalism and the West,* William L. Holland, ed. (New York: The Macmillan Company, 1953), pp. 274–275.

[28] C. Northcote Parkinson, "The Pre-1942 Singapore Naval Base," *United States Naval Institute Proceedings,* LXXXII, No. 9 (1956), 950.

conquered. It is a usual British practice to claim that military defeats were in reality epic delaying actions. Perhaps it is more accurate to view the fall of Malaya and Singapore as "the worst disaster and largest capitulation in British history."[29] The British were clearly unprepared for war, as compared with the Japanese, in numbers and quality of aircraft and in the state of training of their troops and their commanders.[30]

The British had not succeeded in mobilizing the people of Malaya against the Japanese. During the occupation, however, the Japanese pursued racial policies based on expediency, which attempted to mobilize some sections of the local population in their favor. Because of the war with China they were already committed to being anti-Chinese in Malaya. The Chinese were equally committed, and the resistance movement consisted mostly of Chinese, among whom Communists were the best organized. The Japanese, however, took advantage of Indian nationalist aspirations by recruiting for the Indian National Army, intended to take part in the liberation of India. Policy towards the Malays was more equivocal. On the one hand the four northern, largely Malay, states of Kedah, Perlis, Kelantan, and Trengganu were transferred to Thailand. On the other hand, under Japanese military government, some Malays in the civil service were promoted to posts higher than those they had occupied under the British. The Japanese also encouraged Malay nationalist movements which they thought they could control. Among these was the KMM (Union of Malay Youths), a left-wing group under the leadership of Inche Ibrahim bin Yaacob, founded in 1937 to advocate independence for Malaya and union with Indonesia. Later KMM was reconstituted as KRIS (People's Association of Peninsular Indonesia).

The fighting in Malaya led to destruction of tin-mining equipment and the means of communication. Later in the war the export industries came to a halt because of a lack of Japanese ships to transport their products. Food shortages, disease, and inflation marked the continuation and the end of the occupation.

[29] Sir Winston Churchill, *The Second World War* (Boston: Houghton Mifflin, 1950, and London: Cassell, 1951), IV, 81.

[30] *Second Supplement to the London Gazette of Friday, the 20th of February, 1948* (London: H.M.S.O., 1948), paras. 690–691. This contains the despatch of the British Commander, General Percival, published six years after the event.

❧

SUGGESTED READINGS

Cowan, Charles Donald. *Nineteenth Century Malaya: The Origins of British Political Control*. London: Oxford University Press, 1961. The standard work.

Emerson, Rupert. *Malaysia, A Study in Direct and Indirect Rule*. New York: The Macmillan Company, 1937. A classic. The "Malaysia" in the title is not the present Malaysia; the book compares Malaya with the former Netherlands East Indies.

Gullick, John Michael. *Indigenous Political Systems of Western Malaya*. London: The Athlone Press, 1958. Deals with native rule on the west coast.

Gullick, John Michael. *Malaya*. London: Ernest Benn, 1963.

Jones, Stanley Wilson. *Public Administration in Malaya*. London: Royal Institute of International Affairs, 1953. Concerned more with constitutional history than with administration.

Kennedy, Joseph. *A History of Malaya, A.D. 1400–1959*. London: The Macmillan Company, 1962.

Mills, Lennox A. *British Malaya, 1824–1867*. Singapore: Methodist Publishing House, 1925. A pioneering work. Still of value.

Owen, Frank. *The Fall of Singapore*. London: Michael Joseph Ltd., 1960. Critical of the British management of the campaign.

Parkinson, C. Northcote. *British Intervention in Malaya, 1867–1877*. Singapore: University of Malaya Press, 1960. The origins of British intervention and of indirect rule.

Percival, Arthur Ernest. *The War in Malaya*. London: Eyre and Spottiswoode, 1949. The story of the British defeat told by the commanding general.

Purcell, Victor. *The Chinese in Malaya*. London: Oxford University Press, 1948. A classic by a former member of the Malayan Civil Service.

Purcell, Victor. *The Chinese in Modern Malaya*. Singapore: Eastern Universities Press, 1960. A shorter version of the previous book brought up to date.

Purcell, Victor. *The Memoirs of a Malayan Official*. London: Cassell and Company, 1965. Useful on the Chinese in Malaya.

Swettenham, Sir Frank. *British Malaya*, rev. ed. London: George Allen and Unwin, 1948. By a British administrator who spent a lifetime in Malaya and rose to the highest position in the civil service.

Tregonning, Kennedy G. *A History of Modern Malaya*. Singapore: Eastern Universities Press, 1964.

Winstedt, Sir Richard Olof. *Malaya and Its History*, 5th ed. London: Hutchinson's, University Library, 1958. By a British civil servant who made a deep study of Malay history and language.

Winstedt, Sir Richard Olof. *A History of Malaya*. Singapore: Marican and Sons, 1962. An enlarged version of a previous long journal article.

❧ 3 ❧

Malaya and Singapore
after 1945

Malaya — Problems of a Plural Society

Until the Japanese occupation British rule had largely prevented open expressions of racial tensions and antagonisms. In the process of government the élites, or near-élites, of each racial group dealt with the British rather than directly with each other. This tendency was accentuated by the different forms of government for different parts of Malaya — Straits Settlements, Federated, and Unfederated States — which only the British were in a position to coordinate. There were no elections and no political mass movements. Malaya was an extreme example of a plural society.[1] Its ethnic groups were also divided, largely along the same lines of cleavage, by religion and by language. They also had specialized roles in the productive process. Rupert Emerson stated the position before independence in a striking way. "Divided from each other in almost every respect, the peoples of Malaya have in common essentially only the fact that they live in the same country."[2]

Before the war the existence of a plural society caused the mechanics of government to be somewhat complicated; for instance, the existence of large numbers of unassimilated Chinese made it necessary to set up a special "Chinese Protectorate." But it also made the *political* aspects of British rule simpler. It was taken as axiomatic that there could be no self-government in such a society. The government

[1] J. S. Furnivall, *Colonial Policy and Practice* (Cambridge: Cambridge University Press, 1948), p. 304.
[2] In the foreword to F. H. H. King, *The New Malayan Nation* (New York: Institute of Pacific Relations, 1957), p. v.

could not represent "the people," because there were no "people."[3]
Even in 1945 "the development of nationalism in Malaya seemed
twenty-five years behind the rest of Southeast Asia."[4]

It would be incorrect to say that the British pursued a policy of
"divide and rule."[5] They did not need to divide; the divisions were
already there. Nor were they committed to opposition to one of the
races in Malaya (as the Japanese were committed to being anti-
Chinese during their occupation). They tried to hold a balance between the races, at the same time having a sentimental attachment
to the Malays as the "original" inhabitants. The British failure lay
rather in not perceiving that colonial regimes are by their nature
transient, and in failing to foresee the consequences of large-scale
immigration. With hindsight we can see that the British should either
have placed more restrictions on immigration, or should have done
something during the "no politics" period between the wars to help
to build up a political system for a plural society.[6]

In creating a self-governing state from a colonial plural society the
problem presented by the Chinese was of an infinitely more complex
order than that of the Indians. The number of Indians in Malaya
was relatively smaller, and the concern with the politics of India of
those who stayed was not of major importance. The only exception
was the interest shown by some Indians during the occupation in the
Japanese proposals to liberate India. When India won independence
in 1947, her government encouraged Indians who had become permanent residents in other countries to be good citizens of these
countries. But, with the Chinese, the fear was that the Western impact
had produced two nations in one country, Malaya, one of which was
merely an extension of the Chinese nation in China itself. This fear
was accentuated by the overseas influence of the nationalist movement in China, which was expressed in the founding of the Kuomintang in 1912. When this nationalist movement penetrated to
Malaya, it did not specifically aim at its annexation as a nineteenth
province of China.[7] But after the Kuomintang (KMT) became the
Chinese Government it relied on the Overseas Chinese for money,
especially after the start of the Sino-Japanese War. It also worked

[3] Furnivall, p. 489.

[4] John Kerry King, *Southeast Asia in Perspective* (New York: The Macmillan Company, 1956), p. 43.

[5] Cf. R. S. Milne, "Politics and Government," in *Malaysia: a Survey*,
Wang Gungwu, ed. (New York: Praeger, 1964), p. 328.

[6] T. H. Silcock, "Forces for Unity in Malaya," *International Affairs*,
XXV, No. 4 (1949), 460.

[7] Png Poh Seng, "The Kuomintang in Malaya, 1912–1941," *Journal of
Southeast Asian History*, II, No. 1 (1961), 15.

hard to keep the Overseas Chinese patriotic towards China, claiming that all Chinese overseas were citizens of China, even if they had been born overseas. The British were naturally suspicious of such a policy, and banned the KMT in Malaya in 1930, although the ban was modified shortly afterwards. It was only after the Japanese invasion of Malaya, when China and Britain became allies, that KMT activities in Malaya ceased to be a source of friction between the two countries. The Chinese Communist Party worked to some extent through the KMT, but it also concentrated on certain Middle School students and trade unionists. Anti-Japanese guerrilla activities were largely conducted by Chinese Communists, who formed the nucleus of the Malayan People's Anti-Japanese Army (MPAJA) with some British assistance.

When the Japanese surrendered, detachments of the MPAJA were in effective control of some parts of the country, and it took some time to disarm them. Incidents and fighting took place in several states, in which racial resentments sharpened during the occupation were given free rein.

The nature of Malay nationalism is more elusive than that of Chinese nationalism in Malaya. Malay nationalism was not primarily an "extension" of anything else. But to what degree was it self-generated, to what extent a blending of native and external elements? Malay nationalism was certainly partly inspired from abroad. In one sense it took the form of pan-Islamic loyalty to the Caliph of Turkey, head of the Sunni religious sect, before the Caliphate was ended by Ataturk in 1924. It was also affected through the small, but influential, number of Malays who went to study in Cairo and by nationalist movements in Indonesia. In its first, or religious, stage Malay nationalism was expressed through an increasing number of clubs and religious schools and in a growth of Islamic literature. However, it was not until later that the religious stage was followed by an economic and social stage and, from about 1937, by a political stage.[8]

The key to understanding the nature of Malay nationalism is that whatever external influences existed could find expression only through the existing Malay social structure. Before the war this was overwhelmingly feudal and conservative. In Indonesia a new élite developed earlier, which was middle-class and Western-educated.[9] But in Malaya, in spite of the influence of a few who had been Arabic-educated, Malay leadership was largely confined to the English-educated, and primarily to those of royal blood who had attended the

[8] Radin Soenarno, "Malay Nationalism, 1900–1945," *Journal of Southeast Asian History,* I, No. 1 (1960), 17.

[9] *Ibid.,* 28.

élite Malay College at Kuala Kangsar. The presence of large numbers of Chinese and Indians and the British policy of "protecting" the Malays had prevented the growth of an economic middle class (as in the Dutch East Indies) which might have headed a substantial radical nationalist movement. In some of the states towards the end of the nineteenth century a professional religious hierarchy was built up with British support. This became identified with rural-centered Islam and the traditional ruling class, an alliance of traditional forces that was unbreakable.[10] Consequently an intellectual nationalist Malay might have no love for the old feudal system, but might still be unwilling to see it swept away if any step towards constitutional reform were to give political power to non-Malay groups. A few Malay nationalists, such as Inche[11] Ahmad Boestamam, Inche Ibrahim bin Yaacob and Dr. Burhanuddin, felt differently and rejected the existing social order, working through such organizations as KMM, KRIS and, after the war, the Malay Nationalist Party (MNP). But their numbers were small. In general, when exposed to the shock of change, or proposed change, the Malays instinctively turned towards their traditional leaders.

Malayan Union

This tendency was well illustrated soon after the war ended. When the British took over again in Malaya they proposed, and set up, a new type of government, Malayan Union, to include all the Malayan peninsula except Singapore.[12] The exclusion of Singapore was economically unjustified; union with Malaya could have been reconciled even with the retention of its large entrepôt trade, as was attempted inside Malaysia, 1963–1965. However, Malaya and Singapore continued to use the same currency and maintained close commercial and

[10] W. Roff, "Kaum-Muda-Kaum Tua: Innovation and Reaction among the Malays, 1900–1941," in *Papers on Malayan History*, K. G. Tregonning, ed. (Singapore: Journal of Southeast Asian History, 1962), pp. 187–188.

[11] "Inche" (Sometimes "Enche" or "Che") is the equivalent of "Mr." "Tuan" is used instead of Inche before the name "Syed" ("Sayid"), a name borne by descendants of the Prophet, Muhammad, and before the title, "Haji," a title given to one who has made the pilgrimage to Mecca. "Dato" is a title conferred by a state or by the Head of State, corresponding roughly to a British knighthood. It is not hereditary. "Tun" is a non-hereditary title which can be conferred only by the Head of State, and ranks higher than Dato.

In 1966 it was announced that in the future the federal title, Dato, would be changed to "Tan Sri" to distinguish it from the title of the same name conferred by a state.

[12] *Malayan Union and Singapore* (Cmd. 6724) (London: H.M.S.O., 1946).

banking links. Politically, the separation of Singapore may have been intended to please the Malays by leaving out an area with a population which was over three-quarters Chinese. The British may also have wished to safeguard their Singapore naval base from objections by a future government of an independent Malaya. But there was no great controversy over the exclusion of Singapore. The provisions which excited real opposition were those relating to the new Union of Malaya. They embodied a move towards direct rule by the British, compared with the prewar system which was largely indirect; they also improved the position of the non-Malays politically. The Malay Rulers were to lose their sovereignty to the British Crown, which would be represented in Malaya by a British governor. They would retain their thrones, and their personal residences and allowances, but the chief function of each Ruler would be merely to preside over an Advisory Malay Council, dealing mainly with laws on the Muslim religion.[13] The citizenship proposals provided that citizenship could be acquired by having been born locally (in Malaya or Singapore) or having resided locally for a certain period of time. Application for citizenship could be made after a shorter period, if an oath of allegiance were taken. The provisions were to be the same for Chinese, Indians, and others as they were for Malays.[14] In any future system of democratic elections this would increase the voting power of non-Malays compared with the Malays. Non-Malays would also be given access to some branches of the civil service which had not been open to them previously. These provisions struck at the privileged position of the Malays, as opposed to the other races, at a time when racial feelings had been intensified by the occupation. Also, as has been remarked already, in any situation of racial stress the Malays looked towards their own feudal élite. But, by the Malayan Union proposals, the highest members of this élite, in the person of the Rulers, were to be downgraded along with the mass of the Malays. Insult was added to injury by the methods the British used to have the proposals accepted by the Rulers. A special representative, Sir Harold Mac-Michael,[15] was sent out to get a "shotgun" signature, consenting to the Malayan Union proposals, from each Ruler in turn. The shotgun

[13] On the Rulers' objections, see Max Seitelman, "Political Thought in Malaya," *Far Eastern Survey,* XVI, No. 11 (1947), 128.

[14] The British Secretary of State spoke of "the need to promote the sense of unity and common citizenship which will develop the country's strength and capacity in due course for self-government within the British Commonwealth." (*House of Commons Debates,* Vol. 414, Col. 255, October 10, 1945.)

[15] *Report on a Mission to Malaya* by Sir Harold MacMichael (Kuala Lumpur: Malayan Union Government Press, 1946).

consisted in the representative's power to recommend the deposition of a Ruler, if his conduct had been unsatisfactory during the Japanese occupation. The Rulers signed, but a series of explosions followed in both London and Malaya. The London explosions consisted of letters to *The Times,* written by the "old Malaya hands," in retirement, the British administrators whose names summarized the history of British rule in Malaya over the previous seventy years, including Swettenham, Maxwell, Winstedt, and Clementi. The detonations in Malaya were more surprising. The Japanese occupation had shown that the British were not omnipotent. The Malays were shaken out of their political apathy and their state particularism. The intensity of feeling was shown by the fact that even Malay women took part in demonstrations of protest. Opposition was at first concentrated in the Peninsular Malay Movement of Johore, which after some maneuvering become a national body, the United Malays' National Organization (UMNO), in May, 1946. Both were organized by Dato Onn bin Ja'afar, a civil servant who became Chief Minister of Johore.[16] UMNO used its influence on the Rulers, and eventually they too protested, by refusing to attend the installation ceremony of the first Governor of the Malayan Union. The British had gravely underestimated the opposition to their plan to drop the fiction of indirect rule and to simplify government in Malaya.

Non-Malays were mostly apathetic about the scheme, but some organizations, like the left-wing Malayan Democratic Union (MDU), objected that non-Malays should have been consulted before the proposals were introduced.

The Federation Agreement, 1948

The weight of the Malay protests persuaded the British that they had moved too far and too fast in attempting to dismantle and refashion the old apparatus of government. After all, the existing traditional structure, depending on the Rulers, District Officers and the headmen, was basically a *Malay* structure. If the position of the Malays were downgraded too drastically, an entirely new structure would need to be devised. At the same time the British did not give up two of their original objectives, the creation of an effective central government and some form of citizenship for which non-Malays as well as Malays could qualify.[17] But there were significant differences in the new approach. Provisions were made for consultation of inter-

---

[16] Ishak bin Tadin, "Dato Onn, 1946–1951," *Journal of Southeast Asian History,* I, No. 1, 65–68.

[17] Great Britain, Colonial Office, *Federation of Malaya: Summary of Revised Constitutional Proposals* (Cmd. 7171) London: H.M.S.O., 1947), p. 2.

ests through a Working Committee consisting of representatives of the government, the Rulers and UMNO, and a Consultative Committee, on which non-Malay communities were represented, to which the Working Committee's proposals were submitted. Also, no direct attack was made on the sovereignty of the Rulers. The Malayan Union scheme, which removed their sovereignty, lasted only two years, and the new "Federation of Malaya" came into existence in 1948, created by the joint action of the British King and the nine Rulers.

By the Federation of Malaya Agreement,[18] the central government consisted of a British High Commissioner, an Executive Council, and a Legislative Council. The High Commissioner had the delicate task of safeguarding both "the special position of the Malays" and also "the legitimate interests of other communities."[19] The Legislative Council had official members and a larger number of unofficial members, to be nominated by the High Commissioner. It was intended that, in time, some of the latter would be elected. At state level there was a corresponding structure consisting of the Ruler, an executive council and a legislative body, the Council of State, with both official and unofficial members. Some important functions, such as land and education, were allocated to the states. But, in the tradition of indirect rule, the Rulers undertook to accept the advice of the High Commissioner except in matters relating to the Muslim religion or the custom of the Malays.[20] The federal Legislative Council could also pass laws on subjects within the field of state functions, for the purpose of ensuring uniformity between states. And, financially, the bulk of state revenue came not from taxes but from grants-in-aid voted by the Legislative Council. Additional provisions for central coordination were the High Commissioner's responsibility for "the safeguarding of the financial stability and credit of the Federal Government,"[21] and the existence of British civil servants, transferable from federal to state employment.[22] Not only was government highly centralized; it was also *colonial* government, in the last resort directed by the High Commissioner who was responsible to the Colonial Office in London.

Other features of the scheme of government from 1948 on, including provision for a Conference of Rulers, may be found in the Federation Agreement. The citizenship provisions were complex, but

[18] (Kuala Lumpur: Government Press, 1948).
[19] Federation of Malaya Agreement, para. 19(d).
[20] *Ibid.*, paras. 5 and 8.
[21] *Ibid.*, para. 19(c).
[22] T. H. Silcock, *The Commonwealth Economy in Southeast Asia* (Durham: Duke University Press, 1959), pp. 66–67.

in effect were decidedly stricter for non-Malays than the Malayan Union proposals. Some of them applied almost exclusively to Malays (including persons who had come from Indonesia): for instance those who were subjects of the Ruler of any state. Some provisions covered British subjects (including Chinese and Indians), who had been born in Penang or Malacca and who had resided in the Federation for fifteen years. Most Chinese and Indians could qualify only on their own birth in the Federation and their father's (in some cases, parents') birth and length of residence in the Federation; their own birth there combined with their length of residence; their length of residence in the Federation. In the last case citizenship was not automatic, but could be acquired by application, if the applicant was of good character, declared his intention of residing permanently in the Federation, and had an "adequate knowledge" of Malay or English. These requirements were not easily met. In 1949 it was estimated that only about 375,000 of the Chinese residents in the Federation (just under a fifth) had become federal citizens.

The Emergency

The year 1948 marked a new stage in constitutional development. Guerrilla fighting broke out, which had profound economic, social, and political implications. During the occupation the Malayan Communist Party had been active in the MPAJA, and it was only with difficulty that the MPAJA was disbanded at the end of 1945. But in 1948 the Communists decided to resort to armed violence, thus creating "the Emergency," which lasted for twelve years and cost directly about 11,000 lives. Among the reasons which induced the Communists to resort to "direct action" was their failure to penetrate and control the trade unions by peaceful means. They had attempted this kind of penetration immediately after the war, but the government had reacted by amending the Trade Union Ordinance, among other things disqualifying from office in the unions any person who had not been employed for at least three years in the industry concerned or who had been convicted of any serious crime, such as extortion. Other reasons for the choice of direct action may have been the improvement in the rice supply since the end of the war and the influence of constitutional reform in attracting moderate opinion to support the government.[23]

The Emergency set the government a difficult problem. The number of active rebels was under 10,000, but their guerrilla tactics enabled them to kill and destroy during raids and then to disappear

[23] The British Minister of State for Colonial Affairs (*House of Lords Debates,* Vol. 159, Col. 334, November 10, 1948).

into the jungle. Although the existing troops and police in Malaya were not trained to meet such tactics, the rebellion failed for a number of reasons. Malaya had no border with a Communist state through which reinforcements could be sent, although comparative immunity existed on the Thai border, because of lack of adequate concerted anti-Communist efforts between Malaya and Thailand. In the later stages the Communists became desperate and indiscriminate in their efforts and resorted to terrorism, which, in the long run, turned some of the population against them. Moreover, the Communists were overwhelmingly *Chinese*. The MCP claimed that "the Malayan revolution is, in its present stage, under the leadership of the proletariat, whose base is the combined strength of the workers and peasants: this is an anti-Imperialist anti-feudalistic national revolution, carried out by the people of various races and classes. It has a national character because it opposes the rule of alien imperialism, demands the right of self-determination and the realization of national liberation."[24] But, racially, this claim was totally inaccurate. If a hard core of rebels was attracted to communism largely because it was *Chinese* communism, for precisely the same reason Malays and Indians were repelled by it.

The rebels' defeat also resulted from a number of actions by the government, some of them military, such as the employment of more and better-trained troops, others social and political, such as measures to improve relations between the various ethnic groups and to achieve independence. The most striking single operation was the establishment of "New Villages," largely inhabited by Chinese. The rebels had been obtaining food from Chinese "squatters," many of whom had settled on the land when tin mines and other enterprises had closed down during the war. If the squatters were left where they were, mainly on the jungle fringes, it would be impossible to prevent them from being coerced by the rebels into supplying food. The solution chosen was the gigantic operation of moving about half a million people, including about a fifth of the entire Chinese population, to over 550 "New Villages." Settlement in the villages was concentrated, which made it easier to defend them, although it made farming operations more difficult for the inhabitants.

The main impact of the Emergency was over by about 1955, although it was not formally declared to have ended until 1960. However, later events showed that the Communists, although defeated in battle, had not been eliminated.

[24] Gene Z. Hanrahan, *The Communist Struggle in Malaya* (New York: Institute of Pacific Relations, 1954), p. 101, quoting a Communist publication with the English title, *Strategic Problems of the Malayan Revolutionary War*.

Towards Independence

It might be thought that the Emergency would have put back the attainment of independence for Malaya. But in fact the Malayans used the Emergency as an argument in favor of independence, maintaining that the Communist charge that the rebels were fighting against "imperialism" would lose its force if the government were Malayan and not British. An essential condition of independence, however, was the existence of a political party to whom the British could hand over the government on independence. In view of the racial composition of Malaya it was necessary that this party should represent at least the two major races.

At the beginning of the Emergency in 1948 there was a well-established party, the UMNO; it was entirely a Malay party. Just as the Malayan Union proposals had stimulated the formation of UMNO, so the proposed Federation of Malaya Agreement aroused organized opposition. A mixed bag of organizations joined to fight the Agreement, which they viewed as representing primarily the interests of the British and the Rulers. The new grouping included the left-wing, pro-Indonesian Malay Nationalist Party (MNP),[25] the Malayan Democratic Union (Singapore intellectuals), the Chinese Associated Chambers of Commerce, a number of Communist organizations, and the Malayan Indian Congress (MIC). This alliance called itself the All-Malaya Council of Joint Action (AMCJA). The AMCJA was too heterogeneous to last for long as a single front. A purely Malay grouping, called PUTERA after its initials in Malay, standing for "Central Force of the Malay people," was then formed; based on the MNP it worked together with the AMCJA and the Chinese Associated Chambers of Commerce to put forward alternative constitutional proposals.[26] However, when the Federation of Malaya Constitution came into force in 1948, the AMCJA broke up. When the Emergency was announced some of the member organizations of AMCJA and PUTERA were outlawed. The MDU dissolved, and in 1950 the MNP was banned.

The eventual major partner of UMNO, the Malayan Chinese Association (MCA), was formed in February, 1949. Its president was a respected Straits Chinese, Tan Cheng Lock, who had also headed the short-lived AMCJA. The MCA had several different roles. Immediately, it could provide a rival focus for Chinese loyalties apart

[25] See Burhanuddin Al Helmy, "Towards Tanah Melayu Merdeka," *Merdeka Convention, Papers and Documents* (London, 1957).

[26] Ian Morrison, "Aspects of the Racial Problem in Malaya," *Pacific Affairs*, XXII, No. 3 (1949), 245–246.

from the Communists. Socially, it raised funds to help with the resettlement of the Chinese squatters. Looking beyond the immediate future, it was a respectable body which could see to it that Chinese interests were fully taken into account in any future constitutional changes.

The political activities of the MCA were encouraged by the British, who also attempted to bring the leaders of the main communities together in the "Communities Liaison Committee" (CLC). Dato Onn, the president of UMNO, who had been active in the CLC, tried to go even further. At first he tried to work for the inclusion of non-Malays as members of UMNO,[27] but, on encountering resistance, in 1951 he resigned the presidency of UMNO and founded the Independence of Malay Party (IMP). This body was supported by an impressive number of organizations and individuals, including leaders of the MCA, members of the Communities Liaison Committee, the Malayan Indian Congress and several labor and trade union groups. It was also smiled upon by the British. In spite of the important role Dato Onn had played in founding UMNO, it survived his departure and chose as its new president, Tengku [Prince] Abdul Rahman, brother of the Sultan of Kedah. Although Tan Cheng Lock joined IMP, the bulk of the MCA remained indifferent. The municipal elections held in Kuala Lumpur in 1952 saw the decisive defeat of the IMP. The UMNO and the MCA formed a purely local *ad hoc* alliance against the IMP, and defeated it by nine seats to two. This arrangement was continued in later local elections, resulting in further victories for the Alliance. Confident prophecies were made that this intercommunal alliance would not last, but it did. A national Alliance organization was set up in 1953. Communal divisions in Malaya were so deep that it was impossible to form successfully a single non-communal *party;* but they were not too deep to destroy an *alliance* of communal parties. In the next few years the wheel turned full circle. Dato Onn had abandoned the declining IMP and had founded the, in effect, Malay-communal Party Negara. On the other hand, the Alliance, which by 1954 included the UMNO, the MCA, and the MIC, showed at a number of local elections that it had enough support from all the different communities to qualify as the prospective government when the British handed over power. It also benefited from the fact that Negara, which was strong in the Legislative and Executive Councils, became identified with the British-controlled government.

Steps had already been taken towards giving Malayans more political responsibility when the "Member" system was introduced in the

27 Ishak bin Tadin, 81 ff.

Legislative Council in 1951. This "quasi-ministerial" system had made nominated members of the Council responsible for various departments and functions of government, such as education and health and spokesmen for them in the Legislative Council. In the following year all these members were included in the Executive Council. This was a usual transitional stage towards independence from British rule, a rehearsal, as it were, for building up an executive which would be responsible for the legislature. Agitation by the Alliance[28] forced the British to make the big concession that the fifty-two members of the Legislative Council elected in 1955 should form a *majority* of the Council (52 out of 98); the nonelected members, apart from the Speaker, consisted of three ex-officio members (the Chief Secretary, the Attorney-General and the Financial Secretary), the nine Mentri Besar (Chief Ministers) of the Malay States and one representative from each of the two Settlements, and thirty-two appointed members.[29] It was unprecedented for a British territory to advance directly from a wholly nominated Legislative Council to one with an elected majority.[30]

At the first general elections, 1955, the Alliance won 51 out of the 52 seats.[31] Tengku Abdul Rahman, who had led the party, was appointed Chief Minister and formed a Cabinet.

The 1957 Constitution

The Alliance victory was followed by a Constitutional Conference, held in London early in 1956 and attended by representatives of the Rulers and the Alliance. It was decided there that Malaya should become fully self-governing and independent within the Commonwealth by August, 1957, if possible, and that a Constitutional Commission should be appointed to draw up a draft constitution.[32] The Constitutional Commission consisted of Lord Reid, an English judge, as chairman and one member each from Britain, Australia, India, and

[28] H. Miller, *Prince and Premier* (London: Harrap, 1959), pp. 147–161.

[29] Twenty-two for "scheduled interests" (commerce, planting, mining, trade unions, etc.), three for racial minorities, seven nominated. [*Report of the Federation of Malaya Constitutional Commission* (Kuala Lumpur: Government Printer, 1957), paras. 30 and 32.]

[30] F. G. Carnell, "Constitutional Reform and Elections in Malaya," *Pacific Affairs*, XXXVII, No. 3 (1954), 228–229.

[31] See pp. 96–97.

[32] The transitional arrangements until independence are given in L. A. Mills, *Malaya: A Political and Economic Appraisal* (Minneapolis: University of Minnesota Press, 1958), pp. 98 ff. British willingness to grant independence may have been influenced by the fact that Malaya, whose exports were substantial earners of United States dollars, intended to stay inside the British Commonwealth and the sterling area.

Pakistan. It published its *Report* in 1957. Organizations and individuals, 131 in all, submitted memoranda to the Commission. But the submissions of the Alliance had exceptional importance in view of its prospective role as the future government, compared with, say, the representations made by the World Fellowship of Buddhists, Selangor, or the Central Electricity Board. Indeed, the Commission, in its *Report*[33] indicated its particular indebtedness to the Alliance for their memorandum and their verbal explanations of it. The Alliance, in particular the UMNO and the MCA, had hammered out proposals which represented, in effect, a "bargain" over the relative constitutional position of the two major races.[34] Only one single memorandum was submitted to the Constitutional Commission by the Alliance, in spite of the strains and stresses which inevitably existed between its component parts.

However, the Constitutional Commission's proposals were not accepted in their entirety. Changes were made after consultations between the British government, the Rulers, and the Alliance. In effect, concessions were made to Alliance, and in particular to UMNO, views.[35]

Independence (*merdeka*) was proclaimed on August 31, 1957. The Constitution which came into force on that date generally resembles that of Britain or of India. It is "parliamentary," as opposed to presidential, in that the Ministers, or Cabinet, sit in the legislature and are responsible to it. In fact, although this is not laid down in the Constitution, the Ministers belong to a single political party, the party which has won a majority of the seats in the lower house of the legislature. Therefore normally any powers conferred on "Parliament" by the Constitution are in fact exercised by the majority party through its control of a parliamentary majority. Like Britain and India there is a nonpolitical Head of State (Yang di-Pertuan Agong), who on most subjects acts on the advice of his Ministers; a legislature composed of two houses, one of them directly elected; a neutral civil service; an independent judiciary.[36] Unlike Britain, but

[33] (Kuala Lumpur: Government Press, 1957), para. 9.

[34] The process is described in T. H. Tan, "The Struggle of the Alliance for the Independence of the Federation of Malaya," *Merdeka Convention, Papers and Documents.*

[35] The main alterations made in the Constitutional Commission's recommendations are indicated in *Federation of Malaya Constitutional Proposals* (Kuala Lumpur: Government Press, 1957). For the main debate on the Constitution, see *Legislative Council Debates* (Second Session) October, 1956–August, 1957, July 10 and 11, 1957, cols. 2838–3030.

[36] Cf. the features of the Constitution as stated in the Yang di-Pertuan Agong's speech on the opening of Parliament, *Straits Times,* September 12, 1959.

like India, the Constitution is *federal*. In practice, however, the powers of the central government are considerable compared with those of the states. The decision to form a federation was almost certainly dictated by the existence of the Rulers and by the desire to avoid a repetition of protests similar to those voiced against the Malayan Union Scheme of 1946. A number of bodies, such as the National Land Council, are provided for in the Constitution with the object of ensuring coordination between the federal government and state governments.

The Constitution may be amended, with some exceptions, by the approval of at least two-thirds of the total number of members of each house.[37] The courts are guardians of the Constitution, as in the United States. If the courts declare that a law is contrary to a provision of the Constitution, that law is invalidated, in spite of its having been passed by the federal parliament or by a state legislature.

There are some special features of the Constitution which are not found in other countries. Some of these, such as the Conference of Rulers and the method of choosing the Head of State, result from the need to fit the Rulers into the framework of constitutional democratic government. But the features of most interest are those which embody the "bargain" between the UMNO and MCA, and which set out the political framework, or rules, within which the racial groups are to operate. One broad assessment of the situation was that the price to be paid by non-Malays for full participation in the political activities of the Federation was acceptance of certain forms associated with Malay traditions.[38] This is certainly a part of the arrangement. The functions assigned to the Rulers, the choice of Islam as the state religion,[39] the decision that from 1967 the national language, Malay, should be the sole official language[40] were part of "the bargain." In exchange, non-Malays benefited from further relaxation in citizenship provisions, which had already been altered in favor of non-Malays in 1952. Citizenship by operation of law was now extended to any person born in the Federation after August 31, 1957 (Independence Day).[41] This recognized at last the claim of the Chinese to be citizens

[37] Article 159(1) and (3).

[38] F. H. H. King, *The New Malayan Nation*, p. 13.

[39] The Constitutional Commission had recommended that there should not be a state religion (*Proposals*, para. 169). In practice, the provision does not yet seem to have been of major importance.

[40] Unless Parliament provided that English could continue to be used after 1967 [*Constitution*, Article, 152(2)].

[41] By the Constitution (Amendment) Act 1962 a restriction was imposed in that at least one parent must have been ordinarily resident in the Federation at the time of the child's birth.

by virtue of *jus soli*, not retrospectively but only for those born after Independence Day. It was also extended, with qualifications, to any person whose father was a citizen at the time of his birth. Provisions for acquiring citizenship by other means were also made easier; for example, the requirement that an applicant should know Malay was waived for a period of one year after the date of independence.[42] These measures would increase the voting strength, and therefore the political power, of the Chinese. An important feature of the "bargain" was not explicitly stated in the Constitution. The Chinese were to continue to play their dominant role in business, free from the hindrances or persecution to which they had been subjected in some other Southeast Asian countries.

In addition, however, the Constitution made provision for the "special position of the Malays." Article 153 states that it "shall be the responsibility of the Yang di-Pertuan Agong to safeguard the special position of the Malays and the legitimate interests of other communities. . . ." The Yang di-Pertuan Agong (acting in practice on the advice of the government) may therefore reserve for Malays such proportion as he may think reasonable of (a) positions in the public service of the Federation; (b) scholarships, exhibitions and other similar educational or training privileges or special facilities given or accorded by the federal government; and (c) permits or licenses required by federal law for the operation of any trade or business. Elsewhere in the Constitution (Article 89) there is provision to preserve, as a Malay reservation, land which before independence was a Malay reservation in accordance with state law. Such a law can now only be amended by a special and difficult process.

Article 153 is phrased in very broad terms. But it has actually been used only to *continue* policies which were already in force before independence, for instance, as regards admission into some branches of public service and for particular types of licenses, such as those for road haulage and hired passenger vehicles.[43]

At first sight the existence of Article 153 appears to be strange. Why was it necessary to make constitutional provision to protect the Malays when they were the largest racial group in Malaya and constituted a majority of the electors? The answer is not contained in

[42] The provisions and later changes are summarized in J. M. Gullick, *Malaysia* (London: Benn, 1963), Appx. 1, and H. E. Groves, *The Constitution of Malaysia* (Singapore: Malaysia Publications, 1964), ch. XI. For the complications of citizenship affecting Singapore during the negotiations on Malaysia see Chapter 3, below. On deprivation of federal citizenship see Groves, pp. 173–177.

[43] *Report of the Federation of Malaya Constitutional Commission*, paras. 163 ff.

the Constitution. At the root of Article 153 is the problem of achieving an approximate short-run "balance of power" between the races. The Malays have not yet acquired any appreciable degree of *economic* power in Malaya. Only the least developed, or "peasant" sector of the rural economy is primarily Malay. At the same time relaxation of citizenship provisions is increasing the voting strength and political power of non-Malays. It may be argued, therefore, that until Malay economic power is substantially greater, the bulk of the Malays will not be sufficiently confident that a genuine long-term balance of power would exist between the races if the protection of Article 153 were to be removed. According to this approach, the article "is aimed to do no more than correct the imbalance in the living conditions and lives of the people in this country. . . ."[44]

Probably the most contentious aspect of the provisions to safeguard the special position of the Malays is their *duration*. The Constitutional Commission recommended that the matter be reviewed after fifteen years,[45] but the Constitution itself did not include this proposal. Some members of political parties with a high proportion of non-Malays, have attacked Article 153 as giving an unfair, because possibly permanent, advantage to the Malays. They would have preferred this subject not to have been included in the Constitution at all, or, failing this, that a time limit should have been specified.

Two objections to Article 153 may be mentioned. One is that, since there are many poor Chinese and Indians as well as many poor Malays, any constitutional protection which is given should be on the ground of economic weakness rather than racial origin.[46] This argument is economically sound, but completely ignores the racial basis of politics in Malaya and the circumstances in which the Constitution was drawn up. The second objection is that the protection given by Article 153 is inadequate and liable to abuse, for example by Malays taking up licenses which they do not use themselves but hand over to non-Malays in exchange for money.[47] This objection is well taken in emphasizing that in the long run the economic position of the Malays will be substantially improved, not by provisions such as those in Article 153, but rather by the progress of the rural development plan

[44] Tengku Abdul Rahman, *Dewan Ra'ayat Debates,* IV, No. 2, April 28, 1962, col. 449, and V, No. 3, May 28, 1963, cols. 357–362.

[45] *Report,* para. 167.

[46] S. M. Huang-Thio, "Constitutional Discrimination under the Malaysian Constitution," *Malaya Law Review,* VI, No. 1 (1964), 12–13. See also Tan Phock Kin (Socialist Front), who said he would support Malay privileges if they would eliminate poverty, but not if they would make rich Malays richer, *Dewan Ra'ayat Debates,* IV, No. 2, April 28, 1962, col. 449.

[47] Huang-Thio, 14–15.

and by increasing the supply of Malay entrepreneurs.[48] But these are *long-run* measures, and in the interim, to satisfy the Malays that a fair balance between the races does exist, something along the lines of the provisions of Article 153 seems to be necessary. This brings the argument back to the contentious point about the duration of these provisions.

It is worth noting that Article 153 has also in fact been invoked to safeguard the legitimate rights of *non-Malays*. The Tengku referred to it before the fifteenth assembly of UMNO in defending his intervention when the governments of Perak and Penang wanted to withdraw *padi* (rice) dealers' licenses from non-Malays in order to give them to Malay cooperative societies.[49]

To say that a rough "balance" was achieved between the conflicting claims of the various communities is not to claim that equality has been achieved in every sphere. It is easy to point to apparent inequities, which affect *some* communities in *some* respects. But when the whole scene is surveyed, in its social, economic, and political aspects, it becomes clear that a kind of short-term rough justice between the claims of the communities has in fact been attained. The problem of keeping a racial balance was accentuated by the new elements introduced when Malaysia was formed.

Fundamental Liberties

The Constitution states that every citizen has the right to certain freedoms, notably those of speech and expression, of peaceable assembly, of forming associations [Article 10(1)]. But immediately, in the same Article, there is the qualification that Parliament may impose restrictions on these rights for a number of reasons, including grounds of security or public order. Part XI of the Constitution spells out more fully the circumstances in which Parliament may act in this way. The act imposing restrictions must recite that "action has been taken or threatened by any substantial body of persons, whether inside or outside the Federation" to do a number of things, including exciting disaffection against the Yang di-Pertuan Agong or the government, or promoting feelings of ill will and hostility between different races or other classes of the population likely to cause violence [Article 149(1)]. Under this part of the Constitution laws or ordinances may be passed which provide for "preventive detention," that is, imprisonment without trial, a restriction on another article of the Constitution which states that no person shall be deprived of his life or personal liberty save in accordance with law [Article 5(1)]. There

[48] See Chapter 13, pp. 231–234.
[49] *Straits Times,* August 24, 1962.

is no public appeal against such detention, but there is some safeguard in that a person detained must be informed of the grounds for detention, allowed to make representations against it and to have these representations heard by a three-man advisory board. If the person is a citizen, he may not be detained longer than three months, unless such an advisory board has considered any representations he has made and has made recommendations on them to the Head of State.[50] Restrictions on freedoms have been imposed by a number of acts and ordinances, notably the Internal Security Act (1960, amended 1962), the Sedition Ordinance (1948), the Public Order (Preservation) Ordinance (1958) and the Prevention of Crime Ordinance (1959).[51]

By Article 150 provision is made for a Proclamation of Emergency. Under it the executive may promulgate ordinances having the force of law, which may, however, be annulled by resolutions passed by both houses of Parliament. It is stated that none of the ordinances so made shall be invalid because of inconsistency with the Constitution's provisions on fundamental liberties. Some of the powers conferred in this Article are sweeping; for instance, the federal Parliament could legislate on nearly all matters which the Constitution allocates to the states, and elections could be suspended. In practice, although there was a State of Emergency in force until 1960 and again from September, 1964, onwards, few really drastic measures were taken, although local elections were suspended in 1965. However, emergency powers were once again invoked, in Sarawak, September, 1966, to justify the passing of a constitutional amendment which led to a change of government (p. 145, below).

Clearly the fundamental liberties provided for in the Constitution have been subject to severe limitations, expressly provided for in the Constitution itself. In any case, since independence the times have been abnormal, and there was hardly any interval between the end of the danger from internal Communist rebellion (1960) and the beginning of Confrontation by Indonesia (1963). It is to be hoped the government will be as swift in removing restrictions on fundamental liberties as it was in imposing them, now that Confrontation has officially ended.

[50] Article 151. In any action he takes, the Head of State must act on the advice of his ministers.

[51] Groves, chs. XII and XIII. Perhaps the most comprehensive restrictions are included in the Internal Security Act, passed after a Constitutional Amendment in 1960; its provisions replaced those of the Emergency Regulations Ordinance of 1948, temporarily kept alive by Article 163 of the Constitution.

Singapore, 1945–1963

When Singapore was separated from Malaya after World War II, it posed quite a different kind of political problem. Over three-quarters of the population was Chinese, and there was no traditional Malay framework of government on which to build the institutions for self-government. Indeed, from Britain's point of view, the practicability of self-government could not be taken for granted. The population had not yet reached one million, and even if political independence were to be achieved, Singapore and Malaya (its hinterland) were inevitably economically interdependent. It also became clear, as democracy was gradually introduced into Singapore, that extensions of the franchise had the effect of increasing the proportion of Chinese-educated voters, of whom some were Chinese chauvinists or extreme socialists or both. It truly became "impossible to gain control of the machinery of the government in Singapore without making some concession to Chinese ideology."[52] How in these circumstances could the British, who wished to retain the use of their Singapore naval and military base, consider granting complete independence? The problem was so complex that at one time or another the most ingenious and fantastic solutions were put forward — one local politician suggesting that Singapore should become the headquarters of the United Nations with a kind of "international enclave" status. The advance towards self-government, up to the final step of complete independence, was made in the usual British colonial way. An increasing proportion of the members of the Legislative Council were "unofficial" instead of official, and an increasing proportion of the unofficials were directly elected. Elected members, or "commissioners," were also introduced into the *municipal* government of the *city* of Singapore. The potential electorate for choosing the elected members of the Legislative Council was probably about a quarter of a million persons, mostly Chinese, who were British subjects, not alien immigrants. But at the first two elections (1948 and 1951) only a fraction of the electorate registered — about 20 per cent in the latter election. The vast majority of the Chinese, and in particular the Chinese-educated, voters had not yet registered, and this was reflected in the composition of the members elected to the Council, who were mostly moderates. In 1953 a Constitutional Commission (the Rendel Commission) was set up. It recommended a Legislative Assembly of thirty-two, of which twenty-five would be elected. The

[52] T. H. Silcock, "Singapore in Malaya," *Far Eastern Survey*, XXIX, No. 3 (1960), 35.

leader of the largest party in the Assembly would be Chief Minister, and he would nominate himself and five other members of the Assembly as Ministers on the executive "Council of Ministers." The British Governor could overrule the Assembly but these powers were to be used only in exceptional circumstances. To improve the voting turnout, registration for elections was to be compulsory.[53]

The new Constitution implementing these proposals came into force in 1955. The election which followed, in April, 1955, was not decisive. The most successful party, the Labour Front,[54] won ten seats but only just over a quarter of the vote. Its leader was David Marshall, a Singapore-born lawyer of Iraqi-Jewish extraction. As a lawyer, Mr. Marshall was particularly effective in defense, but he now devoted himself with enthusiasm to prosecuting British colonialism. Also prominent in the Labour Front was Lim Yew Hock, leader of a large trade union group, the Trade Union Congress. The moderate Progressive Party, which had previously been the largest party, won four seats, the Democrats, backed by the Chinese Chamber of Commerce, two. Among the other successful candidates were three from the People's Action Party (PAP). At the head of the PAP was a group of Straits Chinese and Indians, including some Communists or near-Communists, who had previously been imprisoned under Emergency Regulations. Its leader was Lee Kuan Yew, a Cambridge-educated lawyer of great intellectual ability, whose approach to politics was more scientific and calculating than Marshall's. The party had some trade union support and was also strongly organized in the Chinese Middle Schools.

The Labour Front formed a government, precariously, with the help of the small Malay Union Alliance (a coalition of UMNO and MCA) and some nominated and official members of the legislature. Its period of office, 1955–1959, was a confused period for Singapore in which three major struggles took place, sometimes simultaneously: the Labour Front against the British government; the PAP against the Labour Front; the Communists and fellow-travellers against the rest inside the PAP leadership.

In the first of these struggles Marshall failed to get the independence terms he wanted from the British. In view of Singapore's strategic importance and the uncertain prospects for stable government in the future, they were unwilling to hand over defense and internal security to the extent that Marshall desired. He resigned as

[53] *Report of the Constitutional Commission* (Singapore: Government Press, 1954), para. 10.

[54] For its origins see S. Rose, *Socialist Parties in Southern Asia* (London: Oxford University Press, 1959), pp. 208 ff.

Chief Minister in 1957, and his successor, Lim Yew Hock, reached an agreement with the British. An internal security council would be set up to deal with questions affecting the maintenance of public safety and public order. It would consist of three British members, plus three from Singapore and one from the newly independent Federation of Malaya. Two other important features of the new Constitution were the provision that "persons known to have been engaged in subversive activity should not be eligible for election to the first Legislative Assembly of the new state of Singapore" and that aliens who had lived in the colony for ten years could be registered as citizens if they took an oath of loyalty and gave up their allegiance to any foreign state. This provision added about 300,000 Chinese to the electoral rolls.

For many years the Communists had been active in the Chinese Middle Schools, both among teachers and "students" — who might be well over twenty years old and might have remained in school purely for the purpose of organizing Communist study groups.[55] The PAP supported this movement. At least among the younger Singapore Chinese-educated, it replaced the Chinese Chamber of Commerce as the acknowledged voice of social and political authority. Attempts were made by the government to increase financial support for, and also control over, the schools, but strikes and rioting occurred under the Marshall and Lim Yew Hock governments. Lim Yew Hock took tougher action against the rioters than Marshall, but this had the unfortunate consequence of alienating many Chinese-educated Chinese who thought that he was attacking Chinese education, as such. A bus strike was converted into a major political event by one of the PAP's chief trade union leaders, Lim Chin Siong. The PAP non-Communist leaders, on the other hand, appreciated the need to win the votes of the Chinese-educated away from the Communists. But, in order to do so, it was necessary to play the perilous game of working with the Communists. In August, 1957, at the Third Party Conference they were temporarily outmaneuvered when Communist elements took over control of the party executive. Shortly afterwards, however, when the Lim Yew Hock government arrested and detained the top Communists in the party, they managed to regain control.

At the 1959 election the PAP won an impressive majority in the Legislative Assembly (43 seats out of 51) over its right-wing rivals, the Singapore People's Alliance, the Liberal-Socialists and the UMNO-MCA.[56] For a time its success obscured the tensions between the

[55] Stanley Spector, "Students and Politics in Singapore," *Far Eastern Survey*, XXV, No. 5 (1956), 65–73.

[56] See p. 201, below.

Communist and the non-Communist leadership. But these tensions soon came to the surface. The non-Communist PAP leaders, before taking office as a government, were committed to obtaining the release from detention of the party's pro-Communist leaders; these were their own past rivals, and potential future rivals, for control of the PAP. An attempt was made to insulate the released detainees,[57] from the effective process of government by making them "Political Secretaries." But they remained politically, if not governmentally, active, particularly in the trade unions and among organizations of rural dwellers.

The non-Communist PAP leaders were shaken by the results of two successive by-elections in May and July 1961. The first resulted from the expulsion from the PAP of Ong Eng Guan. Ong had been mayor of Singapore before the City Council was abolished in 1959, and according to himself had originally been one of a "triumvirate" at the head of the party.[58] In the PAP government Ong was made a Minister, but his more important functions were soon taken away from him. After Ong's expulsion the question of his effectiveness as a Minister was overlaid by an exchange of personal attacks between him and the party leaders. Ong resigned his seat, Hong Lim, and fought it again at the subsequent by-election, partly on the issue of complete independence for Singapore as opposed to union with Malaya. The government was decisively defeated by 7,747 votes to 2,820. Most of Ong's electoral support was probably personal, based on his appeal to the largely Hokkien population in the constituency. But the substantial defeat was unexpected by the government, and raised general doubts whether the PAP was now the almost irresistible force that it had seemed to be immediately after it had won the 1959 election. Two other members of the Legislative Assembly joined Ong's new United People's Party (UPP). Soon after Hong Lim the Malaysia proposal alarmed the pro-Communists in the PAP, because in Malaysia the central government would necessarily have control of internal security. The prospect of a completely independent Singapore in which a future pro-Communist government would be free of any controls, except its own, over internal security, would vanish.[59] The pro-Communists therefore agitated for local control over internal security and the release of all political detainees. This agitation coin-

[57] For the statement signed by them on release see Lee Kuan Yew, *The Battle for Merger* (Singapore: Government Printing Office, 1961), Appx. 9.

[58] United People's Party, *Full Text of Memorandum submitted to British Labour MP's* (Singapore, May 18, 1963).

[59] On whether or not in 1961 the British would have tolerated a Barisan government, see Lee Kuan Yew, pp. 38–44.

cided with a second by-election in the Anson constituency, at which Marshall, now chairman of the Workers' Party, attempted to re-enter the Assembly. The PAP pro-Communists threw their weight behind Marshall, and he narrowly defeated the PAP candidate.

Shortly afterwards the pro-Communists split from the PAP and formed a new party, the Barisan Sosialis. Either from ideological conviction or because they feared that the PAP could no longer win the next general election, thirteen of the Legislative Assembly members left the party and joined the Barisan. The PAP now had a precarious majority of one in an assembly of fifty-one. It was only by the skillful use of the Malaysia issue that the PAP leadership avoided further fatal defections[60] and survived to win the Singapore Assembly elections in 1963.

SUGGESTED READINGS

Federation Malaya Official Year Book, 1962. Chapter XXII, "The Emergency." Kuala Lumpur: Government Press, 1962. A good factual account, reprinted, with some revisions, from the Year Book for 1961.

Hanrahan, Gene Z. *The Communist Struggle in Malaya.* New York: Institute of Pacific Relations, 1954. Well documented.

Hickling, R. H. *An Introduction to the Federal Constitution.* Kuala Lumpur: Government Information Services, 1960. A useful introduction.

King, John Kerry. "Malaya's Resettlement Problem," *Far Eastern Survey,* XXIII, No. 3 (1954), 33–40. Deals with the origins of the New Villages.

Lee Kuan Yew, *The Battle for Merger.* Singapore: Government Printing Office, 1961. The Singapore Prime Minister's account of his fight against communism and for merger with Malaya.

Mahajani, Usha. *The Role of Indian Minorities in Burma and Malaya.* New York: Institute of Pacific Relations, 1960.

[60] An additional PAP member joined the Barisan, and another died. However, the PAP won back one member of Ong Eng Guan's United People's Party, reducing its Assembly strength to himself and one other member. On nearly all issues affecting Malaysia the PAP could count on the votes of the Singapore Alliance members.

Miller, Harry. *Prince and Premier*. London: George G. Harrap and Sons, 1959. A biography of Tengku Abdul Rahman. The only adequate biography of any Malaysian political figure yet published.

Mills, Lennox A. *Malaya, a Political and Economic Appraisal*. Minneapolis: University of Minnesota Press, 1958. Good on economics and on the politics of Singapore in the mid-fifties.

Purcell, Victor. *Malaya, Communist or Free?* London: Victor Gollancz, 1953. A polemic with the British General Templer as chief target.

Pye, Lucian W. *Guerrilla Communism in Malaya*. Princeton: Princeton University Press, 1956. A psychological approach to communism and Communists in Malaya.

Report of the Federation of Malaya Constitutional Commission. Kuala Lumpur: Government Press, 1957. Sometimes known as the Reid Commission after its chairman. With some alterations the basis of the 1957 Constitution.

Robinson, John Bradstreet Perry. *Transformation in Malaya*. London: Secker and Warburg, 1955. Informative on resettlement and the New Villages.

Silcock, Thomas H., and Ungku Abdul Aziz. "Nationalism in Malaya," in *Asian Nationalism and the West*, William L. Holland, ed. New York: The Macmillan Company, 1953. The best account in existence of the confused evolution of immediate postwar politics in Malaya.

🌿 4 🌿

The Borneo Territories, The Formation of Malaysia

The Borneo Territories

Before Malaysia was proposed officially in May, 1961, there was a good deal of ignorance about the Borneo territories in Malaya and Singapore. Some who should have known better had only two main assumptions: that basically the territories were like Malaya, but that they were "less developed." Brunei, which, in its internal affairs, does not come within the scope of this book, was viewed as being different: partly because it was ruled by a Sultan, descended from an ancient line, while Sarawak and North Borneo were British colonies, and partly because of the fabulous revenues Brunei derived from oil. There was some excuse, perhaps, for ignorance about North Borneo. While Sarawak occupies the northwestern part of the island of Borneo, and, as the crow flies, is not too far from Singapore or from southeastern Malaya, the east coast ports of North Borneo are almost as close to Hong Kong.

The similarities and dissimilarities between the Borneo territories on the one hand, and Malaya and Singapore on the other, will become clearer later. But, as an introduction to the Malaysia proposal and its consequences, it is worth considering the extent to which the territories were in fact "underdeveloped" in 1961. It is suggestive, for instance, that in the *Annual Reports* of Sarawak, published a few years ago, some twelve pages are devoted to "pre-history" but only two pages to "history" (since 1400 A.D.).

As far as national income per capita is concerned, the Borneo territories were not too far behind Malaya. According to the "Rueff

Report" (1963)[1], in 1961 annual per capita income in Sarawak was about M$550 and in North Borneo about M$700, compared with about M$800 in Malaya, and M$1,300 in Singapore. It should be remembered that even the Sarawak figure is higher than that for Thailand or the Philippines. However, in an important sense the occupational distribution of the population suggests that the Borneo economies were "less developed" than those of Singapore or Malaya. In each of the Borneo states about 80 per cent of the population is engaged in agriculture, forestry, or fishing, compared with 58 per cent in Malaya and only 8 per cent in Singapore. On the other hand, manufacturing and construction account for 20 per cent of the labor force in Singapore, 11 per cent in Malaya, but only about 6 per cent in the Borneo states. Trade, transport, and other services employ about 70 per cent in Singapore, 30 per cent in Malaya, and 13 per cent in the Borneo states. Another index of development is the proportion of land under settled cultivation. In Sarawak and North Borneo it is only about 3 per cent, compared with about 17 per cent in Malaya. In spite of the low figure of 3 per cent, the population of the Borneo states is so small that there is actually more land in use *per person* than in Malaya.

Of course, these figures are averages, and do not indicate the variations in population distribution in the two states. Nor do they convey the difference in their economic *prospects*. The soil in North Borneo is better than in Sarawak, partly because it has not been exhausted by the native "slash and burn" technique, practiced at too frequent intervals. Rubber, timber, and pepper are Sarawak's chief exports, but none of the rubber estates is large, and, outside the government's Rubber Planting Scheme, the rubber planted by smallholders is of very low standard.[2] In 1961 North Borneo, with a smaller population than Sarawak, had higher foreign exchange earnings. Almost half of these came from timber, of which there are vast reserves, the rest mostly from rubber and copra.[3]

In both territories difficulties of physical communication are serious. In Sarawak, apart from air travel, the main means of communication are the large muddy rivers with their numerous tributaries which

[1] *Report on the Economic Aspects of Malaysia,* by a Mission of the International Bank for Reconstruction and Development (Kuala Lumpur: Government Press, 1963), pp. 1–2. Three Malayan dollars equal one United States dollar, approximately.

[2] *Sarawak Development Plan, 1964–1968* (Kuching: Government Printing Office, 1963), p. 3.

[3] *Report on the Economic Aspects of Malaysia,* p. 104.

flow northwest into the South China Sea. By their very existence they cut off the possibility of land communication on a large scale. Consequently, Sarawak is, *par excellence*, the country of the outboard motor. Indeed, during electoral campaigning a major item of expense is fuel for outboard motors. When the government issues a handbook designed to promote virtuous behavior by the citizens, urging them to report thefts from neighbors' houses instead of standing idly by, the item which is being stolen (chosen to create the feeling of greatest deprivation in the reader's heart) is an outboard motor. North Borneo does not have the same extensive maze of rivers and streams as Sarawak. For communications it depends mainly on its roads, which it plans to extend substantially, as well as on its famous railway, now almost a legend as well as a means of communication.

In one respect both North Borneo and Sarawak were undeniably underdeveloped in 1963 in relation to Malaya. Only about 25 per cent of the population over ten was literate, compared with over 50 per cent in Malaya. This figure was inflated by the fact that over 50 per cent of the Chinese were literate. Among the rest, only about 17 per cent were literate. More remarkable were the small numbers who had completed a university or technical college course in 1960. If only "natives" are considered, and Chinese, Europeans, Indians and others are excluded, the numbers were only four for North Borneo and nine for Sarawak.[4] These low numbers to some extent limited the pace of political and constitutional advance. More important, they set a limit to the replacement of expatriate civil servants by qualified natives.

Another, less obvious, aspect of "development" may be considered. From the point of view of a nation's stability, it is important that cultural cleavages should not be so deep that communication between groups is prevented. There should be some national beliefs or symbols which can be shared by all groups. The ethnic patchwork in the Borneo territories is almost terrifying in its complexity. In Sarawak a 1953 ordinance considered it necessary to list the races indigenous to Sarawak and therefore to be regarded as natives: Bukitans, Bisayans, Dusuns, Dayaks (Sea), Dayaks (Land), Kadayans, Kalabits, Kayans, Kenyahs (including Sabups and Sipengs), Kajangs (including Sekapans, Kejamans, Lahanans, Punans, Tanjongs and Kanowits), Lugats, Lisums, Malays, Melanos, Muruts, Penans, Sians, Tagals, Tabuns, Ukits, "and any admixture of the above with each

[4] See also T. H. Silcock, *Fiscal Survey Report of Sarawak* (Kuching: Government Printing Office, 1956), p. 3.

other."[5] To the expert[6] the ways of life of these various groups are distinctive. To be sure, some of the groups are very small in number. The Cobbold Commission on Malaysia conscientiously attempted to ascertain the views of the 2,800 Bisayahs and the 2,000 Kelabits. Yet considerable cleavages are apparent, even if only the more numerous native groups are considered in each territory: in Sarawak, Malays, Melanaus, Ibans (Sea Dayaks) and Land Dayaks; in North Borneo, Dusuns, Muruts, and Bajaus. For instance, there is an important religious cleavage in both. In Sarawak, Malays and some Melanaus may roughly be equated with the Muslim population, and the other races with non-Muslims. Indeed, in a loose sense, many persons are called "Malays," not because of their ethnic origins, but simply because they are Muslims. This usage is reminiscent of the medieval Crusades, when all the Crusaders became known as "Franks," simply because they were Christians. Another possible source of cleavage is that when some of the present areas of Sarawak were under the rule of the Sultan of Brunei, the non-Malays sometimes suffered from Malay domination. This is still alleged, but also often denied, to be a cause of anti-Malay feeling among other natives. In North Borneo the largest native group, the Dusuns, constitute about one third of the total population, and are almost entirely non-Muslim. But 38 per cent of the population is Muslim, the largest single group being the Bajaus. A complicating factor is that many of the Dusuns now prefer to call themselves Kadazans, believing that the former name, meaning a country-man or a yokel, was colonial and degrading.[7] But a minority, maintaining that "Kadazan" is the name of merely one subgroup of the Dusuns, prefer to keep the original name. Perhaps the most convincing evidence that, for the major groups at least, ethnic divisions still retain their importance, is the fact that when political parties were at last formed in both territories they tended to take shape largely along communal lines.

In comparison with Malaya, the variety of native races and the difference in their religions (Muslim, Christian, or other) is striking. But one racial factor is common to the Borneo territories *and* Malaya: the Chinese. In Sarawak they constitute about 31 per cent of the population, in North Borneo, 23 per cent. In each, and particularly in Sarawak, their rate of increase is higher than that of the other

[5] *Report of the Commission of Enquiry, North Borneo and Sarawak* (Kuala Lumpur: Government Press, 1962), p. 106, subsequently referred to as the "Cobbold Report," after the name of its chairman.

[6] E.g., Tom Harrisson (ed.), *The Peoples of Sarawak* (Sarawak: distributed by the Curator, Sarawak Museum, 1959).

[7] K. G. Tregonning, *North Borneo* (London: H.M.S.O., 1960), pp. 82–83.

races. As a study of the Chinese in Sarawak has pointed out, no single economic group can be labelled "Chinese," although for the sake of simplicity one may point to two main groups, the urban Chinese, who are mostly merchants and middlemen, and the rural Chinese, who are primary producers, many of them rubber planters.[8]

From 1841 to 1946 the Brooke family, whose style of government is described below, ruled Sarawak. Descriptions of Sarawak under the Brookes were lyrical about the idyllic state of race relations which existed. But after 1945 it became evident that the laissez-faire elements in Brooke rule had led to a dangerous situation. The Chinese had intermarried more with other races in Sarawak (and North Borneo) than in Malaya. But, for several reasons, many of them were even more divided from the rest of the population than in Malaya. The Chinese system of education had been left to develop on its own, without aid from the government and without reference to the other communities or to the task of building up nationhood. Some Chinese were educated in English by mission schools. But the Chinese-educated, whose knowledge of English was slight, had the frustration of trying to obtain employment in surroundings where Chinese was of limited value in most jobs. The schools were infiltrated by Communists who took advantage of Chinese patriotism and chauvinism. After 1946, there was more state intervention, for instance through grants, but it was not until 1961 that the decisive step was taken of announcing that in the future the medium of instruction in all government-aided secondary schools would be English. Chinese Middle Schools which did not agree to convert to English would lose their grants. As a result, eleven of the sixteen government-aided secondary schools which taught in the medium of Chinese were converted.[9] A further Chinese source of grievance was land.[10] The amount of good land available was small, and this was largely earmarked for natives. When party politics and elections at last came to Sarawak these grievances were partly responsible for the rise of a mainly Chinese radical, Communist-infiltrated, party, the SUPP (Sarawak United People's Party).

[8] Ju-K'ang T'ien, *The Chinese of Sarawak* (London: London School of Economics, n.d.), pp. 20–21.

[9] *Borneo Bulletin,* August 12, 1961. See also, *A Guide to Education in Sarawak* (Kuching: Sarawak Information Service, 1961); D. McLellan, *Report on Secondary Education* (Kuching: Government Printing Office, 1959); *Sarawak Annual Report 1962* (Kuching: Government Printing Office, 1963), p. 150.

[10] *Sarawak Gazette,* May 31, 1955, pp. 97–101; Michael B. Leigh, *The Chinese Community of Sarawak, a Study of Communal Relations* (Melbourne: University of Melbourne [mimeo.] 1963), pp. 23 ff.

The Chinese in North Borneo were in a happier position. No detailed analysis of the relative situation of the Chinese in the two territories has been made, but several reasons may account for the contrast. Compared with Sarawak, the number of Chinese was smaller and a higher proportion of them settled on the land, because legal restrictions on the ownership of land were less strict. A tougher line was taken by the government at an early date on subversion in schools, and outstanding dissentients were shipped off to their ideological home. Perhaps most important of all, North Borneo's greater economic prosperity compared with Sarawak provided a "cushion" against racial antagonisms.

This account may indicate the complexity of the racial and religious background in both territories in 1961. When Malaysia was proposed, the task had to be faced of building a new nation when two of the constituent parts, Sarawak and North Borneo, were nowhere near nationhood themselves.

The description given of economic and social development must now be supplemented by considering the course of political and constitutional development. The extremely indirect nature of British rule in the Borneo territories helps to explain the slow rate of political development. The northern parts of Borneo, as well as some adjacent island territories, were under the rule of the Sultans of Brunei, who became Muslims in the fifteenth century, and whose family tree once enlivened the time of travelers at Brunei airport. But difficulties of communication were so great that, even at the height of the Sultans' power, they never really controlled the island's vast hinterland of mountains and rivers. In addition, as has been pointed out, the peoples over whom they ruled were heterogeneous ethnically, and the majority were not Muslims. There were also the usual family and dynastic quarrels. One of these led to the death of the twenty-second Ruler, Sultan Mohamed Alam, early in the nineteenth century, who was informed, according to one account, that he would be killed by strangulation. He prophesied that if, after death, he fell to the right this would be a favorable omen for Brunei, but that if he fell to the left, it would be an evil omen. The dead Sultan fell to the left. Some might dispute that the prophecy was correct. With the finding of oil early in the nineteenth century and Brunei's present riches from that source, which ensure that its revenues are three times its expenditures, it might seem that, whatever its recent political troubles,[11] Brunei is now, a least economically, extremely fortunate.

However, from an immediate point of view the dead Sultan's prophecy was accurate. Brunei's weakness and internal dissension led

[11] See pp. 185–186, below.

to the setting up of European outposts on Brunei's territory, which eventually swallowed up the whole of Northern Borneo, except for a tiny area in the middle which the Sultans retained.

The European incursions followed roughly the same pattern as in Malaya; Portuguese were followed by Dutch and Dutch by British. In the late eighteenth century the British made an abortive attempt to establish a settlement at Balembangan, but by 1804 they had finally given this up. Thirty-five years later a young Englishman, James Brooke, first came to Borneo. At this time the Sultan was having difficulty in pacifying rebels who had been driven to revolt by the harsh rule of his governor. When Brooke returned in the following year, in exchange for achieving a settlement with the rebels, he was rewarded by being installed as Rajah of Sarawak, in 1841. This was the beginning of the rule of the famous "White Rajahs." For a time Brooke's position was precarious, but he maintained it with the support of the British navy. In 1846 the British claimed the island of Labuan, and the Sultan of Brunei ceded it to the British Crown, at the same time concluding a treaty of friendship and commerce. Sarawak was recognized as an independent state by the United States in 1850, and the British in effect granted recognition by appointing a British consul in 1864. In 1888 Sarawak formally came under British protection. At the same time the Rajahs were expanding their territory. By the time of the last expansion in 1905 the country was over twenty times its original size.

The acquisition of Sarawak was, if the support of the British navy is set on one side, a one-man venture. The founding of the other British territory was less personal and less romantic. It was also much more complex. It was preceded by the failure of the American Trading Company of Borneo, based on a concession granted by the Sultan of Brunei. A settlement was founded but was quickly abandoned. A few years later a survivor of the American Trading Company, J. W. Torrey, collaborated with William Cowie, a Scottish gunrunner who had been leased an area for a trading company in Sandakan Harbor by the Sultan of Sulu (now in the southern Philippines), and the Austrian consul in Hong Kong, Baron Overbeck. A series of negotiations in 1877 and 1878 with the Sultans of Brunei and Sulu resulted in the transfer of a large part of the northeast of the island of Borneo. The arrangement with the Sultan of Sulu was subject to conditions, among them the payment of a certain sum annually. (The exact nature of the arrangement has been questioned by the present government of the Philippines. In its claim to Sabah [North Borneo] it maintains, among other things, that the territory was not *ceded* by the Sultan of Sulu, but only *leased*.) Eventually the interests of Overbeck, Torrey, and Cowie were bought by Alfred Dent and his brother,

British financiers, who had originally provided backing for Overbeck. Dent transferred his rights to a Provisional Association, which in 1882 was replaced by the British North Borneo (Chartered) Company. The Charter gave the enterprise a certain degree of status in its operations. From the British government's point of view it ensured some control; for instance, it was laid down that the Company would always be British and that it would undertake to abolish slavery in its territories. It amounted to a very indirect version of indirect rule, and served as a warning to European powers not to try to annex North Borneo. In 1888 the new state became a British protectorate, at the same time as Sarawak and Brunei. This made British control a little less indirect: for instance, it was provided that the relations between the state and all other states, including Brunei and Sarawak, were to be conducted by the British government.

Sarawak: Constitutional and Political Development

From the British government point of view, the Brooke regime in Sarawak was an example of indirect rule. From the point of view of the White Rajahs themselves, technically their rule was direct. But the object was much the same as with British indirect rule elsewhere — to preserve the native way of life from external shocks. The last Ranee of Sarawak conveyed Brooke attitudes vividly when she wrote, in the early 1920's: "Outside the gates the ogre 'Progress' stirs and stretches — 'Open up,' he cries, 'open up your country, expand, and let the exploiters in.' But the Rajah looks back upon the toil of those before him, he looks at Sarawak as it is today. He looks around him at other countries, and sees the world-wide abuse of the word — 'Progress.' To those who would introduce such 'progress' he offers no welcome. But to those whose sense of duty to the country and its people is as keen as his own, and who would develop it on the broad principles of the Brooke traditions, the Rajah ever extends an inviting hand."[12] Some Chinese immigration was permitted, but heavy European investment was discouraged. Government was paternalistic, with many decisions made by the Rajahs themselves, who were always accessible to the people. There was a small civil service, composed of European officials and a Malay élite. Social services were minimal. Not only was economic development stunted by the absence of appreciable amounts of foreign capital, there was no pos-

[12] Her Highness the Ranee of Sarawak, *Sarawak* (Singapore: Methodist Publishing House, 192?), p. 58. For a statement of the views of the second Rajah on "native" and "European" principles of government see S. Baring-Gould and C. A. Bampfylde, *A History of Sarawak under its Two White Rajahs, 1839–1908* (London: Sotheran, 1909), pp. 313–314.

sibility of a change in this policy, except after a long time lag, because of the absence of provisions to educate the natives to play a part in an economically developing society. Constitutionally, as far as internal rule was concerned, the Rajahs were sovereign. There was a Supreme Council, later supplemented by a Committee of Administration, to advise the Rajah, but neither of these had any executive powers. The Council Negri, a national body representing the people, had even less power. Consisting of the leaders of the various racial communities, its meetings were intended, not to advise or influence the Rajahs, but rather to promote intercommunal understanding. On the eve of the Japanese invasion, in 1941, the third Rajah promulgated a Constitution. Ostensibly, this was to celebrate the centenary of Brooke rule, but there may also have been some pressure from the British government.[13] The composition of the Supreme Council and the Council Negri were made more specific and their powers were apparently increased. The Supreme Council was to consist of the Chief Secretary and the Financial Secretary ex officio plus other members appointed by the Rajah for a three-year period, drawn from either the civil service or the Council Negri. The Rajah, who was to be president of the Council, was now supposed to exercise his former absolute powers only with the advice of the members. The only exception was his power to nominate the members of the Council itself. The Council Negri was to be a larger body, consisting of both officials and unofficials, the latter intended to represent various racial and interest groups. No legislation was to be passed or public money spent without the approval of the Council Negri. The Rajah could veto legislation, but not if the Council passed a bill on three separate occasions. These provisions, together with "nine cardinal principles," stating the rights, duties, privileges, and responsibilities of the people of Sarawak, had an impressive appearance. But they contained no approach to popular elections, and it is a fair criticism to say that the previous autocracy was not removed but merely disguised. "The Rajah had in fact surrendered his absolute power to a bureaucracy which he himself nominated."[14]

Shortly after the end of the Japanese occupation Sarawak was ceded to Britain (1946). This apparently sudden move had been perhaps to an extent foreshadowed in 1941, when an agreement had been made for Britain to appoint a representative with an influence

[13] Liang Kim Bang, "Sarawak, 1941–1957" in *Number Five: Singapore Studies on Borneo and Malaya* (Singapore: Department of History, University of Singapore, 1964), pp. 14–15.

[14] Steven Runciman, *The White Rajahs* (Cambridge, England: University Press, 1960), p. 251.

on the *internal* policy of Sarawak. The main reason given for cession in 1946 was that the burden of rehabilitation, reconstruction, and development would be too heavy for the Brooke regime and could be better undertaken if Sarawak became a British colony. The situation was complicated by the reluctance of the Rajah's relatives, and possible successors, to agree to cession. The succession disputes of the Brookes were a little reminiscent of those of their predecessors, the former Sultans of Brunei, although not as bloody. Another complication was that the proposal for cession was passed by only a narrow margin in the Council Negri. Without the votes of the Europeans on the Council the proposal would have been defeated by one vote. The Chinese members were in favor, hoping that the country would be opened up and that there would be more attractive opportunities for trade. The natives in the Council, apart from the Malays, split their votes evenly. The Malays, however, showed a slight majority against. Indeed, the first notable signs of political consciousness among the Malays of Sarawak arose on this issue, resembling in a way the feeling stirred up among the Malays in Malaya by the Malayan Union proposals. But there was not the same solidarity of Malay feeling in Sarawak. The Malays in favor of cession joined the Young Malay Association, while those who were opposed joined the Malay National Union of Sarawak.

Although Sarawak had been handed over to Britain, there was no great constitutional advance for some time. On cession, the Supreme Council and Council Negri, as constituted in 1941, were maintained. A British Governor was substituted for the Rajah. In exercising his powers he was obliged to consult with the Supreme Council, with a few exceptions. But, unlike the situation under the Rajah according to the 1941 Constitution, sovereignty and the ultimate power of control lay with the Colonial Office in London. The main constitutional changes occurred in local government, where provision was made for a number of district councils, and the Kuching Municipal Council, which after a time were elected on a limited franchise. The introduction of democracy at grass roots level was linked with a new Constitution, enacted in 1956, which took effect in the following year.[15] It embodied the principle, which lasted even beyond the creation of Malaysia in 1963, that a proportion of the members in the higher organs of government would be elected by the members in a lower tier of government. So the Supreme Council contained ten members, three ex officio, two nominated and five elected from the members of the Council Negri. The Council Negri, in turn, out of forty-five

[15] Liang Kim Bang, pp. 19–21.

members, had twenty-four elected at a lower level, namely from five Divisional Advisory Councils, the Kuching Municipal Council, and the Urban District Councils of Miri and Sibu. The Divisional Advisory Councils were elected by the bottom tier, the District Councils. The District Councils, which provided all the democratic elements in the entire system, were chosen directly by the people, either by secret ballot, or, in the rural areas, at traditional gatherings.

North Borneo: Constitutional and Political Development

The course of events in North Borneo to some extent resembled that in Sarawak. Until the beginning of the nineteenth century there was an expansion of the territories originally occupied until it became clear that North Borneo and Sarawak were in competition for the remaining lands of the Sultan of Brunei, which at one time appeared likely to be partitioned between the competitors. An alternative solution, that cession of territory by Brunei would cease and that the Sultan would be bolstered by the presence of a British Resident, was eventually adopted in 1905, when Brunei had shrunk to minute proportions.[16] The island of Labuan was put under Company rule in 1889. In 1906, however, it was taken back for direct rule by the Crown. This change represented the Colonial Office's revenge for the dismissal of the Governor by a strong-minded member of the Company's court, the same William Cowie who had been one of the original adventurous band to whom the Company owed its birth. This dispute illustrates the more complex power situation in North Borneo, in comparison with Sarawak. The degree of control exercised by the Company's court in London depended largely on the respective strength of personality of the chairman, or other leading figures, in the court, and the Governor on the spot.

In 1883 the Governor formed an Advisory Council, with six members, five official and one unofficial. The Court apparently desired that the unofficial member should be Chinese or a native. But the Chinese preferred to have their own Council; they acquired one in 1890, and it therefore became the practice for the unofficial member to be a European. The Advisory Council ceased to meet in 1905. It was revived in the shape of a "Legislative Council" in 1912, with seven official and four unofficial members. The four represented the Chinese, the planters on the east coast and on the west coast, and the business community. Chinese representation was later raised to two.

[16] K. G. Tregonning, *Under Chartered Company Rule* (*North Borneo, 1881–1946*) (Singapore: University of Malaya Press, 1958), p. 45.

These political advances were imposed from above. They did not result from pressure from below: "the privileges about to be conferred will be specially welcome, because they have not been the result of popular agitation."[17] Indeed, until the war criticism of the government was more likely to come from the Rubber Planters' Association or the Chinese Chambers of Commerce than from the Legislative Council.

As with Sarawak, it was decided that the devastation resulting from the war was too great to repair under a continuation of the prewar regime. Consequently, in 1946 North Borneo, together with Labuan, became a British Colony. Provisional arrangements were made for an Advisory Council and later for a smaller Executive Council to advise the British Governor. A new Constitution was drawn up in 1950. Roughly on the same pattern as Sarawak, there was an Executive Council, consisting of three ex-officio members, two official members and four nominated members; there was also a Legislative Council, comprising, in addition to the Governor, three ex-officio members, nine official members and ten nominated members, including four natives.[18] This was a distinct advance on the prewar Legislative Council, which had fewer unofficial members and no native members. More important, under the Chartered Company there was a distinct limit to the amount of unofficial representation and the degree of "democracy" which could be introduced. But, as a colony, there were precedents for further constitutional advance, leading eventually to independence. Further advances were made in both the Executive Council and the Legislative Council. On the eve of the Malaysia proposal, important changes came into effect (April, 1961), after which the number of unofficial members in the Legislative Council exceeded the remainder. At the same time, compared with Sarawak or with many other British colonies then in existence, North Borneo was far behind.[19] It had not yet reached the stage at which some of the unofficials were elected, either directly or indirectly. It was not until after the formation of Malaysia had been agreed upon that steps were taken to hold the first election in North Borneo, at district level.

The Malaysia Proposal

The first public authoritative Malayan proposal for a Federation of Malaysia, consisting of Malaya, Singapore, North Borneo, Sarawak, and possibly Brunei, was made by Tengku Abdul Rahman on May 27,

[17] *Ibid.,* pp. 65–66, quoting an unofficial member.
[18] M. H. Baker, *North Borneo, the First Ten Years, 1946–1956* (Singapore: Malaya Publishing House, 1962), p. 40.
[19] *Ibid.,* p. 67.

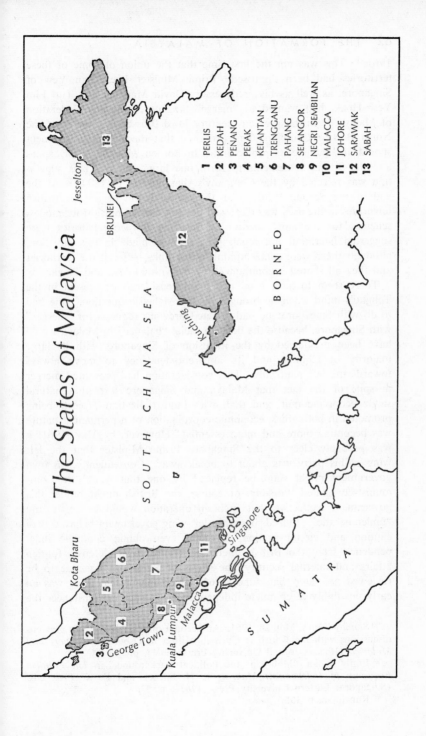

The States of Malaysia

1 PERLIS
2 KEDAH
3 PENANG
4 PERAK
5 KELANTAN
6 TRENGGANU
7 PAHANG
8 SELANGOR
9 NEGRI SEMBILAN
10 MALACCA
11 JOHORE
12 SARAWAK
13 SABAH

SOUTH CHINA SEA

BORNEO

SUMATRA

Jesselton

BRUNEI

Kuching

Kota Bharu

Kuala Lumpur

Malacca

George Town

Singapore

1961.[20] This was not the first time that the union of some of these territories had been discussed. Prime Minister Lee Kuan Yew of Singapore, as well as his predecessors David Marshall and Tun Lim Yew Hock, had wanted to "merge" Singapore with the Federation of Malaya.[21] In the previous century Lord Brassey, a director of the North Borneo Company, had proposed that the British government should amalgamate its protectorates in Borneo with the Malay states and the Straits Settlements to form one large colony. This suggestion was rejected by the Company's shareholders in 1894.[22] At the end of the Second World War the consolidation of all the British territories in the area was discussed but not carried out. More modest schemes for the amalgamation of just the Borneo territories were suggested later, but not much progress was made in this direction, although there were some administrative links between the territories and they all shared a common currency with Malaya and Singapore.

There seem to have been two main considerations present in the Tengku's mind when he brought up the Malaysia question. One had to do with Singapore: he had rejected previous requests for "merger" with Singapore, because the delicate racial "balance" in Malaya would have been prejudiced by the inclusion of Singapore, with its large majority of Chinese and its apparent tendency to move always towards the left politically. This consideration had prevented merger in spite of the fact that Malaya and Singapore formed a natural single economic unit, and that, with industrialization projects being promoted in both areas, economic coordination of a permanent nature was becoming more and more essential. However, by May, 1961, it was probably clear to the Singapore Prime Minister that the left wing of his party was about to break away. Consequently, his own government might soon be replaced by one that would be Communist-dominated. Possibly, of course, the British might render this government ineffective, but such an operation would be costly and "undemocratic." Indeed, if such a left-wing government behaved with caution and circumspection, it might even obtain complete independence from the British, including control over defense, foreign affairs and internal security; the status of Singapore was due to be reviewed not later than June, 1963, which meant that there was an early possibility of complete independence. In such circumstances the

[20] *Sunday Times*, May 28, 1961. An account of possibly relevant previous discussions with the British is given in Milton E. Osborne, *Singapore and Malaysia* (Ithaca: Cornell University Press, 1964), pp. 13–14.

[21] Emily Sadka, "Malaysia: the Political Background," in *The Political Economy of Independent Malaya*, T. H. Silcock and E. K. Fisk, eds. (Singapore: Eastern University Press, 1963), p. 33.

[22] Runciman, p. 195.

prospect of a "Cuba" (only relatively nearer and relatively more populous) was considerable. Previously the Federation government had considered it dangerous to take Singapore *inside* Malaya. Now, it seems, the Tengku had been persuaded by the Singapore Prime Minister that it was even more dangerous to keep it *outside*. "National Security" and "our mutual economy," said the Tengku, demanded that the two countries should work together. "We must prevent a situation in which an independent Singapore would go one way and the Federation another."[23]

The inclusion of the Borneo territories was not so urgent, but it did promise to solve two problems at once. To some degree the addition of the indigenous inhabitants of these territories would "balance" the Singapore Chinese majority. This argument should not be overstressed; the indigenous peoples were indeed more numerous than the Chinese in the Borneo territories, but the majority of them were neither Malays, nor Muslims. However, the Malays in Malaya looked on the indigenous races as being their "brothers," and hoped that they could be persuaded to support Malaysia, and also the Alliance Party. There may be truth in the allegations that the British originated or encouraged this part of the Tengku's plan, although to call the entire scheme a British plot would be an exaggeration. In 1961 North Borneo and Sarawak were economically and politically unready for independence on their own. There would also be an internal security problem after independence in Sarawak. "In the absence of some project like Malaysia, the Chinese, with their rapidly increasing population and their long start over other races in education, could expect, when independence came, to be in an unassailable position in Sarawak. This, in turn, could put the Communists, with their highly developed organization, to work on the fears and frustrations of the great body of non-Communist Chinese, in an equally unassailable position."[24] In the light of subsequent events it appears that there might also have been an external threat to the territories from Indonesia. Nevertheless, in spite of their underdeveloped condition and the fact that there was little internal demand for independence, the Indonesian campaign for West Irian and the general hardening of opinion against colonialism all over the world made early independence desirable from a broad "public relations" point of view.

Apart from Malaysia the only other possibilities would have been

[23] Tengku Abdul Rahman, *Dewan Ra'ayat Debates,* III, No. 16, October 16, 1961, cols. 1590–1613, and V, No. 6, August 12, 1963, cols. 669–683. In the 1961 debate the Tengku expressed uneasiness about the inclinations of some Singapore Chinese towards Chinese chauvinism or communism. Similar fears were voiced by members of UMNO during the next two years.
[24] The "Cobbold Report," p. 8.

to join Indonesia, which aroused little enthusiasm, or to form a union of Borneo states. A single independent state, however, would have to face the same problems that had beset the individual territories. There would have been the same probability of Communist infiltration, via the Chinese, referred to above. Moreover, the new state would have been economically viable only if Brunei had joined and shared its revenues with the two other territories. Later events showed that this could not have been taken for granted.[25]

Curiously, the arguments in favor of disposing of the Borneo states through the creation of Malaysia strongly resemble some which were urged to support the inclusion of West Irian in Indonesia. "Such historical and cultural ties as Western New Guinea has had all point in this direction. It is difficult to see that anyone would gain from the creation of yet another unviable and essentially miniature state. Since further continuation of even the best-intentioned and enlightened type of colonial rule is increasingly unlikely in the international atmosphere of the 1960's, there seems to be only one course left. Nor is it logical to advance the popular newspaper argument that the Papuans are different from 'Indonesians' in racial and cultural terms. It is highly unrealistic to talk as though there was *an* Indonesian race or unitary culture pattern. . . ."[26]

Against the Malaysia proposal was the absence of any great immediate economic advantages to be expected from Malaysia, except for the prospect of development loans from Malaya and Singapore to the other territories and the hope that the Malayan rural development schemes would be extended to Borneo. The distances between some of the territories and the lack of extensive communications between some of them, even between North Borneo and Sarawak, were also an obstacle. Nevertheless, the areas had similar systems of government and administration (although at different levels of development), a *lingua franca* in Malay, and a common currency. In all the circumstances the Malaysia proposal seemed to be a workable, if intricate, solution.

Between May, 1961, and the birth of Malaysia over two years later, a series of discussions and investigations took place on the possible terms of federation. For the sake of clarity, four main stages may be distinguished as far as North Borneo and Sarawak are concerned.

[25] On the possibility of the Borneo states constituting a viable independent country see T. E. Smith, *The Background to Malaysia* (London: Oxford University Press, 1963), pp. 43–46.

[26] Robert C. Bone, Jr., *The Dynamics of the Western New Guinea (Irian Barat) Problem* (Ithaca: Cornell University, 1962, 2nd printing), p. x. Of course such arguments could also be used to support the inclusion of the Borneo territories in Indonesia!

First, the project was discussed by leaders of the five states (Malaya, Singapore, North Borneo, Sarawak, Brunei) at the Commonwealth Parliamentary Association Regional Meeting, held at Singapore, July, 1961. This led to the formation of a Malaysia Solidarity Consultative Committee of the Association, which by February, 1962, had produced a memorandum supporting Malaysia and indicating some general conditions for federation.[27] Second, following a visit to London by the Tengku in October, 1961, a Commission of Enquiry was set up, with Lord Cobbold as chairman, two other members nominated by the British government, and two members nominated by the government of the Federation of Malaya. Its terms of reference were to ascertain the views of the peoples of North Borneo and Sarawak on Malaysia, to assess these views and to make recommendations accordingly. Third, after the Cobbold Commission had reported favorably, the detailed working out of the terms of federation was assigned to an Inter-Governmental Committee under Lord Lansdowne.[28] The final stage consisted of a round of negotiations in London in July, 1963, just before Malaysia was formed.

The Singapore sequence was rather different. Singapore was represented on the Malaysia Solidarity Consultative Committee, but was outside the scope of the Cobbold Commission or the working party under Lord Lansdowne. By November, 1961, the Tengku and Lee Kuan Yew had arrived at an understanding on certain points, which was put on record in the form of a White Paper.[29] But even a few weeks before Malaysia was formed (September 16, 1963) a number of important issues, such as the allocation of tax revenues, had not been decided, and there were some last-minute sessions of poker-like bargaining. Negotiations with Brunei were also conducted outside the "Cobbold-Lansdowne" framework. In the end Brunei decided to stay outside, although it was not entirely clear what the main obstacle was. Apparently it was either the retention of oil revenues by Brunei, although Malaya offered substantial concessions on this score, or the precedence which the Sultan of Brunei would have vis-à-vis the other Rulers, which would determine his eligibility to be chosen Yang di-Pertuan Agong.

When agreement had been reached among the four states, and with the British, the government of Malaya amended the Constitution

---

[27] Reproduced in the "Cobbold Report" as Appendix F.

[28] *Malaysia Report of the Inter-Governmental Committee* (Kuala Lumpur: Government Press, 1963).

[29] *Memorandum Setting out Heads of Agreement for a Merger between the Federation of Malaya and Singapore* (Cmd. 33) (Singapore: Government Printing Office, 1961).

accordingly by passing the Malaysia Act (1963). It also passed an Immigration Act relating to entry to North Borneo and Sarawak, because the type of federation agreed upon was unusual in that it provided for restrictions on immigration into these two states from the rest of the new Federation. In deciding that Malaysia should be brought about by amendment of the existing Constitution of Malaya rather than by the adoption of a new Constitution, the main consideration may have been to ensure that the continuity, Malaya-Malaysia, should not be questioned internationally: "in no sense is it a new State that has come into being but the old State has continued in an enlarged form and with a new name.

"There has been no severance of the continuity of the existence of the old State nor has it been brought to an end in any way.

"No question therefore arises concerning its continuing membership of the United Nations still less the credentials of its representatives."[30]

This insistence on continuity did not give any loophole to Indonesia, once she had declared her hostility to the new Federation, which would help her in persuading other nations to withhold recognition of Malaysia or to question Malaysia's membership in the U.N.

Before indicating the main features of the agreement, as embodied in the amendment to the Constitution of Malaya, something should be said about the attitudes of the peoples of the Borneo territories. The Cobbold Commission made the following assessment, inexact but probably realistic, in the middle of 1962. About one-third of the population was in favor of Malaysia, and another third also in favor, provided that conditions and safeguards on various points were obtained. "The remaining third is divided between those who insist on independence before Malaysia is considered and those who would strongly prefer to see British rule continue for some years to come. If the conditions and reservations which they have put forward could be substantially met, the second category referred to above would generally support the proposals. Moreover, once a firm decision were taken, quite a number of the third category would be likely to abandon their opposition and decide to make the best of a doubtful job. There will remain a hard core, vocal and politically active, which will oppose Malaysia on any terms unless it is preceded by independence and self-government; this hard core might amount to near 20 per cent of the population of Sarawak and somewhat less in North Borneo."[31]

[30] Dato M. Ghazali bin Shafie, Permanent Secretary to the Ministry of External Affairs, letter to *Straits Times,* September 25, 1963. Dato Ghazali had been a member of the Cobbold Commission.
[31] "Cobbold Report," p. 50.

As late as October, 1962, three Borneo parties — the Sarawak United People's Party, the Party Rakyat of Brunei, and the National Pasok Momogun Party of North Borneo — opposed Malaysia in a memorandum to the United Nations Committee on Colonialism, stating that they would prefer a federation of the three Borneo territories by themselves.[32] But scrutiny of the results of the local government elections in the two territories, in late 1962 and in 1963, led a U.N. Malaysia Mission to state that participation in the new Federation was approved, "by a large majority of the people."[33] This conclusion is probably correct,[34] and may indicate that a shift of opinion had occurred in favor of Malaysia in the year or so following the Cobbold Commission's investigations. The change may have resulted largely from the Malayan Alliance Party's having helped to organize the pro-Malaysia ethnically based parties which won the elections in North Borneo and Sarawak. On another level it may be accounted for by the fact that some of those who had been opposed did decide "to make the best of a doubtful job." If independence outside Malaysia was not attainable then federation as a part of Malaysia with safeguards was, to the overwhelming majority, preferable to union with Indonesia or (for North Borneo) with the Philippines.

The safeguards desired by various groups of the indigenous peoples are discussed below. Some of them are alleged to have their origins in distrust of Malay rule, dating back to resentment against cruelties and injustices suffered in previous times under the Sultans of Brunei. It was by no means self-evident to the indigenous inhabitants that colonialism could be practiced only by white men. This was difficult for some Malay members of the government of Malaya to understand, because they looked upon the non-Chinese inhabitants of the territories, whether Malays or not, as brothers. The Tengku found it necessary to give an assurance on this point. "When the Borneo territories become part of Malaysia, they will cease to be a colony of Britain, and they will not be a colony of Malaya — I thought I had made it clear — they will be partners of equal status, no more and no less than the other States now forming the Federation of Malaya. Where does he get the idea that by taking in the Borneo territories, we would colonize them? The days of imperialism are gone and it is

[32] *Straits Times,* October 2, 1962.

[33] *United Nations Malaysia Mission Report* (Kuala Lumpur: Department of Information, 1963), para. 245. See also p. 190, below.

[34] But it has been said that in Sarawak "there were many extraneous issues interjected that cut across the pro-Malaysia and anti-Malaysia division" (Robert O. Tilman, "Elections in Sarawak," *Asian Survey,* III, No. 10, 517).

not the intention of Malaya to perpetuate or revive them."[35] The British attitude was that, while approving of Malaysia, any suggestion that the new Federation had been forced on the Borneo territories would lay the British open to the charge that they had betrayed their responsibilities and the trust which the indigenous peoples had placed in them. They felt the same paternalistic but moral concern for the future of the natives of the territories which they had previously felt for the Malays in Malaya. Therefore they wished to move more slowly than the Malayans. Commenting on the Cobbold Commission proposals, the British members saw many of them "as objectives which should be progressively worked towards, and where possible introduced, during a transitional period, whereas they are seen by the Malayan members as recommendations which should start to take effect immediately on the creation of Malaysia."[36]

The Malaysia Agreement and its Provisions

As far as the Borneo territories are concerned, distinctive provisions of the Malaysian Constitution are those which have to do with the Head of State, language, religion, immigration, and the special position of the natives.[37] It was decided that the position of Head of State for each of the two Borneo territories should be open to members of all communities. Because the choice was not restricted to Malays (or at any rate to Muslims), these Heads of State would be in the same constitutional position as the Governors of Penang and Malacca in that they would not be eligible to become Yang di-Pertuan Agong. Although this decision did apparently widen the range of choice of Head of State, it meant also that North Borneo and Sarawak could never become more closely identified with Malaya by providing the symbolic figure of Supreme Ruler.

The language issue was essentially a matter of the relative place of English and Malay. The arrangement by which Malay was to become the sole official language of Malaya by 1967 was not acceptable to Sabah and Sarawak, because the time for a changeover to Malay from English would then have been too short. Accordingly, a delay of ten years was provided for, until 1973, just as a ten-year period had previously been allowed, from 1957 to 1967, before English could cease to be an official language in Malaya. As a result,

[35] *Dewan Ra'ayat Debates*, IV, No. 3, April 28, 1962, cols. 451–452.

[36] "Cobbold Report," p. 91.

[37] On the legislative powers of the two states generally, see Malaysia Act, Fourth Schedule, Part I, Lists IIA, IIIA. This corresponds to Ninth Schedule, Lists IIa, IIIa of the federal Constitution of Malaysia. Future references to the Malaysia Act will be followed by a number in square brackets giving the corresponding Article of the federal Constitution.

the representatives from the Borneo territories may use English in the federal Parliament until 1973, and it may also be used until then in the courts of the two states and on appeals from them. It may also be used until that time in the two Legislative Assemblies or for other official purposes.[38] The provision about the language to be used in the federal Parliament may create some anomalies. After 1967, Malayans who have been English-educated must use Malay in Parliament, while representatives from the Borneo territories, whose acquaintance with English may be much less profound, will still be permitted to speak there in that language. It is possible that for the whole of Malaysia 1973 may replace 1967 as the date when Malay is to become the sole official language. Apart from the provision about the federal Parliament, even 1973 may not be the terminal date for English inside the two Borneo states. Any act affecting its use in the courts of one of the states, or on appeal from them, or in one of the states in the Legislative Assembly or for other official purposes, is not to come into operation *until it has been approved by an enactment of the legislature of the Borneo state concerned.*[39]

Although Islam was the religion of the Federation of Malaya and continues to be the religion of the new Federation of Malaysia, it is not the religion of the states of Sabah or Sarawak. Some practical consequences of this are spelled out in the new Malaysian Constitution. No act of Parliament providing financial aid for Muslim institutions or instruction in the Muslim religion, with reference to a Borneo state, shall be passed without the consent of the state Governor, in effect the consent of the state government; moreover, when federal grants are made for Muslim religious purposes elsewhere in Malaya, proportionate grants will be made for social welfare purposes to Sabah and Sarawak.[40]

The provisions on immigration are unusual for a federal state. The Borneo states seem to have been fearful that large numbers of persons would be attracted to them from overcrowded and densely populated areas in Singapore and Malaya. These fears were expressed in the Malaysia Solidarity Consultative Committee Memorandum and also in other representations to the Cobbold Committee. It is not clear to what extent these fears were well grounded, but at any rate they were met in the Malaysia Act and in the complementary Immigration Act. The provisions are complex but may be summarized as follows. Generally, control over immigration into the new Federation from outside, or between the Borneo states or a Borneo state and the rest of the Federation, is a federal matter. But where it is a

[38] Malaysia Act, Sec. 61 [161].
[39] Malaysia Act, Sec. 61 (3) [161(3)].
[40] Malaysia Act, Sec. 64 [161C].

question of immigration into a Borneo state, with a few exceptions in effect that state has a veto on entry and residence.[41]

Other provisions affecting the Borneo states concern the position of the natives. Article 153 in the Constitution of the Federation of Malaya was to apply (with the substitution of references to natives of one of the Borneo states for the references to Malays) to reservations of positions in the public service in the two states and to scholarships and so on.[42] Reference is made elsewhere to changes in the structure of the courts and the provisions for elections to Parliament and the Legislative Assemblies. The relatively large number of seats given to the Borneo territories in the federal Parliament was intended to be yet another reassurance to the natives that they would not be dominated by Malaya. There are also financial provisions on special grants to the Borneo states and additional sources of revenue assigned to the states. These were to be subject to review, in the first instance after five years.[43]

The constitutional provisions for Singapore's powers and functions were also different from those of the states in the Federation of Malaya.[44] Some related to the topics just discussed with reference to the Borneo states, for instance, language. But other provisions were peculiar to Singapore. Unlike any other state, Singapore was given control of education, labor, and other subjects. It would have been political suicide for any Singapore government to have attempted to conform to the Malayan pattern of education and to have removed the possibility of state-subsidized secondary education in the medium of Chinese. Similarly, Singapore labor laws were substantially more favorable to workers than Malaya's; it would have been retrogressive and unpopular to have assimilated them to Malaya's.

The question of Singapore citizenship was complex and confusing and, after Malaysia had been proposed by the Tengku, it had led to acrimonious debate between the Singapore government and its political opponents, chiefly the Barisan Sosialis. The root of the problem was that, before Malaysia, the qualifications for obtaining Singapore citizenship had been much less strict than the corresponding qualifications for obtaining citizenship of the Federation of Malaya. Consequently, if the new Federation applied the Federation of Malaya citizenship criteria to Singapore, only about two-thirds of the Singa-

[41] Malaysia Act, Sec. 60 (1) [9(3)]. See also the Immigration Act, 1963.

[42] Malaysia Act, Sec. 62 (2) [161A].

[43] Malaysia Act, Secs. 45–47 [Tenth Schedule and Articles 112C and 112D].

[44] See Malaysia Act, Fourth Schedule, Part II [Ninth Schedule, Lists IIB and IIIB].

pore adult citizens would qualify.[45] This arrangement would have caused great discontent, and would have been regarded as an example of anti-Chinese discrimination. On the other hand, if qualifications for Singapore citizenship were to be less strict than for citizenship in Malaya, the Federation of Malaya government feared that Singapore politicians and voters might move into Malaya and upset its political "balance." The solution adopted was to continue the system by which Singapore laid down its own conditions for citizenship and to say that such "Singapore citizens" would have parity of status with "federal citizens." There was, however, one important consequence of this choice of terminology; only Singapore citizens could run for a legislature or vote in Singapore, and only federal citizens could run for a legislature or vote in Malaya. However, citizens of one could campaign in the territory of the other. These provisions were important, because they limited the strategy of a party, established in one of the two territories which wanted to expand into the other.[46] The restrictive aspects of the citizenship provision must be considered along with the low number of seats (15) allocated to Singapore in the Malaysian federal Parliament. To be sure, this low figure was explained by saying that the number of Singapore seats should be small because Singapore retained control over education, labor, and so on. But, taken in conjunction with the citizenship arrangement, the net result was to "insulate" politics in Malaya to some degree from the impact of Chinese votes in Singapore.

The financial relations between Singapore and the Federation of Malaya were eventually embodied in a White Paper,[47] given legal force by the Malaysia Act. There were two main aspects of the negotiations: the respective roles of the Singapore and the Malaysian federal governments in collecting taxes and the divisions of revenues between them; the provisions for a common market[48] and the co-

[45] The majority by birth, a smaller number by registration. See also Malaysia Act, Secs. 23–34 [14–31].

[46] E.g., the PAP when it decided to enter candidates for the 1964 federal election. For a restatement of the citizenship provisions for the whole of Malaysia, as contained in the Malaysia Act, see H. E. Groves, "The Constitution of Malaysia — the Malaysia Act," *Malaya Law Review*, V, No. 2 (1963), 255 ff.; H. E. Groves, *The Constitution of Malaysia* (Singapore: Malaysia Publications, 1964), ch. XI.

[47] *Agreement between the Governments of the Federation of Malaya and Singapore on Common Market and Financial Arrangements* (Cmd. 27 of 1963, Federation of Malaya), reprinted as "Annex J" of the *Malaysia Agreement* (Kuala Lumpur: Government Printer, 1963). For the financial arrangements with the Borneo states, see Chapter 5, p. 79.

[48] On the relation between the common market issue and the financial issue see Osborne, pp. 50–61. See also *Report on the Economic Aspects of*

ordination of tariffs. In the short run Singapore was anxious to
minimize the damage to her entrepôt trade. In the longer run, unless
she reached an agreement on a common market with Malaysia, her
industrialization plans would be frustrated because of her small internal market. As the date fixed for Malaysia drew nearer, the bargaining on the terms became more intense and acrimonious. In-
credible as it may seem, the early negotiations do not seem to have
resolved a fundamental point — which government should collect
income tax in Singapore.[49] New issues came up late in the discussions. The Federation of Malaya government persuaded the Singapore government to make a loan, interest-free for the first five years,
to the Borneo governments. In turn, the Singapore government
stipulated that in any projects financed by that loan 50 per cent of the
labor should be recruited from Singapore. However, this condition
had rather tenuous constitutional status, having taken the form of
an agreement signed on the back of an envelope by the Tengku and
Mr. Lee during a session of the final negotiations at the Ritz Hotel
in London.[50] Mr. Lee's "toughness" during the negotiations probably
had two main purposes, apart from his desire to get the best possible terms for Singapore. In view of the forthcoming Singapore
general elections he wished to create the image of a politician who
was not afraid to stand up to the Tengku and the British in defense
of Singapore's interests. By choosing finance as his ground, he was
also striking at the Federation of Malaya Finance Minister, Tan Siew
Sin. It is perhaps relevant that Mr. Tan was the president of the
MCA, and that Mr. Lee was desirious of replacing the MCA, by his
own PAP, inside the Alliance Party.

As it happened, Malaysia was not formed on the planned date of
August 31, 1963, the anniversary of Independence Day (1957). Indonesian and Philippine objections resulted in postponement until
September 16. Singapore, Sarawak, and North Borneo (henceforward
called "Sabah") were opposed to the delay and maintained that, since
British control ended on August 31, they were "independent" between
then and September 16.[51] A further attempt to prevent the formation of Malaysia came from the government of the state of Kelantan
on September 10, when it instituted a legal action to have the Malay-

Malaysia, by a Mission of the International Bank for Reconstruction and
Development (Kuala Lumpur: Government Press, 1963), chs. III, IV, and
V.

[49] Lee Kuan Yew, *Singapore Legislative Assembly Debates,* XX, No. 6,
June 10, 1963, cols. 613–620.

[50] *Ibid.,* July 10 and 24, 1963; *Malaysia Agreement, Exchange of Letters*
(Singapore: Government Printer, 1963).

[51] *Straits Times,* August 22 and 23, 1963.

sia Act declared null and void or to have it declared not to be binding on Kelantan.[52] The action failed, and Malaysia came into existence on September 16, 1963.

Evidently Malaysia is a much looser form of federation than Malaya was. This is clear from the existence of a number of subjects, such as citizenship, religion, the constitution and jurisdiction of the High Court, where the powers of the Borneo states are different from those of the other states; on these subjects the Constitution of Malaysia may not be amended without the concurrence of the state concerned.[53] The comparative looseness of the new Federation and the lack of uniformity of powers among the states may be distressing to the constitutional purist. Even in the former Federation of Malaya, where the Constitution provided for a high degree of centralization, the diversity of outlook was so great that the prospects for the development of a truly national consciousness were necessarily long-term. The relative autonomy of the new units in Malaysia makes such a development even longer-term for the new Federation. Nevertheless, the arrangements made, or something close to them, were essential if Malaysia were to come into existence at all, except by force. It is indeed necessary that in "future constitutional arrangements the Borneo people can have a big say in matters in which they feel very strongly."[54] The Constitution of Malaysia tried to do just this in framing the constitutional provisions for the Borneo territories and also, in a rather different way, for Singapore.

SUGGESTED READINGS

Baker, Michael H. *North Borneo, the First Ten Years, 1946–1956.* Singapore: Malaya Publishing House, 1962. Comprehensive, dealing with political, social and economic aspects.

Geddes, W. R. *The Land Dayaks of Sarawak:* A Report on a Social Economic Survey of the Land Dayaks in Sarawak Presented to the Colonial Social Science Research Council. London: Her Majesty's Stationery Office, 1954.

Groves, Harry E. *The Constitution of Malaysia.* Singapore: Malaysia Publications Ltd., 1964. Greatly facilitates reference to the Constitution.

Liang Kim Bang. "Sarawak, 1941–1957," and Lee, Edwin. "Sarawak in the Early Sixties," in *Number Five: Singapore Studies on Borneo*

[52] Groves, *The Constitution of Malaysia,* p. 132.
[53] Malaysia Act, Secs. 66 and 69 [161E and 161H].
[54] "Cobbold Report," p. 114, quoting the Tengku.

and Malaya. Singapore: Department of History, University of Singapore, 1964. Mainly of constitutional and political interest.

Malaysia Report of the Inter-Governmental Committee. Kuala Lumpur: Government Press, 1963 ("the Lansdowne Report"). A detailed scheme of the arrangements for Malaysia.

Osborne, Milton E. *Singapore and Malaysia.* Ithaca: Cornell University, Department of Asian Studies, 1964. Well documented. Also good on internal politics in Singapore.

Papers on Financial Arrangements, submitted by the Federation of Malaya and Singapore for consideration by the Inter-Governmental Committee and Related Documents, (Misc. 4 of 1963) Singapore: Government Printer, 1963.

Payne, Pierre Stephen Robert. *The White Rajahs of Sarawak.* London: Robert Hale, 1960. Critical of Brooke rule.

Report of the Commission of Enquiry, North Borneo and Sarawak. Kuala Lumpur: Government Press, 1962 ("the Cobbold Report"). Contains much general information on the territories in 1962.

Runciman, Steven. *The White Rajahs.* Cambridge, England: Cambridge University Press, 1960. Sometimes rather tolerant of the Brookes.

Sadka, Emily. "Singapore and the Federation: Problems of Merger," *Asian Survey,* I, No. 8 (1961), 17–25.

Smith, T. E. *The Background to Malaysia,* London: Oxford University Press, 1963. A useful introduction to the whole Malaysia question.

Starner, Frances L. "Communism in Malaysia: a Multifront Struggle," pp. 221–250 in *The Communist Revolution in Asia; Tactics, Goals and Achievements,* Robert A. Scalapino, ed. Englewood Cliffs, N.J.: Prentice-Hall, 1965.

Tilman, Robert O. "Malaysia: The Problems of Federation," *The Western Political Quarterly,* XVI, No. 4 (1963), 897–911.

Tregonning, Kennedy G. *Under Chartered Company Rule.* Singapore: University of Malaya Press, 1958. Covers the history of North Borneo from 1881 to 1946.

Tregonning, Kennedy G. *A History of Modern Sabah (North Borneo) 1881–1963.* Singapore: University of Malaya Press, 1965. A second edition, updated, of the preceding book.

Tregonning, Kennedy G. *North Borneo.* London: Her Majesty's Stationery Office, 1960. A general account.

United Nations Malaysia Mission Report. Kuala Lumpur: Department of Information, 1963. Includes good background information on the political development of the Borneo territories.

van der Kroef, Justus M. "Communism and Chinese Communalism in Sarawak," *The China Quarterly,* No. 20 (1964), 38–66.

❦ 5 ❦

Federal-State Relations

The Constitution and Federalism

If there had been no Rulers in Malaya, and if an outcry had not followed the abortive attempt at centralization through Malayan Union in 1946, it is questionable whether the 1957 Constitution would have been federal. The Philippines, with a larger population, with considerably more difficulties of communication, and with the model of the United States to imitate, rejected federalism when it drew up its Constitution. To be sure, Malaya contains a number of different ethnic groups and, superficially, this might be regarded as an argument for having a federal system, after the pattern of, say, Canada. But, with the exception of the northeast coast states, Kelantan and Trengganu, where over 90 per cent of the population is Malay, the races are not concentrated in separate self-contained areas in Malaya. If anything, apart from the Northeast the main division is between town (Chinese) and country (Malays) and this would be an impracticable basis for drawing state boundaries in a federation.

The solution which was adopted deferred to the existence of the Rulers and to traditions of indirect rule in that a federal *form* of state was adopted. But the balance of power lay heavily with the central government. The *Report* of the Constitutional Commission had recommended the "establishment of a strong central government with the states and settlements enjoying a measure of autonomy."[1] The Constitution which went into effect stressed the first of these requirements rather than the second.

In the first place, the minor role of the states is shown by their restricted control over amendments. Generally speaking, the Constitution may be amended by an Act of Parliament supported on both

[1] *Report of the Federation of Malaya Constitutional Commission* (Kuala Lumpur: Government Printer, 1957), para. 3.

the second and third readings by the votes of not less than two-thirds of the total number of members of each house. Some amendments, mostly of a minor character, do not even need the two-thirds majority, but may be effected by the procedure for an ordinary parliamentary act. The ordinary process could also be used for an amendment made for or in connection with the admission of any state to the Federation or its association with the states thereof, or any modification made as to the application of the Constitution to a state previously so admitted or associated.[2] No part of the amendment process specifically gives a role, and a check, to the states as such. Apart from the Borneo states (since the Constitution was amended on the formation of Malaysia), the only exception to the general rule that a particular state does not have a "veto" to protect itself against unwelcome constitutional amendments, is that the physical boundaries of all the states are fixed, and may not be changed without the consent of that state, expressed in a law passed by the legislature of that state.[3] It is true that some of the members of the Senate are nominated by the states, but there has not yet been any evidence that they have acted as supporters of states' rights when constitutional amendments are considered. Also, a limited range of amendments cannot take effect without the consent of the Conference of Rulers, but these are restricted to the powers of the Rulers themselves and the privileges of the Malays.[4] It is only in the new Constitution of Malaysia, that, as far as the Borneo states are concerned, the state itself must consent to amendments on certain subjects before they can be passed. The Governor of the state concerned must concur, and he is required to act on the advice of the state government.[5]

The Constitution does not make any explicit provision for secession. Certainly there could not be any "unilateral" secession, just because a particular state desired it. One authority believed, however, that "new" states admitted to the Federation — that is, Singapore, the Borneo states, and any others subsequently admitted — could be dissociated from the Federation by an Act repealing, by a two-thirds majority, the constitutional amendments by which they were admitted.[6] On August 9, 1965, Singapore's separation from Malaysia

[2] Article 159(4)bb. But note the qualification in Article 161E.

[3] Article 2(b). It has been suggested that some clauses which concern federal-state relations, such as 71(3), 71(4), 74, 76(4), and 80, should be capable of amendment only with the approval of the states (R. H. Hickling, "The First Five Years of the Federation of Malaya Constitution," *Malaya Law Review*, IV, No. 2 [1962], 202–203.

[4] Article 159(5).

[5] Article 161E and H.

[6] H. E. Groves, *The Constitution of Malaysia* (Singapore: Malaysia Publications, 1964), p. 152.

was effected by a constitutional amendment, which was passed in each house without any opposing vote.

The Constitution does not divide the power to legislate between the federal government and the states in the same way as does the United States Constitution, which lists a number of federal powers with the residual powers remaining in the states. The Constitution of Malaya, and Malaysia, follows the pattern of the Indian Constitution in having three lists: federal, state, and concurrent.[7] Any residual powers are given to the states,[8] but the three lists are so comprehensive that this provision is of no practical consequence.

A glance at the lists is sufficient to show that the federal government has more substantial powers by far than the states. The main powers retained by the states are over the development of natural resources, namely land (including mining), agriculture, and forestry, but it will be seen later that the federal government is also concerned with land. Even the additional powers given the Borneo states are not so important, although when Singapore was a part of Malaysia, 1963–1965, its powers over education, labor, health, and social security placed it in a position of "semi-autonomy" not approached by the other states. It should also be noted that the federal government enjoys "preference" in the concurrent list. If there is any clash between a federal law and a state law on an item in the concurrent list, the federal law overrides the state law, even if it was passed after the state law. There are a number of other clauses in the Constitution, permitting the federal Parliament to legislate on matters which appear in the list of state functions,[9] for instance, when concluding treaties with other countries, for promoting the uniformity of state laws, and so on. The most important of these provisions is probably that in Article 150. After a declaration of Emergency, the federal Parliament may make laws with respect to any matter on the state list, except matters of Muslim law or the custom of the Malays, or with respect to any matter of native law or custom in a Borneo state. This mechanism was used, in September, 1966, in dealing with a constitutional crisis in Sarawak.

The federal government, as opposed to the federal Parliament, has a number of controls over the states. Among others, the agricultural and forestry officers of the states, except the Borneo states, are required to accept professional advice from the federal government in respect to their duties.[10] A measure of *indirect* control also results

[7] Ninth Schedule.

[8] Article 77.

[9] Listed in Groves, pp. 135–137.

[10] Articles 94 and 95E(4). See also *Legislative Council Debates* (Second Session) October, 1956, to August, 1957, cols. 2923–2924 (Inche Abdul Aziz bin Ishak).

from the fact that some of the officials working for the states and on their civil service establishment are actually employees of the federal government, dependent in the last resort, on it for promotion.[11] The federal government may also undertake inquiries and surveys in the states.[12] It controls borrowing by the states.[13] Also, while a Proclamation of Emergency is in force, the executive authority of the federation extends to any matter within the legislative authority of a state and to the giving of directions to the government of a state or to any of its officers.[14]

Cooperation between the federal government and the states is ensured in a number of ways. In some respects the onus for cooperation is so placed on the states as almost to approximate federal "control." Thus, the executive authority of a state is to be so exercised as to ensure compliance with any federal law applying to that state and so as not to impede or prejudice the exercise of the executive authority of the Federation.[15] There are also two policy-making bodies, on which both the federal government and the states are represented, whose policy decisions are binding on both federal and state governments. Their policy decisions are not, however, binding on the Borneo states, whose representatives do not have the right to vote. These bodies are the National Land Council and the National Council for Local Government.[16] A third organization, the National Finance Council, although constituted on similar lines, is not empowered to make policy which is binding on the federal government or the states.[17] A number of other provisions exist for ensuring harmony between federal and state governments in which the emphasis is on cooperation rather than on control.[18]

When viewed as a whole, the powers of the federal government over the eleven "original" states are truly formidable. Yet the federal Prime Minister on one occasion lamented that the "ultimate" weapon was missing. In September, 1961, he deplored the fact that the Trengganu state government, which was inactive and did not call meetings of the state Assembly and the state Executive Council as often as it should, could not be adequately disciplined by the federal government, which had no power to suspend the state government

[11] See pp. 152 and 158, below.
[12] Article 93.
[13] Article 111(2).
[14] Article 150(4).
[15] Article 81.
[16] Articles 91, 95A(5) and 95E.
[17] Article 108.
[18] Groves, pp. 140–142.

and take over its functions,[19] as the Indian federal government is empowered to do — and has actually done — in India.

The financial arrangements of the Federation underline the centralizing tendencies of the Constitution. Just as the powers of the states are small as compared with those of the center, so are the states' budgets small compared with the federal budget. Total state revenue (or expenditure) is only just over a quarter of federal revenue (or expenditure).[20]

Not all the expenditures from the state budgets, small as they are, are paid for out of revenues raised by the states themselves. Roughly a third of state revenue comes from federal grants.[21] The state sources are numerous, ranging from revenue from mines and forests and from various licenses to treasure trove.[22] But without grants they would be insufficient. The federal government's grants to the states consist principally of the capitation grants, based on state population, of a road grant calculated on road mileage, and, mainly of benefit to Perak and Selangor, a share of the export duty on tin produced in a state.[23]

The provisions for the Borneo states are different and too complex to sketch except in outline. They have extra scope for levying taxation, in the form of sales taxes, and both are assigned import and excise duties on petroleum products and export duty on timber and other forest products, and the revenue from fees and dues on ports and harbors, except federal ports and harbors. They both receive capitation and road grants, and each individually, has a grant, calculated from a formula. After five years (1968) each of these grants may be renegotiated, but they cannot be abolished until 1974.[24]

Federal-State Relations in Practice

The best guarantee of happy federal-state relations does not lie in any constitutional provisions but rather in the harmonizing influence of membership of the same party. One instance of informal coordination via the party machinery was that after both the 1959 and 1964 elections in Malaya the person appointed to head the executive in each Alliance-controlled state in Malaya, the Mentri Besar, or Chief Minister, had to be approved by the (Alliance)

---

[19] *Straits Times,* September 20, 1961.

[20] For the eleven states of Malaya (*Malaysia Official Year Book, 1963* [Kuala Lumpur: Government Printer, 1964], p. 513).

[21] *Ibid.*

[22] Article 110(1) and Tenth Schedule Part III.

[23] Articles 109 and 110 and Tenth Schedule Parts I and II.

[24] Article 112 and Tenth Schedule.

Federation Prime Minister. Even the Political Secretaries to the Mentri Besar and Chief Ministers must be similarly approved.[25] Another party device for helping coordination is to hold a meeting of the federal Cabinet together with the Mentri Besar and Chief Ministers of the states controlled by the Alliance. The importance of *party* in ensuring cooperation between the states and the central government is so well known that it has become a common argument at elections. During the 1964 election in Penang, the (Alliance) Chief Minister warned the electors that there was no point in their voting for the Socialist Front: even if the Front won a majority in the state, the Alliance was bound to be in control of the federal government, and the federal grants, on which Penang so largely depended, would be cut. To drive the point home the Chief Minister of Penang cited the example of Kelantan. Kelantan has been under a PMIP (Pan-Malayan Islamic Party) government since 1959, and therefore provides the best example of a state controlled for a long period by a party other than the one in power at the federal level. Some of the disputes between the Kelantan state government and the federal government have, in themselves, been of minor importance. For instance, the state government's opposition to Malaysia took the form of deciding that September 16, 1963, and the following day would *not*, as in other states, be public holidays, and even after that day for some time the state flew a flag with an eleven-pointed (Malaya) star rather than a fourteen-pointed (Malaysia) star. Nevertheless, disputes on such apparently minor issues reflect a deep-seated division of opinion on substantial matters of policy and on the interpretation of the meaning of "cooperation" between federal and state governments. The PMIP point of view, stated by the party leader, Dr. Burhanuddin, was that some states were not getting a fair allocation of money for rural development "because of political sentiments."[26] But Tun Razak, the federal Minister of Rural Development, speaking with reference to land, thought that the Kelantan government had been unfair. The federal government wanted to help in every way possible, but the PMIP government had refused to cooperate.[27]

Perhaps the most serious example of a lack of cooperation between the federal and the Kelantan governments concerns land policy. Most of the responsibility for opening up new land for settlement has been given to the Federal Land Development Authority (FLDA). In the Constitution land is one of the subjects in the state list. Presumably,

[25] *Straits Times,* May 6, 1964.
[26] *Ibid.,* April 21, 1961.
[27] *Ibid.,* February 4, 1962.

if the Federal Land Council formulated explicitly a land policy empowering the FLDA to extend its operations to Kelantan (or any other one of the original eleven states of Malaya), then, irrespective of the wishes of the state government, this policy could be put into effect, if necessary, by force. So far, however, this situation has not arisen. Consequently, the main inducement for Kelantan, or any other state in Malaya, to allow the FLDA to operate in its territory, is that these operations benefit mainly[28] the inhabitants of the state and are paid for out of federal funds. This is a substantial inducement. However, initially the PMIP government of Kelantan refused to accept it,[29] and proceeded with its own, much less ambitious, land settlement scheme, which had to be financed out of its own meager state funds. To some degree the PMIP state government objection concerned FLDA methods. The FLDA procedure is elaborate; land is cleared for the settlers, and they are then settled on a substantial holding, which will give them a comfortable livelihood, although they have to pay off the debt incurred over a period of years. The Kelantan state scheme is less elaborate, costs less money, attempts to settle more people on a given area, and entails less going into debt on the part of the settler.[30] Behind this difference of opinion on methods, there is also a difference on principle. One reason for the state's refusal of FLDA help, it is said, is that the FLDA does not discriminate between the various races: the PMIP government likes to be free to select Malays as settlers. Also, it has been alleged, the FLDA plan, by which large stretches of land are cleared by contractors, is disliked by the PMIP, because most of the contractors, who benefit from this work are Chinese. The dispute about rival methods of land clearance has been made the subject of political propaganda. The PMIP has represented the withholding of FLDA assistance, except on FLDA conditions, as Alliance Party "pressure" on the state government. The Alliance has countered, since the change of government in Trengganu in 1961, by taking busloads of its supporters from Kelantan to see the extensive FLDA land schemes, newly started just inside Trengganu. Since the general elections in 1964, however, there

[28] "Mainly," because in some states with a large supply of undeveloped land, such as Pahang, land is cleared for the benefit of settlers from more crowded states.

[29] Statement by the Mentri Besar of Kelantan in the State Assembly, *Straits Times,* January 1, 1962.

[30] D. E. M. Fiennes, "The Malayan Federal Land Development Authority," *Journal of Local Administration Overseas,* I, No. 3 (1962), 156–163; Peter Polomka, "$130 Million Plan That Just Gathers Dust," *Straits Times,* August 7, 1963.

has been a distinct change in the atmosphere. The newly appointed Mentri Besar, Dato Mohamed Asri bin Haji Muda, said that the PMIP-controlled state government was ready to cooperate with the federal government in all matters.[31] Later the Kelantan government agreed to accept federal aid for rural development.[32] There was no specific mention of the FLDA, but it was expected that the FLDA would operate in Kelantan soon with the state government's approval.

Another much-discussed object of dispute between the Kelantan government and the federal government was the bridge intended to link Pasir Mas and Tumpat with Kota Bharu. The state government asked for a federal loan but did not agree to submit the plans for the construction of the bridge to the federal Public Works Department. The loan was therefore refused, and the state government proceeded to construct the bridge, at a cost of about $5 million, attempting to finance it entirely out of state funds.[33]

At the same time as it appeared to be cooperating more closely with the federal government, the Kelantan government has gone ahead with a scheme, which, if successful, would reduce its financial dependence on the federal government. During the 1964 election campaign in Malaya it was revealed that the Kelantan government was negotiating a land agreement with a Singapore industrial corporation. In 1965 it was announced that, in return for allowing the corporation to exploit timber resources in Kelantan, the state government would receive over M$50 million in revenue.[34]

Sabah and Sarawak Relations with the Federal Government since Malaysia

Some of the topics on which the people of the Borneo territories felt most strongly during the Malaysia negotiations have become less prominent since. Immigration, for instance, has not been a source of friction. The Borneo territories secured the power to keep out unskilled labor from the rest of the Federation; the new problem has arisen of how to *encourage* the entry of *skilled* labor. However, on occasion it has seemed that there has been some disappointment in the two states, because more has not been achieved since Malaysia. To an extent this is perhaps the result of the idea of Malaysia having

[31] *Straits Times,* July 20, 1964.

[32] *Ibid.,* November 4 and 14, 1964. But the argument about the respective roles of the two governments in rural development continued into mid-1966.

[33] *Ibid.,* March 1, 1962, and June 1, 1962. Criticisms that the manner in which the project was undertaken were not likely to safeguard public funds were made by the Auditor-General in his 1963 report on Kelantan (*ibid.,* December 11, 1964).

[34] Dato Asri, *ibid.,* August 20, 1965.

been "oversold" to Sabah and Sarawak. To bring about Malaysia quickly it was necessary to present a picture of the future which has not yet been realized. Partly because of Confrontation, the development plans in both territories have been slow in coming into operation. The slogan of "Independence through Malaysia," which was used, may also have created confusion in misleading some persons in the territories into believing that a Borneo state could literally be independent while being at the same time inside a federation. It may have been this eagerness for independence which made the Sabah and Sarawak governments declare themselves independent (as did the Singapore government) for the brief period between August 31, 1963 (the date when the British were originally scheduled to hand over control) and September 16, 1963 (the date to which the Federation of Malaya government postponed the beginning of Malaysia in order for the findings of the U.N. Malaysian Mission to be published). One expression, unimportant in itself, of the continued belief in "independence in Federation" occurred at a meeting of the Sabah Legislative Assembly in November, 1964. The Assembly unanimously supported a motion rejecting Philippine claims to the sovereignty of Sabah, which included a reference to "the people of Sabah, in whom alone that sovereignty rests. . . ."[35]

Specific points of federal-state friction have been the appointment of the first Head of State in Sarawak, the "expatriate question," and the use of the Malay language, particularly in education.

The dispute about the appointment of the Sarawak Head of State, the Governor of Sarawak, became public just at the time Malaysia was being formed. The Alliance Party in Sarawak, including the Chief Minister, Dato Stephen Kalong Ningkan, wished Temenggong Jugah anak Barieng, a Dayak and head of one of the Dayak parties in the Sarawak Alliance, to be Head of State. But the Federation Prime Minister claimed that it had been previously agreed that, if the Chief Minister was a Dayak (which Dato Ningkan was), then the Head of State must be a Malay or a Melanau. Partly, the dispute may possibly have occurred because an alternative choice for Chief Minister was a Melanau, and, if he had in fact been chosen, from the point of view of "racial balance" Temenggong Jugah would have been acceptable as Head of State. However, the additional complication existed that, to the federal government, perhaps the image of the Temenggong was rather too traditional and insufficiently modernized for him to be Head of State. A compromise was arrived at by which

[35] *First Legislative Assembly, State of Sabah, First Session, Order Paper,* Monday, November 2, 1964.

a Malay, Datu[36] Abang Haji Openg, was made Head of State, while the Temenggong was given a post in the federal Cabinet with the title, "Minister of Sarawak Affairs."

In detail, the "expatriate question" properly belongs to the chapter on the civil service. But it also has had political implications which profoundly affected federal-state relations. The expatriate question in Malaya, and in Singapore, took the relatively straightforward form of how quickly British officers should be replaced by local officers. But in Borneo, and particularly in Sabah, the supply of qualified local officers available to replace expatriates was very small. Unless expatriates left very slowly, some of them would be replaced by Malayans, not local men. In Sabah the party consisting principally of non-Muslim natives was in favor of slow replacement and a higher proportion of natives taking over: the mainly Muslim native party and the federal government were in favor of quicker replacement, with a higher proportion of Malayans. Those who supported the latter course included Inche Abdul Rahman bin Yaakub (born in Sarawak), who was then Assistant Minister for National and Rural Development, the then Deputy Federal Secretary in Sabah, Yeap Kee Aik, and the Prime Minister himself. The Tengku even went so far as to say that in appointing Ministers to the federal Cabinet from Sabah and Sarawak he was influenced by the consideration that bringing in more Ministers would indirectly bring in British influence.[37] The choice of a State Secretary for Sabah, because of the importance of the post, was the most fiercely contested single appointment, and in December, 1964, nearly led to a complete split in the Alliance Party in Sabah.[38] The expatriate question was also one of the issues on which the Sarawak Alliance split in June, 1966.

Especially in Sarawak, there has also been some dispute on the use of Malay in education. In 1964 there was not a single secondary school in which Malay was the medium of instruction and there was a great shortage of qualified teachers of Malay. Nevertheless, some members of the federal government believe that, even bearing such obstacles in mind, education in Malay should be pushed more vigorously in Sarawak. The question of the medium of instruction became somewhat mixed up with the provision of free primary education in Sarawak, which did not yet exist. An opposition politician even suggested that, if the federal government were to provide money for free primary education in Sarawak, it might do so only on the condition

[36] An old Malay hereditary title, not to be confused with "Dato."
[37] *Ibid.*, August 13, 1964.
[38] See p. 105, below.

that Malay be more widely used.[39] In August, 1965, the Minister of
Education announced that free primary education would be provided
in all government and government-aided schools in Sarawak (and in
Sabah) as from January 1, 1966. The central government would not
arbitrarily impose its plans on any state government, but the governments "will have to consider very seriously how we can bring
closer together the federal and state system."[40] During the crisis which
occurred in the Sarawak Alliance, June and July, 1966, some fears
were expressed that Malay might become the only official language
before 1973. This possibility was denied by the new Chief Minister,
Penghulu Tawi Sli.

There are two possible views on the course of federal-state relations in the Borneo states since 1963. One is that, in spite of all the
safeguards provided for the Borneo states in the Constitution, the
existence of a federal government necessitated a certain degree of
centralization; in the face of Confrontation, the pace of centralization has had to be stepped up a little. The other view is that centralization has proceeded too fast, even allowing for Confrontation; the
safeguards in the Constitution are now not as strong and reassuring
as they once seemed. "Some may think all we need to show federal
presence here is that we fly more flags and forget our status as a
State in the federal system or government. But this is not so, and
you know this cannot be done overnight."[41]

These different viewpoints were well illustrated by the reactions to
the news of Singapore's separation from Malaysia in August, 1965.
In both territories shock and surprise were expressed at the sudden-
ness of the move. In Sarawak the Sarawak United People's Party, an
opposition party, called for a referendum on whether or not Sarawak
should remain in Malaysia. But the possibility of secession was not
raised by any of the parties in the Sarawak government. For one
thing, Sarawak was so short of finance for development that from an
economic angle secession simply could not be contemplated. But in
Sabah the United Pasok-momogun Kadazan Organization (UPKO)[42]

[39] *Straits Times,* May 28 and June 25, 1964. This suggestion was apparently confirmed by a ministerial statement which linked free primary
education with "conformity to the national educational policy" (*Government Press Release,* December 15, 1964).

[40] *Straits Times,* August 4, 1965.

[41] Dato Donald Stephens, then Chief Minister of Sabah, *ibid.,* April 6,
1964.

[42] United Pasok-momogun Kadazan Organization, formed by the union
of the United National Kadazan Organization (UNKO) and National Pasok
Momogun Party in June, 1964.

and its leader, Dato Stephens, raised the question of whether the relations between Sabah and the federal government should not be re-examined to take account of Singapore's departure.[43] In itself this request was perfectly reasonable, as would have been a similar request from Sarawak. Malaysia had been formed less than two years before by the union of four territories on the basis of a most complicated arrangement of exceptions, checks and balances. It could not be assumed that, after Singapore had become independent, everything else would remain the same. The racial proportions of the population of Malaysia and the balance of party strengths were now obviously different. But the federal government reacted strongly against Dato Stephens' suggestion. It may have feared that he really was hinting at secession. The Tengku, on a visit to Sabah, warned that any attempt by Sabah to secede from Malaysia constitutionally or by armed rebellion would fail.[44] Dato Stephens resigned from the federal Cabinet on the same day, and retired from politics altogether in the following November. Later, Tun Razak, the federal Deputy Prime Minister, while on a tour of Sabah, agreed that "the administrative machinery by which the two governments could liaise together should be improved," although he did not agree that the terms on which Sabah had entered Malaysia should be re-examined.[45]

Dato Stephens' party, the UPKO, had already taken up the stand of a states' rights party against its nominal ally, the United Sabah National Organization (USNO), which was closely identified with the federal government.[46] Logically, therefore the UPKO was likely to react the way it did to the sudden secession of Singapore, just as the Alliance government, in a tense situation, predictably reacted to what may have seemed to it to be a first step by Sabah towards secession.

The Cabinet changes in Sabah (December, 1964) and Sarawak (June, 1966) by which Dato Stephens and Dato Ningkan, respectively, were forced out of office have also been regarded as examples of the federal government's power, exercised through the party system. The removal of Ningkan, however, was achieved by working through the Malaysian Alliance machinery, not the Sarawak Alliance machinery, and, later, by passing a constitutional amendment.[47]

---

[43] *Straits Times,* August 17, 1965. Dato Stephens' case is stated comprehensively in the *Sabah Times,* September 6, 1965.

[44] *Sunday Times,* August 22, 1965.

[45] *Straits Times,* September 8, 1965.

[46] See p. 105, below.

[47] See pp. 103 and 145, below.

6

Political Parties, Elections, and Interest Groups

Malayan Parties

By the time of the 1955 elections in Malaya the early postwar political organizations had disappeared, leaving the Alliance Party and the Party Negara as the chief contenders. Since then the Party Negara has declined almost to insignificance. The parties which hold Malayan seats in the federal Parliament now are the Alliance, the Labour Party (formerly part of the Socialist Front), the Pan-Malayan Islamic Party, the People's Progressive Party, the United Democratic Party, and the Democratic Action Party.

Because of the communal nature of politics in Malaya all parties face a dilemma. If they do not try to appeal to a particular community or communities, they will lose support to parties which do make this type of appeal. The quick death of Dato Onn's Independence of Malaya Party (IMP) is a terrible warning of the fate awaiting an explicitly noncommunal party. On the other hand, because of the mixed racial composition of the electorate, it would be difficult for a party which appealed to only one community to win a majority in Parliament. The Malays could have done this in 1955 quite easily, because the proportion of non-Malays who had the vote was small, although this would have been entirely counter to the scheme by which the British proposed to hand over power to a government representative of all major races. In Malaya the Malay advantage in the number of electors is now less,[1] although in the federal Parliament it is offset to some extent by the non-Malay native preponderance in the Borneo territories. Nevertheless, the Malays are helped by the favorable weighting which is given to rural constituencies[2] where the proportion of Malays is high. Now that Singapore is out of Malaysia, it would be quite possible for the Malays, in alliance with the Muslim electors in Sarawak and Sabah, to win a majority of the seats in the federal Parliament. Such an alignment, however, of Muslims versus the rest, would indicate that multi-racial parties had completely failed in Malaysia.

It would seem that noncommunal parties cannot hope to survive, while communal parties might have some difficulty in winning a majority. The solution to this impasse was reached, by accident, by the Alliance. The Alliance formula is that a number of communal parties are joined, "at the top," in an intercommunal Alliance.[3] Of the three Alliance communal parties — the United Malays' National Organization (UMNO), the Malayan Chinese Association (MCA), and the Malayan Indian Congress (MIC) — UMNO is the strongest and the MIC clearly the weakest. There is reason to believe that at the top of the structure the personal ascendancy of Tengku Abdul Rahman makes the Alliance Party constitution not a very accurate guide to how the machinery actually works.

As a son of a Sultan of Kedah, the Tengku[4] partly represents the traditional in Malay life, but he is also a Westernized person, as revealed in his undergraduate interest in racing cars, and his present interest in golf. He is probably one of the few political leaders in existence who genuinely does not strive hard after power. He is not attracted by politics as such; "I am not very interested in politics. I am more interested in . . . looking after the welfare and well-being of the people and the nation."[5] Of course, for some time after a country becomes independent the government party can command support just because it is identified with the winning of independence. Additionally the personal appeal of the party leaders can be relied on to rally support. Later, however, some parties develop an ideology. The Alliance Party sometimes denies that it has any ideology. Alter-

[1] At the 1964 general election in Malaya approximately 54 per cent of the electors were Malays and 46 per cent non-Malays.

[2] *Constitution,* Thirteenth Schedule, Part I, 2(c). This provision dates from 1962.

[3] However, direct membership in the Alliance, not via the UMNO, MCA, or MIC, was provided for in 1965 (*Straits Times,* December 20, 1965).

[4] The Tengku's origins and character are described in Harry Miller, *Prince and Premier* (London: Harrap, 1959).

[5] *Straits Times,* September 21, 1962.

natively, it sometimes takes the line that its ideology, while not capable of being summed up as "socialism," "communism," "neo-colonialism," or "capitalism," rests on *development*. The Deputy Prime Minister, Tun Razak, has put this point of view, and has become identified with the drive for rural development. Measures which can be represented as examples of development or welfare have a high place in the Alliance program, but usually the party shies away from anything which can be represented as "socialism."

It is a little difficult, however, for the government of an Asian country which is not completely reactionary to denounce socialism in all its aspects on all occasions. Sometimes certain Alliance "welfare" measures have been equated with socialism. "In industrial development we have adopted the capitalist practice of allowing private enterprise to find its fullest expression. In the sphere of community development and social services we have adopted a programme patterned on the basis of socialistic ideals."[6] There is also an endemic feeling in the Youth Section of the MCA that the Alliance, or the MCA, "ought" to have an ideology. This feeling arises, no doubt, from awareness of the high place given to ideology by the MCA's main rival for the support of Chinese youth, the Labour Party. An argument on "socialism" was also one aspect of the MCA-PAP dispute which took shape late in 1963 and early in 1964. Tan Siew Sin, the national president of the MCA, drew comparisons, unfavorable to Singapore, between the terms for the Employees' Provident Fund in Singapore and in Malaya. "Though we are supposed to be a right-wing government, we are more socialist in practice than many so-called socialist governments."[7]

The strains and stresses inside the Alliance are considerable. Each of the two main partners, the UMNO and the MCA, has to meet the competition of parties appealing to its own community, while trying to keep in step with its Alliance partner. This may result in pressures which tend to disrupt the component party. These are less obvious in the UMNO, perhaps partly because it is in a more secure position, except in Kelantan and, formerly, Trengganu, perhaps because of the dominant personality of the Tengku. The troubles of the MCA have been more open. It has been exposed to charges of having betrayed the Chinese on some aspects of the "bargain," such as lan-

[6] Tun Ismail, speaking in the General Assembly of the United Nations (*ibid.*, October 13, 1959). Cf. Tun Razak's statement, "nothing could be more socialistic than our rural development programme" (*ibid.*, December 25, 1964).

[7] *Ibid.*, January 31, 1964. For an exchange of letters between him and S. Rajaratnam, chairman of the PAP Political Bureau, see *ibid.*, February 3 and 5, 1964.

guage, education, and Malay rights. In 1959 discontent came to a head over the allocation of seats to the MCA in the Alliance choice of candidates for the forthcoming election. The secretary, Too Joon Hing, and some other prominent members left the party, and the president, Dr. Lim Chong Eu, gave up his post, went to England for medical treatment, and later resigned. Some of the former MCA leaders contested the election as Independents. Even after the election, discontent persisted over the government's education policy. It took some time to convince the bulk of the Chinese that the new policy would not be fatal to the study of Chinese language and culture. During that period Too Joon Hing defeated a government candidate at a by-election, largely on the education issue. In the early 1960's the strains were less pronounced. At the party's annual assembly late in 1963 some older members were replaced on important committees by younger ones. But the position of the national president was untouched, perhaps strengthened. Even the entry of the PAP into the federal elections in 1964 did no immediate damage to the party.

Towards the end of 1965 there were increasing tensions inside the Alliance. In the MCA the focus of discontent was the Chinese language issue, which threatened to become almost as explosive as the education issue had been half a dozen years before. Much of the agitation on the language issue in 1965 probably represented a revival of the whole complex question of the place of Chinese tradition, culture, and education in Malaysia. The expected change in the official language in 1967 did not directly concern Chinese; instead of Malay and English being the official languages, from 1967 the only official language would be Malay. Significantly, the threatened resignation of Lee San Choon as chairman of the MCA Youth Section in 1965 seems not to have been because he wanted Chinese to be an official language but because he wanted a "more liberal stand" on the Chinese language, especially as regards education.[8] In September, 1965, leaders of MCA state branches supported the stand taken by the MCA central working committee, that Chinese should not be an official language, but at the same time called for "a more general and wider use of the Chinese language by all Government departments and statutory bodies."[9] The prominence of the Chinese language issue in late 1965 may have reflected, to some extent, a reaction against the vigor with which Malay was being promoted as the national language.[10] It may also have been partly attributable to the ferment

[8] *Straits Times,* August 18, September 4, and September 8, 1965.
[9] *Ibid.,* September 14, 1965.
[10] See pp. 239–242, below.

stirred up by the "Malaysian Malaysia" policies of the People's Action Party in its incursion into politics in Malaya, even though the PAP had not advocated that Chinese should be an official language.[11] One of the Alliance reactions to the agitation was to set up an "Alliance Action Committee" composed of representatives of the UMNO, MCA, and MIC, one of whose major tasks was to make recommendations on the Chinese education and language problem.[12]

Inside the UMNO there have also been signs of dissatisfaction with the party's official policy. One of these was the resignation of Dato Syed Ja'afar Albar as secretary-general of UMNO after the separation of Singapore, indicating that he, and no doubt others in the party, would have preferred that a tougher line had been taken with Singapore.[13] Another was the increasing prominence of the Malaysian Afro-Asian People's Solidarity Organization, led by an UMNO member of Parliament, Dr. Mahathir bin Mohamed, which was distinctly more "anti-colonialist" and pro-Indonesian in its pronouncements than was Malaysia's official foreign policy.[14]

The Socialist Front, which existed from 1957 to 1965, was also built on an Alliance-type "formula": parties which were largely communal were linked at the higher levels. The communal aspect was less obvious than in the Alliance. The Front's structure was sometimes justified by saying that the component parts were necessary to cover urban and rural areas, respectively. It is significant, however, that, even with the assistance of ideology (which the Alliance Party lacks), communal differences still had to be recognized by the use of a structure resembling that of the Alliance. The antecedents of the parties which formed the Front are complex. But the Front itself dated from 1957, when the Labour Party and the Party Ra'ayat came together. In March, 1964, the National Convention Party, newly founded by Inche Abdul Aziz bin Ishak, joined it as a third component. Broadly, the Party Ra'ayat is based on the rural areas and consists mainly of Malays. The Labour Party is for the most part urban and Chinese. The National Convention Party is also mostly rural and Malay, based mainly on the parts of Selangor nearest to Inche Aziz's former state constituency, Morib. The Labour Party is stronger and better organized than Party Ra'ayat; for example, the latter has often had difficulty in finding good Malay candidates. When the Chinese joined Party Ra'ayat branches in great numbers sometimes the reason was that there is no convenient branch of the

---

[11] See p. 217, below.
[12] *Straits Times,* September 3, 1965.
[13] See p. 219, below.
[14] See p. 196, below.

Labour Party nearby: but sometimes it was with the explicit object of "stiffening" a weak sector of the party's organization.

The Socialist Front was somewhat vague in its proposals for social and economic reform, partly because of struggles among extremists, moderates, and opportunists inside the party. The party favored welfare measures and development, but so does the Alliance. The Socialist Front openly advocated more economic equality in its 1964 election manifesto. "We shall endeavour to achieve by constitutional means an egalitarian society based upon the principle of justice for all." Yet in the same manifesto it made no mention of nationalization of industry. It concentrated much of its fire on colonialism. Foreign business firms in Malaya, which embody the twin evils of capitalism and colonialism, were a particularly attractive target. More recently Dr. Tan Chee Khoon made a sophisticated attack on certain aspects of Alliance economic policy, particularly on the benefits to a few firms in each industry which resulted from the grant of pioneer status.[15] But after Confrontation the party suffered because it was not considered 100 per cent patriotic. Its 1964 manifesto, to be sure, said "we will unite to defend the sovereignty of our country." But not all Socialist Front leaders were outspoken in their opposition to communism, and the image of the party as Communist-infiltrated was intensified by the arrest of such leaders as Inche Ahmad Boestamam (February, 1963) and Inche Abdul Aziz bin Ishak and Inche Ishak bin Haji Mohammad (February, 1965).[16]

Like the Alliance, the Front was far from united on the language question. There was an attempt to restrict its comments on language to noncommunal criticisms, such as saying that secondary education should be free. But some Labour Party members went on record as saying that Chinese and Tamil should be made official languages, which antagonized the largely Malay following of Party Ra'ayat. In December, 1965, the Labour Party and Party Ra'ayat both split away from the Front, leaving it a shadow organization. The main reason for the split appears to have been the language issue.[17]

[15] Speech on the 1964 budget (mimeographed by Dr. Tan Chee Khoon).

[16] Inche Boestamam was alleged to have been concerned in the plans for the Azahari revolt in Brunei, December, 1962. After the 1965 arrests the Socialist Front leaders, and some PMIP leaders, were said to have plotted with the Indonesians to set up a "Malaysian government in exile" [*Straits Times,* February 14, 1963, and March 1, 1965; *A Plot Exposed* (Kuala Lumpur: Government Printing Office, 1965)].

[17] *Straits Times,* December 15, 1965 and January 11 and 13, 1966 (Lim Kean Siew). Since the arrest of Abdul Aziz in February, 1965 the National Convention Party had been moribund.

As its name suggests, the Pan-Malayan Islamic Party is founded on the principles of Islam. Its support is greatest in the northeastern states of Kelantan and Trengganu, where the population is over 90 per cent Malay, where communications with the rest of Malaya have been bad, and where the standard of education provided has been poor. Some of the grievances which lead to support for the PMIP are economic. The party has attacked the existence of Chinese middlemen and moneylenders and the UMNO's mixing with rich Chinese in the higher reaches of the Alliance Party. But the economic remedies proposed by the PMIP are somewhat vague. The party claims that if it came into power it would base its economic policy on the principles of Islam, but that the exact method of applying the principles would have to be worked out. It appears, however, that parts of the economic program might be radical. The PMIP has found support in the teachings of Islam for some kinds of nationalization, for instance, of land and electricity.

The driving force behind the party comes from religion. Economically, some of its beliefs may be radical, but socially it is profoundly conservative. It stands for a strict interpretation of Islam, distrusts progress, and sets a low value on material prosperity. It denounces many Western importations, particularly Western dancing. Much of its strength lies in the fact that the religious teachers on the relatively underdeveloped east coast, who are listened to with the greatest respect by most Malays, are preponderantly pro-PMIP. The party benefits from the view that, in the eyes of Islam, religion and politics are indivisible. As *the* religious party it stands to gain from the effects of a more vigorous propagation of the Faith. To break the hold of the PMIP the short-term tactics of the UMNO are to show, for example by providing mosques, that it is equally devoted to Islam. Its long-term tactics include spreading education to adults through extension classes, administered by the (federal) Ministry of Rural Development.

The third main point about the PMIP is its nationalist aspect. It is purely a Malay party: it is neither ostensibly noncommunal, like the People's Progressive Party or the United Democratic Party, nor is it intercommunal like the Alliance or the Socialist Front. It is unsympathetic to the claims of the other communities in Malaya, and urges the special rights of the Malays as the original "sons of the soil." It is anticolonialist, believing that the colonial powers were not sincere when they appeared to agree to the creation of independent nations in Southeast Asia. It also favors eventual union with Indonesia. Its former leader, Dr. Burhanuddin, and Inche Ishak bin Haji

Mohammad and Inche Boestamam, both of the Socialist Front, were all active in the Malay National Party which advocated a Greater Indonesia before it was dissolved in 1950.

Three main strands in PMIP policy have been indicated by Dr. Burhanuddin: they are nationalism, Islamism, and socialism — reminiscent of the ideas embodied in President Sukarno's "NASAKOM." The element of socialism, says the Doctor, is in nationalism, because nationalism is fundamentally based on the aspiration to build a just society. There are elements of nationalism in socialism, because socialism cannot be built unless pioneered by the nationalist spirit to blaze the path towards freedom from the yoke of colonialism. The elements of nationalism are found in Islam as a basis for the national liberation movement. There is a factor common to these three forces — they are all opposed to colonialism.[18] In the same article Dr. Burhanuddin stated that he was opposed to communism. But sometimes nationalism tends to blind PMIP supporters to the nature of communism. Frequently members of the PMIP will deny that communism represents a serious threat in Indonesia. They cannot imagine that native Indonesians, sons of the soil, can be Communists. Almost by definition, to them a Communist must be a Chinese. Confrontation put a severe strain on the PMIP in view of its hope that eventually Malaya and Indonesia would unite. In the early days of the dispute PMIP leaders urged mediation. Later many of them, while still suspicious of the designs of the Western powers in Southeast Asia, pledged their support to measures to meet Indonesian aggression. But in February, 1965, several leaders, including Dr. Burhanuddin, were arrested for subversion. Two, including Dr. Burhanuddin, were released in March, 1966.

The People's Progressive Party is the present name of the former "Perak Progressive Party," which fought the 1955 general elections. In spite of the change of name, the party has had little success in expanding beyond the boundaries of Perak; indeed, although it controls the important municipality of Ipoh, it has not managed to capture control of the Perak state government. In addition to being regional the party is also personal, in that its driving force comes from two politically talented lawyers, the brothers D. R. and S. P. Seenivasagam. Although sometimes described as a left-wing party, the PPP appeal is not mainly economic. In its 1959 election manifesto it made no immediate radical economic proposals, although it said that "in due course" tin and rubber "will have to be nationalised

18 Dr. Burhanuddin Al Helmy, "Towards Tanah Melayu Merdeka," *Merdeka Convention, Papers and Documents* (London: 1957).

so that the true wealth of the nation can be utilised to secure for the people of Malaya a better standard of living and prevent the workers from being exploited." The main appeal of the party has been to the non-Malays, largely on the issues of language and education. It has urged that Chinese and Tamil should be recognized as "official" languages, although Malay should remain the "national" language. Malay should be a compulsory subject in schools, but non-Malay children should be taught and examined in their own mother tongue. In the name of "equality" the PPP has opposed those measures which provide for the "special position of the Malays." In the municipality of Ipoh, which it controls, it has tried to introduce "multi-lingualism" on signboards and at council meetings. After Confrontation the PPP was a firm supporter of government foreign policy: an important reason for this was dislike of the Indonesian government's treatment of the Chinese in Indonesia.

In 1962 a new party was formed, the United Democratic Party. Behind the UDP was Dr. Lim Chong Eu, the former president of the MCA. The UDP genuinely aspires to be a noncommunal party, but probably most of the votes it received in the 1964 election were Chinese. The party's policy is reflected in its origins, a delayed off-shoot of the MCA. It is not as extreme as the PPP and does not demand complete equality for non-Malays with Malays. It does not seek a complete reversal of the Alliance government's education policy. But it criticizes the *implementation* of Alliance policies, notably in education. It is difficult to see the party gaining much success, unless it can offer a policy sufficiently distinctive from those of the existing parties. At present its strength lies largely in the personality and reputation of Dr. Lim. The party originally had its doubts about the way in which the Malaysia proposal was introduced and managed, but supported the government on external policy after Confrontation.

Elections in Malaya

So far there have been three general elections in Malaya, in 1955 for 52 out of the 98 seats in the Legislative Council, and in 1959 and 1964 for the 104 seats in the federal Parliament. In 1959 and 1964 there were also elections for the state legislatures in Malaya: in the former year they were held at different times during the two or three months preceding the federal parliamentary elections; in the latter year they were held on the same day. Although Malaysia was already in existence in 1964, the Sarawak, Sabah, and Singapore seats in the federal Parliament were not filled by direct election in 1964. They had already been filled indirectly[19] at the time of the formation of Malaysia in 1963. In the future, however, it is the intention that all the seats in the federal Parliament (and in all the state legislatures) shall be filled directly.

Arrangements for holding and for supervising their conduct are in the hands of the Election Commission. Originally this three-man body enjoyed a substantial measure of "independence." However, its powers were reduced in 1962, when its ability to delimit the areas of constituencies was curbed, the final decisions on boundaries being given to Parliament.[20]

Table 2[21] indicates the trend of support for the parties between 1955 and 1964. At the 1955 election the Alliance won a crushing victory. It lost only one seat, and its percentage of the vote, 80 per cent, was more than ten times as great as that of its nearest rival, Party Negara. By 1959 there was a perceptible change. The Alliance had 70 per cent of the parliamentary seats but only just over 50 per cent of the votes. Its losses occurred both in mainly Malay and in mainly non-Malay seats. In Kelantan and Trengganu all the opposition members elected (with the exception of one Party Negara member) were PMIP. Not only did the PMIP win more parliamentary seats than the Alliance in these two states: in the preceding state elections they gained control of the two state legislatures. The Alliance also lost support, and seats, in some areas where there was a large non-Malay vote, mostly in the big towns. The seats lost in Penang and Selangor all went to the Socialist Front, and were mostly situated in the urban centers of George Town and Kuala Lumpur, respectively. Four of the five seats lost in Perak were in or near the town of Ipoh, and fell to the PPP, the fifth going to an Independent. The two Negri Sembilan seats were won by Independents who had formerly been MCA: both were in the town of Seremban. The

[19] Indirect election was chosen in preference to direct election for the Borneo territories, because they were not yet sufficiently developed politically to have direct elections. In Singapore the government's attempt to pass a bill providing for direct elections to Singapore seats in the federal Parliament was blocked by a combination of all the opposition parties.

[20] *Constitution,* Article 113(1) and Thirteenth Schedule, Part II, as amended by the Constitution (Amendment) Act of 1962.

[21] The 1955 figures are for the Legislative Council elections, the 1959 and 1964 figures are for the parliamentary elections. Sources: T. E. Smith, *Report on the First Election of Members to the Legislative Council* (Kuala Lumpur: Government Press, 1955); *Report on the Parliamentary and State Elections, 1959* (Kuala Lumpur: Government Press, 1960); *Report on the Parliamentary (Dewan Ra'ayat) and State Legislative Assembly General Elections, 1964, of the States of Malaya* (Kuala Lumpur: Government Press, 1965).

Table 2

Alliance Votes and Seats, Federal Elections 1955, 1959, and 1964

| | Alliance Percentage of Valid Votes | | | Number of Seats | | | | | |
	1955	1959	1964	1955 All.	1955 Other	1959 All.	1959 Other	1964 All.	1964 Other
Kedah	92.8	65.1	68.6	6	—	12	—	12	—
Perlis	66.8	59.6	63.2	1	—	2	—	2	—
Penang	79.9	44.0	47.3	4	—	5	3	6	2
Perak	70.5	49.6	55.6	9	1	15	5	18	2
Selangor	71.2	44.3	53.9	7	—	9	5	12	2
Malacca	87.9	58.9	66.2	2	—	3	1	4	—
Negri Sembilan	83.9	51.9	59.3	3	—	4	2	6	—
Johore	86.1	65.7	71.7	8	—	16	—	16	—
Trengganu	84.9	37.4	56.5	3	—	1	5	5	1
Kelantan	78.1	31.4	42.9	5	—	1	9	2	8
Pahang	90.0	66.9	71.1	3	—	6	—	6	—
Total	80.0	51.8	58.5	51	1	74	30	89	15

Malacca seat which was lost, again an urban one, was captured by Tan Kee Gak, leader of the "equal rights" Malayan Party. With support eaten away both on the Malay side and the non-Malay side, the Alliance survived as a government with a large majority partly because the opposition parties' policies were too divergent to enable them to form a coalition. Some local deals were made by which one party agreed not to enter a candidate for a certain seat in return for reciprocal treatment elsewhere, but there was no united opposition front.

In the absence of Confrontation the result of the 1964 election might have been different. The Socialist Front might have made substantial gains and perhaps might even have established a claim to be *the* opposition party, both in terms of votes and seats won, and also through the geographic spread of its support over a wide area of Malaya. For a short time it seemed that the Malaysia issue might actually bring together the opposition parties in a coalition, because even some of the parties which were not deeply opposed to Malaysia in principle, such as the UDP, had reservations about the manner in which it had been formed. But the negotiations between the parties broke down. One important reason was Confrontation, which placed a barrier between parties sympathetic towards Indonesia on racial grounds (PMIP) or ideological grounds (Socialist Front) and those parties which were largely dependent on Chinese support (PPP and UDP). In the end there was no closer an approximation to a united opposition front than there had been in 1959. The only result of the negotiations was that Inche Abdul Aziz's newly formed National Convention Party became a component of the Socialist Front.

The chief surprise of the 1964 election in Malaya was the entry of the People's Action Party, the Singapore government party. To be sure, one of the expected results of forming a federation is that there will be increased "interpenetration" of parties from one constituent area to another. It is also true that the PAP had long before announced its intention of eventually entering politics in Malaya.[22] But quite recently it had denied that it would intervene in the 1964 election.[23] When the intervention was announced it was said that it would only be a token one. Candidates were entered for only 11 seats. The explanation given by the PAP for its entry was that the MCA had failed to attract the votes of the Chinese in the urban areas. By entering candidates in some of these areas the PAP would give the electors the chance of voting for a party which was pro-

[22] Lee Kuan Yew, *The Battle For Merger* (Singapore: Government Printing Office, 1961), p. 148, giving a reference to the PAP Manifesto, 1954.

[23] Lee Kuan Yew, *Straits Times,* September 10, 1963.

Malaysia, thus preventing former MCA votes from being lost to the Socialist Front.[24]

Confrontation was overwhelmingly the main issue at the Malayan general election of 1964, and it could not fail to help the Alliance. Opposition parties which seemed to be half-hearted in their support of the government could be accused of being disloyal. On the other hand, if they backed the government's stand, then the government could say that the most patriotic thing to do was to rally behind the Tengku and vote Alliance. The fact that the PAP won only one seat (in Kuala Lumpur) may be explained along these lines. The PAP said it was solidly behind the Tengku and the UMNO on the big issue, Confrontation. Consequently, when the Tengku said that he stood shoulder to shoulder with the MCA, the PAP attacks on the MCA were blunted. In the one or two seats where the effect of the PAP's intervention can be intelligently guessed at, it does seem to have diverted votes from the Socialist Front. In terms of seats the opposition parties lost heavily. The PMIP, although it retained all its seats in Kelantan except one, lost three seats in Trengganu. In the state elections it kept control of Kelantan, with a reduced majority in the state legislature, but the Alliance majority in the Trengganu state legislature (acquired in 1961 when several members changed parties) was confirmed. PPP strength in Perak was weakened, and it lost two out of its four parliamentary seats. The only UDP victor was Dr. Lim Chong Eu in Penang. The Socialist Front retained only two of its eight seats, one in George Town and one in Kuala Lumpur. It would be a mistake, however, to think that the Socialist Front was substantially weaker in terms of grass root support in 1964. Certainly it lost seats. But, even in the face of the Confrontation issue, it won a higher proportion of the votes than in 1959, 16 per cent as compared with 13 per cent, although this was achieved by putting up more candidates than in 1959. On the other hand, the Socialist Front's main rival among the opposition parties, the PMIP, won only 14 per cent of the vote in 1964 compared with 21 per cent in 1959. The Front's largest gains, in the proportion of votes won, were in Malacca, Negri Sembilan, and Johore.

Parties and Elections in Sarawak

Political parties are a very recent growth in Sarawak. When the formation of Malaysia was proposed in May, 1961, only two were in existence, the Sarawak United People's Party (SUPP) and the Party Negara Sarawak (PANAS). SUPP was founded in June, 1959, PANAS in April, 1960. Up to that time the only elections held in

[24] *Ibid.*, March 2 and 3, 1964.

Sarawak had been local ones for District Councils. At the 1959 election for the Kuching Municipal Council SUPP won a majority. But after the Malaysia announcement there was an increase in the number of parties. SUPP was opposed to Malaysia, preferring that Sarawak should become independent by itself; in a union with Malaysia it would merely be incorporated in a larger country, which would not amount to true independence. PANAS, on the other hand, after a brief hesitation, came out in favor of Malaysia. It may be asked why, since there was an anti-Malaysia party and a pro-Malaysia party, the number of parties increased after Malaysia was proposed? The answer is probably that political parties in Sarawak, given the general state of underdevelopment of the country, were bound to be racially based. This had happened in Malaya, which politically was more highly developed. The leadership of the intendedly noncommunal SUPP was mainly Chinese. "Taken as a signal for the beginning of the bid for power by the non-natives at a time when the natives felt themselves not yet in a position to compete, this set in motion the strain in race relations springing from the imbalance in economic power."[25] A kind of chain reaction followed in which each main racial group, and even smaller groups in some cases, founded its own political party or parties. PANAS, although noncommunal in principle, did contain a high proportion of Malay members and Malay leaders. Consequently, the first two parties were followed rapidly by four others: the Sarawak National Party (SNAP), largely Iban, in 1961; Barisan Ra'ayat Jati Sarawak (BARJASA), largely Malay, in December, 1961; the Party Pesaka Anak Sarawak (PESAKA), mainly Iban, in August, 1962; the Sarawak Chinese Association (SCA) in July, 1962. The duplication of parties among the Chinese, the Malays, and the Ibans may be accounted for by separate reasons in each case. The SCA owed its origins to the radical stand of the SUPP and the belief that it was Communist-infiltrated, which repelled some right-wing and moderate Chinese. The PANAS leaders were drawn largely from the Malays who had been most in favor of the cession of Sarawak to the British Crown by the Brooke Rajahs. This issue had deeply divided the Malays some fifteen years previously, and BARJASA, the new Malay party, was led by persons who were closely identified with the "anti-cession" faction. The difference between the PESAKA and SNAP parties was largely geographical; the former was based mainly on the Third Division of Sarawak, while the latter's strength lay mostly in the Second Division. Originally some of these parties were not in favor of Malaysia. But by

[25] *Report of the Commission of Enquiry, North Borneo and Sarawak* (Kuala Lumpur: Government Press, 1962), p. 8.

October, 1962, all except SUPP had formed a Sarawak United Front to work, among other things, to bring about the formation of Malaysia. In the intervening period the Alliance in Malaya had been extremely active in promoting the "Malaysia idea," both by sending some of its leaders to Sarawak (and North Borneo) to explain the advantages of Malaysia, and by inviting key political figures in Sarawak to visit Malaya to look at government projects, particularly in the sphere of rural development. Soon politics in Sarawak assumed a pattern similar to Malaya, although more complex. The five pro-Malaysia parties formed a Sarawak Alliance (January, 1963), with Temenggong Jugah anak Barieng (PESAKA) as chairman and Dato Stephen Kalong Ningkan (SNAP) as secretary. The result, as in Malaya, was an intercommunal Alliance, based on communal parties. In April, 1963, however, PANAS, while remaining pro-Malaysia, left the Alliance. One reason for the split was over the nomination of candidates in certain areas for the approaching elections.

The 1963 elections covered a period of about two months, April–June. This was necessary to allow the "polling teams" in rural areas time to go round all the polling stations in their circuit. A feature of the election was the large number of Independents. This reflected the fact, particularly in the remote Fourth and Fifth Divisions where communications were especially difficult, that the party system had not yet put down firm roots. Out of the 429 District Council seats, 73 were uncontested: in 34 of these an Alliance candidate was returned, in 28 an Independent.[26] In the contested seats the total votes were as follows (to the nearest thousand): SUPP, 45,000; PANAS, 28,000; Alliance, 57,000; Independents, 55,000. The total of seats won, in both uncontested and contested seats, was: SUPP, 116; PANAS, 59; Alliance, 138; Independents, 116. After the election, many of the Independents joined a party, in most cases the Alliance. These total figures are of interest in showing the general distribution of support for the parties, and, with intelligent interpretation, in indicating support for Malaysia, or the reverse.[27] But for the elections to the higher tiers of government, which were made indirectly after the District Council elections, what mattered was the *distribution* of support. A party with a minority vote and a minority of the District Council seats, might still gain control of particular Divisional Ad-

[26] *Report on the General Elections* (Kuching: Sarawak Information Service, 1963).

[27] As investigated in *United Nations Malaysia Mission Report* (Kuala Lumpur: Department of Information, 1963). See also K. J. Ratnam and R. S. Milne, *The Malayan Parliamentary Election of 1964* (Kuala Lumpur: University of Malaya Press, forthcoming), chapter on the elections in Sabah and Sarawak.

visory Councils, control of the Council Negri, and a majority of the seats from Sarawak in the federal Parliament. From the District Council results it was clear that the Alliance had won control of the Second Divisional Council, and, with Independent support, the Fourth and Fifth Divisional Councils. But these three Councils returned only a minority of the members to the Council Negri. The Alliance had to exert itself to gain and retain Independent support in order to win control of the Third Divisional Council where it was run close by the SUPP. In the First Divisional Council no single party had a majority: SUPP was in the lead, followed by PANAS and the Alliance. In spite of their policy differences, SUPP and PANAS came to an arrangement to divide the ten seats in the Council Negri, indirectly elected by the First Divisional Council, between them. This was one way of partially correcting the distortions of the electoral system. Without the SUPP-PANAS agreement, SUPP with 24 per cent of the votes in the contested seats and PANAS with 15 per cent of the votes, would not have been represented at all in the Council Negri, or in the federal Parliament. Even with the agreement the Alliance had about three-quarters of the seats in each of these two bodies.

Some comments may be made about later trends. A new party, "MACHINDA," with a name derived from its intended multi-racial coverage, was formed in 1964. Initially, at least, its leaders seem to have come from PANAS. Apart from personality issues, one reason for its foundation may have been a feeling among non-Malays in PANAS that PANAS was becoming a more and more "Malay" party. An eighth party was founded in 1965, based on the Third Division and led by Melanaus but claiming to be multi-racial. The new party joined with PANAS in 1966.

There was a realignment of parties in the Sarawak government in June, 1965. The immediate cause was land legislation which had been introduced to make it easier for Chinese to acquire a legal title to land. However, inside the government there were objections to the proposed legislation from BARJASA and PESAKA. Those who opposed it alleged that some of the provisions were too liberal, that there was a danger that land would become concentrated in the hands of a few, and that natives would regard the legislation as pro-Chinese. On the other hand, the Chief Minister, Dato Ningkan, thought that the opposition inside the government was not based on principle, but was rather a pretext for BARJASA and PESAKA to try to improve their strength in the government at the expense of SNAP and the SCA and to replace himself as Chief Minister. There were several weeks of uncertainty and maneuvering in which BARJASA and a substantial group in PESAKA, led by the secretary-general, Thomas Kana, tried to form a "Native Alliance," consisting of BARJASA, PESAKA and PANAS, to take over the government. The scheme foundered largely because of the opposition of the PESAKA chairman, Temenggong Jugah, who remained loyal to the Chief Minister and succeeded in carrying his party with him. The result was a tactical defeat for BARJASA and a Cabinet reshuffle in which Dato Ningkan remained Chief Minister.[28] PANAS rejoined the Alliance,[29] and was given representation in the Cabinet. The revolt which had failed in June, 1965, succeeded in June, 1966. BARJASA and PESAKA (this time with the support of the Temonggong) nominated Penghulu Tawi Sli to be Chief Minister in Ningkan's place. The nomination was approved by the Malaysian Alliance National Council, and the Governor appointed Tawi Sli Chief Minister. He formed a Cabinet of Sarawak Alliance parties, but SNAP was excluded and went into opposition.

The SUPP has also had problems. Its image is that of a mainly "Chinese" party, and it has had some difficulty in retaining the support of native members. There are also ideological differences in the party. The top leadership of the SUPP, including its chairman, Ong Kee Hui, and its secretary-general, Stephen Yong, is relatively moderate. But some sections have been infiltrated by Communists, and the SUPP is identifiable as the party which gives legal cover to the Clandestine Communist Organization (CCO) named in an exposure of Communist subversion in Sarawak.[30] The party's support has also come from Chinese resentment at government policy on education and on land. The moderate leaders now appear to accept Malaysia, but probably many of the rank and file do not.[31] A split in the party was narrowly averted in 1965 when SUPP, and also MACHINDA, joined the Malaysia Solidarity Convention.[32] The extremists in SUPP were not enthusiastic about joining an organization which contained the PAP but not the Barisan Sosialis or the Socialist Front. At the annual meeting of the central committee of the party, the moderates, including Ong and Yong, found themselves in a minority and walked out.[33] A temporary compromise was arrived at, but in the future

[28] *Straits Times,* June 16, 1965.

[29] *Government Press Release,* June 14, 1965.

[30] *The Danger Within* (Kuching: Sarawak Information Service, 1963).

[31] On a 1964 Council Negri motion condemning Indonesian aggression, most SUPP members voted in favor, but two abstained (*Straits Times,* April 16, 1964). Two months later Mr. Ong said that a large majority of the SUPP now supported Malaysia (*ibid.,* June 23, 1964).

[32] See p. 216, below.

[33] *Straits Times,* June 28, 1965.

there may be an open break into Communist and non-Communist wings, as occurred with the PAP in Singapore. In that event the big question is: Could the moderate leadership capture the bulk, or a sizeable portion, of the mass movement? After SNAP left the Alliance in June, 1966, it seemed quite possible that the party might ally itself with the moderates in SUPP.

Parties and Elections in Sabah

Political development in Sabah was behind that in Sarawak. There were no formally-established political parties in Sabah in May, 1961, yet by December, 1962, when the first District Council elections were held, there were five, joined together to form the Sabah Alliance and all in favor of Malaysia. The five were: the United National Kadazan Organization (UNKO); the United Sabah National Organization (USNO); the National Pasok Momogun Party; the Sabah National Party (SANAP); and the Sabah Indian Congress. The first two of these had the largest membership and the most extensive organization. The main distinction between them was that the second appealed mainly to natives who were Muslims, while UNKO appealed mainly to Kadazans, the largest ethnic group in Sabah, which contained very few Muslims. The Pasok Momogun also had support from non-Muslim natives, but drew its strength mainly from the interior areas far from the towns. It had originally been in favor of independence before Malaysia, but later changed its stand. SANAP was a Chinese party, composed of a union of the former Democratic and United parties, both of which, also, had wanted independence before Malaysia. But, on joining the Alliance, like the Pasok Momogun it changed to support of Malaysia. The Indian Congress represented the very small Indian community.

As in Sarawak, the only direct elections which took place were for District Councils: all the elections to higher-level bodies were indirect. The District Council elections took place in three parts: in December, 1962, March–May, 1963, and April, 1964. Practically all the seats in these District Council elections were won by the Alliance; a few were won by Independents but none by any other organized party. Some members of District Councils were still nominated, not elected. But they had no voice in the elections which took place indirectly from the District Councils, via an intermediate body, to the Sabah Legislative Assembly. Only Alliance representatives were returned to the Assembly and as the sixteen Sabah members to the federal Parliament. The seats in both were divided among the constituent parties of the Alliance, the USNO having the largest share.

Two contrasting views might be taken of the absence of an opposition in Sabah. One of them would rejoice at the absence of a "dan-

gerous" opposition, similar to the SUPP in Sarawak, and would argue
that in a happy country like Sabah party politics would merely dis-
tract the people from the major tasks of development and, while
Confrontation persisted, defense. The other view would point to the
virtues of an organized, responsible opposition as a source of informed criticism and as a possible alternative government. In any
case there are signs that the original absence of an opposition may
not be lasting. A businessman, Peter Chin, who had previously
started the Democratic Party, which later with another party formed
SANAP, founded a new "Social Democratic Party," registered in
January, 1964. Perhaps more significant is the possibility of a split
in the Alliance, particularly between the USNO and the UPKO.[34]
Even during the District Council elections there had been some maneuvering for seats among the Alliance parties. For some seats the
Alliance failed to reach an agreement on which party's choice would
be selected as *the* Alliance candidate, and, under different combina-
tions of party labels, there were in fact contests between representatives of more than one Alliance party, most often between USNO
and UNKO. After the elections some further developments occurred.
There was close competition for new members between the parties,
and they extended their field organization with an eye to the next
elections.

These maneuvers caused a strain inside the Cabinet, which in 1964
led to two reshuffles,[35] in the second of which the Chief Minister,
Dato Donald Stephens (UPKO) was forced to resign and was replaced by Peter Lo (SANAP). Dato Stephens replaced Mr. Lo as
Minister for Sabah Affairs in the federal Cabinet. Among the issues
at stake between the USNO and the UPKO were the role of the
Yang di-Pertuan Negara (the former USNO party leader) and the
question of civil service appointments, particularly that of the Sabah
State Secretary.[36] More generally, the dispute revealed the USNO as
a party which wanted to work closely with the (Muslim) UMNO
and the federal government, while the UPKO took up a stand based
on the rights of Sabah under the Constitution. The dispute was given
an additional twist when Singapore left Malaysia in August, 1965.
The UPKO and Dato Stephens took up the issue that, in the changed
situation, the terms on which Sabah should remain in Malaysia should
be renegotiated.[37] As a result of his differences from his colleagues
in the federal Cabinet on this question Dato Stephens resigned from
the Cabinet.

[34] UPKO is defined on p. 85.
[35] *Straits Times,* June 13, 1964 and December 18 and 30, 1964.
[36] See p. 84.
[37] See pp. 85–86.

In September, 1965, the Yang di-Pertuan Negara, Tun Datu Mustapha bin Datu Harun, resigned his office and was elected president of USNO.[38] Even while he had been Head of State, Tun Mustapha had remained the leading figure in his party. But his formal re-entry into party politics was perhaps a sign that USNO was reorganizing itself in earnest for the state elections, which were expected to take place early in 1966. If the differences between UPKO and USNO continue to grow, the main contest at the state elections will be between these two, nominally allied, parties. Shortly after USNO was strengthened by the return of Tun Mustapha to active politics, UPKO was weakened by the retirement of Dato Stephens from politics, in November, 1965, which was immediately followed by the resignation of the UPKO secretary-general, Peter Mojuntin. The balance between the parties is held by the Chinese component of the Alliance, which so far has tended to support USNO. In 1965 this party, previously called SANAP, merged with a welfare organization, the Sabah Chinese Association, and adopted the latter's name. This move could also be interpreted as a preparation for the 1967 elections. However, a smaller proportion of Chinese will be entitled to vote at these elections than at the previous District Council elections; the qualification to vote will be citizenship rather than residence and this will decrease the proportion of Chinese electors.

The Party System in Malaya and Malaysia

In Malaya the Alliance Party has now won three successive national elections — in 1955, 1959, and 1964. Generally speaking, these elections have been "free" in the sense that the government of the day did not restrict the choice of the voters by force or fraud. The main handicap of the opposition parties (particularly after Confrontation the Socialist Front and the PMIP) has been the arrest and detention of some of their leaders and key party workers. These arrests, and the prevention of demonstrations against the arrests, must have affected these parties more seriously than the small numbers concerned might suggest. Of course, from the government's point of view, because the Emergency ended only in 1960 while Confrontation began in 1963, it has clearly seemed necessary to make arrests where there has been proof of Communist infiltration; Malayan Communist Party documents from as far back as 1958 have urged Communists to work for the Communist Party by infiltrating other parties.[39] In time of national danger such measures are restrictions on democracy which

[38] *Straits Times,* September 18, 1965.
[39] *The Communist Threat to the Federation of Malaya* (Kuala Lumpur: Government Press, 1959), pp. 20–21.

must be accepted in the interests of security. Opposition leaders have frequently complained about the existence of restrictions on the press.[40] To be sure, newspapers are required to have licenses, which may be withdrawn at the discretion of the government and are subject to other controls. But the prevailing newspaper support for the Alliance government is probably traceable more to an alignment of interests between the owners and the government than to direct "control."

The most desirable balance between government and opposition is, of course, a debatable issue. Some opposition leaders, who are entirely free from any suspicion of subversion, feel that sometimes the balance has favored the government too much. Before the start of Confrontation, Dr. Lim Chong Eu appealed to the Tengku, for the sake of parliamentary democracy, to "adopt a fatherly attitude and encourage the growth of a healthy opposition in this country instead of merely condemning other parties as subversive, communal, racialist, chauvinist, or Communist."[41]

However, there are other reasons for the success of the Alliance in Malaya; its prestige as the party which won independence; the personality of the Tengku; the, on the whole, skillful management of UMNO-MCA relations; its rural development program; the fact that, so to speak, it is "fighting on interior lines," while its opponents are even more divided from each other on policy than they are divided from the Alliance. Above all, since Confrontation, the Alliance has benefited from the patriotism of the vast majority of the inhabitants.

Like the Indian party system, the system in Malaya might be termed a system of "one party dominance."[42] The dominant party consists of a number of factions, which nevertheless reach consensus, or agreement, through their sensitive adjustments to pressures from outside. The other parties "do not constitute alternatives to the ruling party. Their role is to constantly pressurize, criticize, censure and influence it . . . and, above all, exert a latent threat that if the ruling group strays away too far from the balance of effective public opinion, and if the factional system within it is not mobilized to restore the balance, it will be displaced from power by the opposition groups."

The formation of Malaysia resulted in some changes in the party system. On the formal level the Alliance parties in Malaysia joined

---

[40] The main provisions are summarized in H. E. Groves, *The Constitution of Malaysia* (Singapore: Malaysia Publications, 1964), pp. 207–209.

[41] *Straits Times*, May 1, 1962. Cf. Dr. Tan Chee Khoon, "What does a political party do when it is denied publications, rallies, processions, and house-to-house canvassing?" (*ibid.*, March 6, 1965).

[42] Rajni Kothari, "The Congress 'System' in India," *Asian Survey*, IV, No. 12 (1964), 1162.

together to form a "grand alliance," the Malaysian Alliance Party. Even before Malaysia the Alliance (in a slightly different form) had been active in Singapore. But after Malaysia, and the PAP intervention in the 1964 election in Malaya, the Alliance and the PAP were competing in each other's territory. The competition was so fierce and so divisive that it could not be accommodated within a democratic framework and Singapore was expelled. However, before this happened, the PAP, along with the UDP, the PPP and two Sarawak parties, SUPP and MACHINDA, had formed the Malaysian Solidarity Convention. Essentially the convention was a protest against a "Malay Malaysia." It fought for a "Malaysian Malaysia," which "means that the nation and the state is not identified with the supremacy, well-being and the interests of one particular community or race."[43] Significantly, apart from MACHINDA, which was a new party, the other parties in the convention all depended heavily on non-Malay, mainly Chinese, support. The convention continued in existence even after Singapore left Malaysia, and carried on a campaign against the government's "denial of fundamental rights" to opposition parties, and in particular its refusal to issue permits for them to hold rallies. But it is doubtful whether the convention can constitute an effective challenge to the Alliance. First, much of the original drive behind the convention came from the PAP, and after Singapore's separation from Malaysia the PAP was no longer allowed to operate there. To be sure, the PAP now has a counterpart in Malaysia, the Democratic Action Party (DAP), which was registered as a political party in March, 1966. But, constitutionally at least, the amount of direct help that the new DAP could receive from the PAP must be limited, and the Alliance government will watch any extra-constitutional activities very closely. Second, when the convention was formed it did not include the strongest opposition party, the Socialist Front. The Front was much less clearly anti-Communist and anti-Indonesian than the parties in the convention. When the Front split into its two constituent parts, the Labour Party and the Party Ra'ayat, in December, 1965, the situation became more fluid. The language issue had been a principal reason for the split in the Front, and the Labour Party and the parties in the convention were all opposed to any sudden decrease in the use of Chinese and Tamil, particularly for education, in 1967. In February, 1966, the PPP and the Labour Party went as far as setting up a joint committee to work out a program for a united front of opposition parties. But it seemed unlikely that any formula could be found which would satisfy both

[43] *Declaration of the Convenors of the Malaysian Solidarity Convention* (Singapore: mimeo., May 9, 1965), Article 6.

the Labour Party and the DAP. The Labour Party said that it differed from the DAP in believing that Malaysia was not formed as a result of the democratic will of the people and in objecting to the use of the Internal Security Act against opposition parties. The DAP, on the other hand, claimed that the Labour Party was pro-Sukarno and had expressed scorn for the convention.[44] If the language issue, or other communal issues, became really acute, this gap between the Labour Party and the DAP might narrow. The MCA might split or disintegrate and party lines might be redrawn on a predominantly racial basis, with the UMNO and the PMIP ranged on one side and the convention and the Labour Party ranged on the other. In such a situation "racial arithmetic," as modified by the line-up in the Borneo territories, would determine the composition of Malaysia's government, and multi-racial parties would be clearly revealed as having failed.

One immediate effect of the formation of Malaysia on the party system was to introduce a block of over thirty Alliance members from the Borneo states into the federal Parliament. However, the Alliance may not continue to benefit from this advantage in the future. SUPP membership in the federal Parliament might increase at the expense of Alliance membership, and splits in the Sabah and Sarawak Alliance Parties could deprive the Alliance of its control of the Borneo parliamentary seats. The nature of the federal system and the relations between federal and state governments have obvious implications for the party system. The powers of the states in Malaya are so weak, compared with the central government, that a party which captures control of a state has a very shaky base from which to conduct operations.[45] It has been pointed out how difficult it was for the PMIP government in Kelantan to carry out its policies because of the hostility of the federal government. The two Borneo states have more autonomy, but, partly because of their relatively late political development, it is unlikely that a party which established itself first in a Borneo state could hope to have much success in penetrating into Malaya afterwards. This is not to say that a party in a Borneo state could not become a member of a *group* of opposition parties, in the way in which the SUPP and MACHINDA became members of the Malaysian Solidarity Convention.

While Singapore was in Malaysia its relative autonomy made it a

[44] *Straits Times,* March 16, 1966 (Lim Kean Siew and Devan Nair, respectively).

[45] See, on Nigerian parties with strong regional bases, Richard L. Sklar, *Nigerian Political Parties: Power in an Emergent African Nation* (Princeton: Princeton University Press, 1963), pp. 499–501.

very strong base for a party which wished to use it as a springboard to enter politics in Malaya. The violence of the Alliance reaction to the attempted penetration of Malaya by the PAP was an indication of how seriously it regarded the threat.

Interest Groups

Until recently the articulation, or expression, of interests in Malaysia has not taken place through bodies organized to voice *particular* interests.[46] For the Malays it has been done through the traditional social structure, which now forms the basis for the existing democratic-bureaucratic structure. The Chinese have until recently expressed their interests through guilds, clan societies, and chambers of commerce.[47]

In Malaya perhaps the best examples of "functionally specific" interest groups are the trade unions. But even they are not free from the influence of communalism. The workers in the towns have been drawn proportionately mostly from the Chinese and the Indians. But, whereas the Indians have taken readily to trade unionism and have provided a high percentage of leaders, the Chinese have been more reluctant. One important reason lies in the use which pro-Communist Chinese made of the labor movement in Malaya after the Second World War. The government reacted by breaking the Communist hold on the unions, and their organization had to be rebuilt.[48] During this time some Chinese workers had been subject to Communist pressure, and others had gathered the impression that the government was hostile to any unions, whether Communist or not. Even in 1961 almost 50 per cent of union members were Indians, while only 17 per cent were Chinese. In recent years the unions have been reorganized. By 1962 there were nearly 300 unions altogether, with about 260,000 paid-up members. Most of the unions are so small that they have been described as "peanut" unions. By far the biggest union is the National Union of Plantation Workers, whose secretary-general is P. P. Narayanan. The largest grouping of unions is the

[46] Cf. Gabriel A. Almond and James S. Coleman, *The Politics of the Developing Areas* (Princeton: Princeton University Press, 1960), pp. 33–38.

[47] William H. Newell, *Treacherous River* (Kuala Lumpur: University of Malaya Press, 1962), pp. 123–124 and 141; Victor Purcell, *The Chinese in Malaya* (London: Oxford University Press, 1948), chs. VIII and X.

[48] S. S. Awberry and F. W. Dalley, *Labour and Trade Union Organization in the Federation of Malaya and Singapore* (Kuala Lumpur: Government Press, 1948); Alex. Josey, *Trade Unionism in Malaya*, 2nd ed. (Singapore: Malaya Publishing House, 1958) chs. 5 and 6; Charles Gamba, *The Origins of Trade Unionism in Malaya* (Singapore: Eastern Universities Press, 1962).

Malaysian Trade Union Congress (MTUC), to which the majority of the unions in government and the private sector are affiliated, and the Congress of Unions of Employees in the Public and Civil Services (CUEPACS), which admits only government unions.

Under the influence of Mr. Narayanan and other leaders of like mind, the unions have so far been nonpolitical, in the sense that they have not affiliated to, and have not supported, particular political parties. Some leaders, however, have been active in parties, mostly in the Socialist Front. In another sense the unions are indeed political, because they play a part in the political process. On occasions their representations have been spectacularly successful, as in 1964 when their opposition persuaded the government to withdraw its proposals to increase the salaries of expatriate officials serving in Malaya.[49] Employers of labor are also organized, the two most powerful bodies being the Malayan Mining Employers' Association and the Malayan Planting Industries Employers' Association.[50]

The chambers of commerce constitute important pressure groups. In addition to the various communal chambers of commerce, since 1962 there has been an intercommunal organization, the United Chambers of Commerce. Because of the dominance of the Chinese in business, a study of the political role of the Chinese Chambers of Commerce in the political process would be of outstanding interest, but unfortunately such a study does not yet exist. It does not require a very searching analysis to see that the Chinese Chambers of Commerce are rather closely aligned with the MCA. In some states there is considerable overlapping of the leading officeholders of the two organizations. This close alignment is obviously useful to the MCA where fund-raising is concerned. In Malacca some members of the Chinese Chamber of Commerce originally supported Tan Kee Gak, president of the Malayan Party. When Mr. Tan fought the 1964 election as an MCA candidate one source of cross-pressures on members of the Chambers was removed. Yet it would be wrong to imagine that the Chinese Chambers and the MCA were in every sense "twins." In at least one important state the MCA does not wish to be associated too closely with the Chamber in the public mind: the image of the Chamber is believed to be too opulent and feudalistic to attract mass votes.

In any Islamic country religion is obviously of at least potential importance in the political process. In Malaya it does not have any great political effect nationally, except that clearly no Malay party

---

[49] *Straits Times,* June 11, 1964.
[50] Paul H. Kleinsorge, "Employers' Associations in Malaya," *Far Eastern Survey,* XXVI, No. 8 (1957), 124–127 and No. 10 (1957), 152–159.

could afford not to support Islam. In the northeastern states of Kelantan and Trengganu, however, cooperation between certain religious teachers and the PMIP greatly strengthens the appeal of the party.

Little is known about the working of farmers' organizations, but it would appear that there has not been much political party activity in them. However, in 1963 an Alliance Minister warned one farming association that it should not allow itself to be used by a new political party for its selfish ends.[51]

Interest groups in Sarawak and Sabah are not yet very highly developed. The main exceptions are Chinese Chambers of Commerce and, in the bigger towns in Sarawak, trade unions. The SUPP controls some of the Chinese trade unions and has exercised influence in the Kuching Chamber of Commerce. The Clandestine Communist Organization (CCO), the underground body run by some extremist members of SUPP, makes use of affiliated groups, such as the Sarawak Farmers' Association and the Sarawak Advanced Youths' Association.[52]

☙

SUGGESTED READINGS

Milne, R. S. "Party Politics in Sarawak and Sabah," *Journal of Southeast Asian History,* VI, No. 2 (1965), 104–117.

Milne, R. S. and K. J. Ratnam. "Politics and Finance in Malaya," *Journal of Commonwealth Political Studies,* III, No. 3 (1965), 182–198.

Ratnam, K. J. "Political Parties and Pressure Groups," pp. 336–345, in *Malaysia, a Survey,* Wang Gungwu, ed. New York: Frederick A. Praeger, 1964.

Ratnam, K. J. *Communalism and the Political Process in Malaya.* Kuala Lumpur: University of Malaya Press, 1965. A study of the communal background to politics with particular reference to the 1959 election.

Ratnam, K. J. and R. S. Milne. *The Malayan Parliamentary Election of 1964.* Kuala Lumpur: University of Malaya Press (forthcoming). This also contains a section on Sarawak and Sabah.

Rose, Saul. *Socialism in Southern Asia.* London: Oxford University Press, 1959. Gives an account of the early left-wing parties.

[51] Inche Mohamed Khir Johari, presumably referring to the National Convention Party (*Straits Times,* July 21, 1963).

[52] For a case history see *Sarawak by the Week,* No. 50/65, December 5-December 11, 1965, pp. 1–4.

Smith, T. E. "The Malayan Elections of 1959," *Pacific Affairs,* XXXIII, No. 1 (1960), 38–47. Contains useful comparative tables on voting.

The Danger Within. Kuching: Sarawak Information Service, n.d. An account of Communist and Communist-infiltrated movements in Sarawak up to 1963.

Tilman, R. O. "Elections in Sarawak," *Asian Survey,* III, No. 10 (1963), 507–518. An analysis of "racial" voting.

Tilman, R. O. "The Alliance Pattern in Malaysian Politics: Bornean Variations on a Theme," *South Atlantic Quarterly,* LXIII (Winter, 1964), 60–74.

Tilman, R. O. "The Sarawak Political Scene." *Pacific Affairs,* XXXVII, No. 4 (1964–1965), 412–425.

7

The Federal Parliament, State Legislatures

The Federal Parliament: Origins

The Parliament of Malaysia is modelled on the British Parliament. It is in Parliament that the laws are made. The Head of State, who corresponds to the British monarch, plays no effective part in making the law. The executive, the federal government, is responsible to Parliament and cannot survive without its support. The legislative power and the executive power are linked, because the members of the executive and the majority of the legislature belong to the same political party. The Parliament of Malaysia, however, differs from the British Parliament in one important respect. The British Parliament is "supreme"; its actions cannot be challenged by a court or by any other body. The Malaysian Parliament is not supreme in this sense. It is bound by the Constitution, and it is possible that some of its actions might be found by a court to be contrary to the Constitution and therefore invalid.[1]

The federal legislature consists of two houses, the House of Representatives, which is popularly elected, and the Senate, which is not popularly elected. The numbers in each of the two houses are laid down in the Constitution. Both these bodies, in their existing form, are comparatively new, and some background is necessary to explain how they evolved as organs of an independent state.

The earliest forerunner of the House of Representatives was the Federal Council of 1909. The (British) High Commissioner presided

[1] The supremacy of the Constitution is declared in Article 4. The power of the courts to determine the validity of legislation is laid down in Article 128.

114

over the entirely nominated Council, which included the four Rulers of the Federated Malay States. In 1927 the Rulers were replaced by four Malay unofficial members. After a temporary "Advisory" Council, 1946–1948, a large and elaborate Legislative Council of seventy-five persons was set up in 1948. In addition to fourteen "official" members who held government positions, there were eleven members from the states and settlements (one each) and fifty unofficial members. This represented a distinct constitutional advance, because the fifty "unofficials" were chosen explicitly to represent particular interests, such as rubber, tin, agriculture, and trade unions. So, in a sense, part of the Council was "representative," although "representation" was not secured through direct elections. In 1951 a device, familiar in countries under British rule which are moving towards independence, called the "Member system," was introduced.[2] Some of the "Members" were civil servants, either British or Malay. The rest were businessmen or professional men of different racial origins, including British. One of the original "Members" was Dato Onn.

A further change occurred in 1953 when the British High Commissioner ceased to be president, and the Council was presided over by an appointed Speaker.

The final stage before a completely elective assembly lasted from 1955 to 1959. During this period the Council had an elected majority, fifty-two out of its ninety-eight members having been elected at the general election of 1955. Independence was won in 1957, but the system was not changed immediately; from 1957 until the general elections of 1959 there was a period when the country was independent, but still had a very high proportion (almost 50 per cent) of nonelected members in the Council. In 1959 the legislature assumed its present form, two chambers named, respectively, the House of Representatives and the Senate.

The House of Representatives (*Dewan Ra'ayat*) is entirely elected as far as the members from Malaya are concerned. The members from the Borneo states (until the first dissolution of Parliament after August, 1968) are chosen by the respective legislatures of these states.[3] The present House of Representatives moved to an attractive modern building in 1963. It employs a staff of about thirty, and has a special committee to supervise their employment and working conditions. Members of the staff perform a wide variety of duties. They range from the erudite clerk (the chief administrative officer of the

[2] See pp. 35–36, above.
[3] Malaysia Act, Sec. 94. The date for the direct elections in a Borneo state may be earlier if the Yang di-Pertuan Agong, with the concurrence of the Governor of the state, so directs.

House) and assistant clerk, who, from their sober dress, might have stepped straight out of the British Parliament in Westminster, to the highly colorful sergeant-at-arms, who is also the macebearer and, in any other context, might be mistaken for an ancient Malay warrior chief.

Procedure in the House of Representatives

The "mechanics" of the House may be quickly described. Like the House of Commons, its shape is rectangular. Unlike the House of Commons, the members have individual seats. The languages of the House are English and Malay. From 1967 onwards Parliament may decide that English may no longer be used in the House (or the Senate). But members from Sabah and Sarawak will be allowed to use English for a period of ten years after the formation of Malaysia (until 1973).[4] There is a system of microphones and simultaneous translation for members and for the press. However, in the official record of the House, speeches are printed in the language in which they are delivered. There is no complete English version or complete Malay version. A bilingual member may use both languages in the course of a speech. For instance, when the Prime Minister is replying during a debate he may use English to answer points made in English and Malay in reply to points made in Malay. In that case his contribution will be printed as it was spoken.[5]

Between one election and another the life of each Parliament is divided into "sessions." A session covers the period between the summoning by the Yang di-Pertuan Agong of a meeting of Parliament at the beginning of one session and its prorogation (dismissal) by him preparatory to the summoning of the next session. Usually a session lasts about a year, but Parliament does not meet continuously during this period. It generally meets for about a week at a time, except for a longer meeting to consider the budget, and then "adjourns." The total number of days on which Parliament sits during a year would, on the average, be between fifty and sixty.

[4] Federal Constitution, Articles 152 and 161.

[5] For this reason some references to debates in Parliament are made to the English newspaper reports of the debates and not to Hansard. Another reason for doing this is the considerable delay between a debate and the publication of the proceedings.

To generalize: UMNO ministers use Malay or English; UMNO backbenchers use mostly Malay; MCA and MIC government members nearly always use English; PMIP members almost invariably use Malay; other Opposition members generally use English. Members from Sabah or Sarawak usually speak in English.

The proceedings of the House are presided over by the Speaker or, in his absence, by the Deputy Speaker. Originally the Speaker had to be a member of the House, but this was changed by an amendment to the Constitution passed in 1964, and in November, 1964, a nonelected member was chosen as Speaker. In presiding, the Speaker applies the Standing Orders of the House, drawn up by the Committee on Standing Orders, and then approved by the House. The Speaker, however, has "residuary powers" over matters not specifically provided for in the Standing Orders. His decisions are final, and cannot be appealed against except upon a substantive motion moved for that purpose.[6] Although the Speaker and Deputy Speaker are elected by the House (and so have to be approved by the government party), they do in fact, as far as is humanly possible, act impartially.

The House's Standing Orders are modelled on those of the British House of Commons. A PMIP member has urged that this model should not be imitated indefinitely and that the orders should be consistent with local conditions and customs.[7] It will probably take time for the orders to be adapted in this way. Ironically, one of the main changes that has been made from the British model is that there are provisions, described below, for limiting debate which is likely to cause hostility or ill will between the various races in Malaya; this provision has sometimes been used to prevent PMIP speakers from developing their arguments.

One of the House's main functions is to legislate by considering and passing bills. In voting on bills, and on other matters, party discipline is very strict, much more so than in the United States. It would be extremely rare for a member of Parliament not to follow the party line in voting. If he deviated more than once or twice he would not be allowed to continue as a member of the party. Members also refrain from criticizing the broad policy of their party in the debates. They frequently urge the particular needs of their constituencies, but their discontent, if any, with party policy on national issues is expressed in private, for example at party meetings.

Between twenty and thirty bills are passed every session, and then transmitted to the Senate. In practice these are all bills introduced by the Government; some are intended to implement the announced policy of the Government party, others deal with relatively noncontroversial matters, such as administrative reforms. It is possible, as in Britain, for a private member to introduce a bill on some subject

[6] S.O.'s 99 and 100.
[7] Zulkiflee bin Muhammad, *Sunday Mail,* September 13, 1959.

which is close to his heart, but no example of this has occurred so far; in November, 1965, Dr. Lim Chong Eu introduced a bill with the Government's permission, which in effect made it impossible for an amendment to the Constitution to be passed in less than a month.[8] Another category of bill may be introduced, the "private bill," intended to affect or benefit some particular person, association, or corporate body. But, although this procedure was used in the Legislative Council, it has not yet been employed in the House of Representatives.

In passing bills there are a number of stages in order to allow consideration both of the principles and the details of each bill. The House follows the British, and not the United States, practice of having a bill considered first by the House as a whole before it is examined in committee. However, there is a significant departure from the British system. In the House of Commons the Committee stage of most bills is taken in a Select Committee with a membership consisting of between 10 and 15 per cent of all members. But it is the normal practice for the House of Representatives to use the Committee of the Whole House for the committee stage of bills. So, after a nominal First Reading, the principles of the bill are debated in the House in the Second Reading, the House itself (sitting in committee) considers the details, and then (when the bill has been reported out of committee) there is a short Third Reading. The only bill which so far has been referred to a Select Committee and then enacted was a Minor Offences Bill in 1960, popularly known as the "Biting Dogs Bill," because one of its provisions concerned the law on hostile encounters between dogs and postmen. Another bill was referred to a Select Committee in June, 1965, but was not proceeded with. From time to time opposition members have suggested that particular bills should be submitted to a Select Committee. But, with the two exceptions mentioned, the Government has rejected these proposals. Referring to the Internal Security Bill of 1960, the Deputy Prime Minister justified the rejection by saying, "Parliament has had a long and thorough debate and the opposition have been given a fair hearing.[9] It could be argued that the failure to use Select Committees was simply a reflection of the fact that the House was a new institution and Malaysia a small country, and that the legislative process had not yet become sufficiently specialized for Select Committees to be part of the normal legislative procedure. The more cynical would

[8] *Straits Times,* November 11, 1965. The bill has not yet been enacted (August, 1966).

[9] *Ibid.,* June 23, 1960.

point to the silence of many Government backbenchers in the House and would go on to say that the Whole House was, in effect, a "Select Committee" in which a limited number of members actually participated, while the rest were merely onlookers.

A special procedure is laid down for dealing with expenditure. Each year there is a Supply Bill, containing estimated financial requirements under various heads of expenditures. There may also be Supplementary Supply Bills for additional expenditure. These bills are considered in a Committee of the Whole House, known as the Committee of Supply. Here, again, the procedure is modelled on the British. In order to keep control of expenditure firmly in the hands of the Government, and to prevent logrolling, it is provided that only Ministers can propose increases in expenditure.[10] However, there are some variations. The system in Malaysia is simpler insofar as the House has only one committee "disguise" when dealing with finance. In Britain, as well as a Committee of Supply, there is also a Committee of Ways and Means. Again, the Government takes up a larger share of the time than British governments do when debating the estimates for expenditure in Committee of Supply. In Malaysia the Opposition does make use of Supply Bills to criticize the Government through the device of moving to reduce a Minister's salary in the estimates. But it is not yet completely established that the Supply days "belong" to the Opposition.

Although little use has been made of committees (other than Committees of the Whole House) for purposes of legislation, there are Select Committees, appointed at the beginning of every session, which perform other functions. The most important of these are the Committee of Selection, the Standing Orders Committee, the Public Accounts Committee and the Committee on Privileges. The Committee of Selection, of which the Speaker is chairman, is responsible for choosing the members to sit on other committees. Reference has already been made to the functions of the Standing Orders Committee. The Public Accounts Committee works closely in conjunction with the Auditor-General, an official who is independent of the executive, and can be dismissed only by the same difficult and unusual procedures needed to remove a judge of the Federal Court.[11] The Committee is charged with examining "the accounts of the Federation and the appropriation of the sums granted by Parliament to meet the public expenditure"[12] and also the reports of the Auditor-General on

[10] S.O. 66(9).
[11] Constitution, Articles 105(3) and 125.
[12] S.O. 77(1).

these accounts.[13] In practice the Committee confines itself mostly to points raised in the Auditor-General's reports and does not do much original "digging" into the accounts. The Standing Orders of the House say nothing about the chairmanship of the Public Accounts Committee. In Britain it has become a convention that an Opposition member is chairman, thus, in conjunction with the part played by the Auditor-General, underlining that the Government is laying the details of its expenditure completely open to impartial, and even hostile, scrutiny. But in the House of Representatives the chairman is always a member of the Government. An Assistant Minister's attempt to justify this, by saying that the Government did not intend to pass its responsibilities over to the Opposition,[14] showed a lamentable lack of appreciation of the principle involved.

To enable Parliament to function properly the Constitution confers certain legal rights and immunities ("parliamentary privileges") on each House and on the individual members. For instance, members are immune from proceedings in respect of things said by them in Parliament. Each House can punish for a breach of privilege, and apparent breaches are referred to the Committee of Privileges.

The only occasion so far on which the Committee of Privileges has acted has arisen from the operations of the Public Accounts Committee. The Committee of Privileges found that an Opposition member of the Public Accounts Commitee, Tan Phock Kin, had made a statement in a debate in the House based on information he had received while a member of that committee, but which had not yet been transmitted to the House. This was held to be a breach of Standing Order 85.[15] The Committee of Privileges recommended that Mr. Tan should be admonished, the House agreed, and this mild punishment was inflicted. In March, 1966, a complaint by Tun Ismail against S. P. Seenivasagam was also referred to the Committee.

The House has functions other than legislation. Chief among these is the function of allowing grievances to be ventilated and providing a forum in which governmental policies can be stated, criticized and debated. One method by which redress of grievances can be sought

[13] The Committee also has to examine such accounts of public authorities and other bodies administering public funds as may be laid before the House. The Auditor-General scrutinizes not only federal Government accounts but also those of state governments and of certain local authorities and public bodies.

[14] *Straits Times*, April 21, 1960.

[15] "The evidence taken before any Select Committee and any documents presented to such Committee shall not be published by any member of such Committee, or by any other person, before the Committee has presented its report to the House."

is by asking Ministers questions in Parliament. Normally fourteen days' notice must be given of questions. When a member hands in questions he may obtain an oral answer by marking them "Oral Reply," but not more than three questions can be marked for "Oral Reply" on the same day. Even questions marked in this way may be given written answers, if the Speaker so directs,[16] for instance because the answer would contain a large amount of statistics. The range of questions asked, even by a single member at a single time, may be wide. In March, 1963, Chan Yoon Onn asked "the Minister for Defence for information on protective measures in Malayan territorial waters followed by a question on post boxes in the trains. How many eggs did the Federation's hens and ducks lay in 1960, 1961, and 1962? And how many goats, sheep, cattle, and pigs were born in the same three years? The Minister of Health is asked to state the percentage of (a) bronchitis, and (b) tuberculosis cases in the Federation during the past ten years; and will he give the figures too for Perak, Selangor, and Negri Sembilan? Cancer research and leucotomy also find a place on the order paper; so do the cases admitted to each mental hospital in the Federation (during the last ten years)."[17] There is a long list of prohibitions on questions of various kinds, for instance on questions referring to proceedings in a committee which have not been reported to the House, questions making charges of a personal character, questions containing any discourteous reference to a friendly foreign country and so on. But when the Standing Orders say that the "proper object of a question is to obtain information,"[18] this does not quite convey the real motives behind asking a question. Often the motive is to bring to public notice information which it is thought will give evidence of maladministration, or even scandal, for which the Government can be held responsible. In this regard supplementary questions may be asked by any member immediately after the reply to the original question. These must be on the same topic as the original question, but the fact that they need not be announced in advance may make them harder to answer than "original" questions.

Opportunities for speaking about a grievance at greater length (for those who are not members of the Government) are provided by Standing Order 17. A member who has given notice at least seven days previously may raise "any matter of administration" on the motion "That this House do now adjourn." On rare occasions it is possible for a member to raise a matter on a motion for the adjourn-

---

[16] S.O. 22(3).
[17] *Straits Times,* March 7, 1963.
[18] S.O. 21(3).

ment on the same day that his request is made. The Speaker, however, has to be satisfied that this is for the purpose of discussing "a definite matter of urgent public importance."[19] Two examples may illustrate the way in which these conditions have been interpreted. In May, 1963, Tan Phock Kin was successful in persuading the Speaker that the cholera outbreak in Malacca fulfilled all the three criteria which were necessary — definiteness, urgency, being a matter of public importance.[20] But three months later the Speaker did not allow D. R. Seenivasagam to use this procedure for making charges of corruption against the Minister of Health. He agreed that the matter was "definite and public," but did not agree that it was "urgent."[21]

The possibility of raising grievances through parliamentary questions and debates on the adjournment is of vital importance in a country, such as Malaysia, which has a parliamentary system of government. Without some approximate equivalent of the investigations of congressional committees, the executive would tend, in time, to go on its way unchecked, and perhaps eventually uncheckable.

Government and Opposition in the House of Representatives

In assessing the work of the House it is important to ask whether a proper balance is struck between the need of the Government to legislate and the need of the Opposition to probe and criticize. The question is complicated by the fact that there is no single "Opposition" with a recognized Leader. Early in 1963 the Opposition parties set up a common front, under the chairmanship of Inche Abdul Aziz bin Ishak, in order to oppose Malaysia in the form proposed by the Government,[22] although this arrangement was not continued in the new House from 1964 onwards. But the Opposition has not been united for long on any major issue, and it is difficult to see how it *could* so be united in view of the wide policy differences between the various parties. In an essentially two-party system, as in Britain, the leaders of the parties in Parliament (or their representatives) get together in order to try to reach gentlemen's agreements on the allocation of time, choice of procedure, and so on. But apparently this rarely happens in the House of Representatives. The Speaker has to act as an intermediary between the Government leaders, on the one hand, and a group of four or five Opposition leaders, on the

[19] S.O. 18.
[20] *Straits Times,* May 24, 1963.
[21] *Ibid.,* August 23, 1963.
[22] *Ibid.,* March 12, 1963.

other. The Speaker's task would be simplified if there were to be a "recognised official Opposition leader in Parliament in future."[23]

The question whether or not the Opposition is given enough scope in the House may be split into two parts. Quantitatively, is the Opposition given enough time? Qualitatively, are there restrictions on certain topics of debate which prevent the Opposition parties from developing an effective attack on the Government? In 1959 and 1960 there were complaints from the Opposition that many of their motions had been left undebated for months.[24] Since then, however, this backlog seems to have been reduced. Sometimes, however, Opposition members have protested when debate has been cut short, as did Lim Kean Siew and D. R. Seenivasagam when the Government moved the closure on the important Malaysia bill after only fifteen hours' debate.[25] It should be noted, however, that the record for the longest speech made in the House, nearly four hours, is held by an Opposition member, the late Inche Zulkiflee.[26]

Lee Kuan Yew complained that he was "denied his constitutional right to reply in Parliament" in June, 1965. He had moved an amendment to the King's Speech (which, in spite of its name, actually consists of a statement of policy by the Government), dealing at length with communal problems and putting forward his party's policy on a "Malaysian Malaysia." Many Government speakers took up points in his argument. "The Singapore Premier asked to be allowed to exercise his right of reply, but was ruled out of order by the Speaker, although he had been privately reassured by the Speaker that he would be given an opportunity to reply.[27]

One of the limitations on the Opposition parties generally (as contrasted with limitations in Parliament) is that they must not resort to unconstitutional means or work in conjunction with Communist Front organizations. On occasion the Government has given a warning in Parliament about the restrictions imposed on Opposition activities by the Internal Security Act.[28] The existence of the Internal Security

---

[23] *Ibid.*, July 16, 1963.

[24] *Ibid.*, December 15, 1959; *Malay Mail,* December 15, 1959; *Sunday Mail,* August 28, 1960; *Straits Times,* September 9, 1960.

[25] *Straits Times,* August 15 and 17, 1963; *Malay Mail,* August 15, 1963. The procedure used was sometimes wrongly referred to as "the guillotine." The guillotine (or allocation of maximum time for debate on different parts of a bill) was used for the 1963 Supply Bill by virtue of S.O. 66(4) (*Straits Times,* December 14, 1962).

[26] *Ibid.*, August 20, 1963.

[27] *The Battle for a Malaysian Malaysia* (Singapore: Ministry of Culture, 1965), pp. 2–4.

[28] E.g., *Straits Times,* December 19, 1962 and March 13, 1963.

Act and the recollection of the arrests made under it (particularly that of the only person who was arrested while a member of Parliament, Inche Boestamam of the Socialist Front in 1963) have a considerable influence on the tone and temper of the House and on the relationship between Government and Opposition.

A more specific check on debate is designed to meet the fact that Malaysia is a multi-racial society and the fear that, beyond a certain point, discussions on racial themes could prove to be inflammatory. A Standing Order provides that it shall be out of order to use "words which are likely to promote feelings of ill will or hostility between different communities in the Federation."[29] Perhaps some rule of this kind is needed. Sometimes tempers have been lost, and shouts have been heard of, "Go back to Arabia" and "China for You." But the present Standing Order is capable of such wide interpretation as to threaten to stifle debate. Commenting on this Standing Order when it was introduced D. R. Seenivasagam said, "If I stand up here and say I want Chinese as the official language, I have no doubt it will cause some ill-feeling among our Malay brethren. On the other hand, when our friends say 'we want Malay reservations' I have no doubt it will cause some ill-feeling among the other races of the country.[30] Mr. Seenivasagam's forebodings were justified. Less than a year afterwards he, and also a subsequent pro-Government spokesman, were warned by the Speaker under this Standing Order when they started to discuss problems of loyalty raised by the report of the Education Review Committee.[31]

Part of the problem derives from the fact that some of the parties are indeed, in one particular sense, "racial," insofar as their main policies reflect the interests of members of particular races. Because of this it is often difficult or impossible to put the case for a better deal without making statements, which, on a broad interpretation, could be held to breach Standing Order 36. It is perhaps significant that when this Order was introduced it was opposed by both the PPP and the PMIP, which might be considered "racial" parties in the sense just described. The PMIP, however, gave the argument an interesting twist by claiming that its policies were, so to speak, *ultra*-communal. "The PMIP wishes to fight for the Malays in this country and make Malay the national language. That is a national issue, not a communal issue."[32]

---

[29] S.O. 36(10). A later addition to this order provided that, if the Speaker was of the opinion that a breach of the Order might ensue, he could disallow a motion or amendment or terminate a debate [S.O. 36(11)].

[30] *Straits Times,* December 10, 1959.

[31] *Ibid.,* August 12, 1960.

[32] *Ibid.,* December 10, 1959.

To sum up: a general Opposition complaint is that the Government does not consult the Opposition enough and does not pay sufficient attention to Opposition suggestions. To be sure, the Government sometimes accepts opposition amendments, even, for instance, on the Internal Security Bill of 1960.[33] But the Opposition has alleged lack of full consultation on some really vital issues, such as the formation of Malaysia.[34] A contrary view is that sometimes there has been unjustified opposition just for the sake of opposing, as when the Tengku's despatch of troops to the Congo and his attempts to mediate between the Indonesians and the Dutch were criticized in Parliament.[35] A final point is that, just as the Opposition is split into several parties, so are its attacks on the Government usually fragmented and uncoordinated. After the 1964 general elections the Opposition was even weaker than before. The Socialist Front and the PPP lost many of their members. The interests of the PMIP extend to only a limited number of issues, and the party has lost the services in Parliament of Dr. Burhanuddin (disqualified from running) and Inche Zulkiflee (killed in a road accident). While Singapore was part of Malaysia, the presence of PAP members improved the quality of debates in the House, although the party supported the Government on so many issues, as a "loyal opposition," that it could hardly be counted as belonging to the Opposition in the strict sense. After August, 1965, when there were no longer any members from Singapore the burden of maintaining opposition in the House fell mainly on the shoulders of D. R. Seenivasagam (PPP) and Tan Chee Khoon (Socialist Front), who were willing to break a lance against the Government on almost any issue and who maintained a generally high level of debate, and Dr. Lim Chong Eu (UDP), a less forceful, but thoughtful and persuasive, speaker.

In the conduct of House affairs, there are evident all the stresses and strains which accompany the transplantation of any alien growth to a new soil. Right from the start an attempt was made to set the correct tone by insisting that members, unless in formal Malay dress, should wear suits in the House. When Parliament first met, six Socialist Front members in shirt sleeves were turned away until they dressed themselves properly.[36] But such precautions have not pre-

---

[33] *Malay Mail,* June 22, 1960; *Straits Times,* June 23, 1960.

[34] Lim Kean Siew, *Dewan Ra'ayat Debates,* V, No. 9, August 15, 1963, col. 1005.

[35] *Straits Times,* April 30, 1962.

[36] *Ibid.,* September 12, 1959. When they pointed out to the Tengku that in the Singapore Assembly shirt sleeves were permitted, he replied, "Singapore is different . . . Malaya is a monarchy." Male Malay dress consists of a cap (*songkok*), a long-sleeved jacket (*baju*), and either a long sarong or an abbreviated sarong and trousers (*sĕluar*).

vented incidents which have done little to enhance the standing of the House, such as the threatened "duel" between two members in which the "weapons" were to have been knives and forks, or the angry feminine verbal exchanges between the head of the UMNO's Women's Section and her predecessor in that position, who had later joined the PMIP.

No detailed analysis has yet been published of the origins and characteristics of the members of the Malaysian Parliament.[37] However, in late 1965 only three of the 144 members were women. Ethnically 74 were Malays, including Melanaus; 43 were Chinese; 21 were natives of the Borneo territories other than Melanaus; six were Indians or Ceylonese. The average age was a little over forty. Very few of the 104 members for seats in Malaya had had only a primary education. The rest were almost equally divided between those whose education had stopped at secondary level and those who had gone on to take either a university degree or a professional qualification. However, among the members from the Borneo territories there were rather more whose education had gone no further than primary level and very few with a degree or a professional qualification; the vast majority had had a secondary education. Occupationally, two-thirds of the members for seats in Malaya were in one of four groups which were almost equally represented: teachers, former government servants, businessmen, lawyers. Malay members tended to come from the first two groups, and a high proportion of PMIP members were teachers, particularly religious teachers. Among the members for the Borneo territories there was a preponderance of former civil servants and of businessmen, the latter overwhelmingly Chinese.

Two comments may be added, based on impressions, not statistics. First, there is a perceptible drop in ability between the Government front benches and middle benches, and again between the middle benches and the back benches. This is subject, of course, to qualification about individuals, for instance, in respect of bright young men on the back benches who have not yet been given their chance of promotion. The gap has become even more marked since the inclusion of members from Sarawak and Sabah, who have not been chosen directly; the qualities of some of them are more obviously "grass roots" than parliamentary. Understandably, their speeches are mostly on the problems of their states, notably on development and education, rather than on questions affecting the whole of Malaysia. Second, it has been claimed that Opposition members do not often

---

[37] The following section is based mostly on information gathered for K. J. Ratnam and R. S. Milne, *The Malayan Parliamentary Election of 1964* [Kuala Lumpur: University of Malaya Press (forthcoming); *Sarawak Who's Who* (Kuching: Information Department, Sarawak, 1964)].

associate with Government members, especially Ministers. One Socialist Front member said, "(T.) . . . was the only Alliance chap with whom I've gone out to have *makan* [food]. You know it's hard to get on with the Ministers — it takes a long time even to be on nodding terms with them."[38]

The Senate

There are fifty-eight members of the Senate (*Dewan Negara*). Twenty-six are elected by the Legislative Assemblies of the thirteen states. Thirty-two are appointed by the Yang di-Pertuan Agong, on the recommendation of the Prime Minister, from among those who "have rendered distinguished public service or have achieved distinction in the professions, commerce, industry, agriculture, cultural activities, or social service or are representatives of racial minorities or are capable of representing the interests of aborigines."[39] The normal term of office is six years, but initially some were appointed for shorter periods so that all the Senators' terms would not end in the same year.

It is difficult to see any clear pattern in the type of person elected by the state Assemblies. The appointed members are easier to group. Through them various interests are represented, as they used to be in the former Legislative Council. The constitutional difference is that the representatives are no longer nominated by the interests themselves. So the sixteen Senators appointed in 1959 included three former Federal Councillors chosen to represent minority races, aborigines, Ceylonese and Eurasians, just as they had done in the Legislative Council. There were two representatives of rubber and several representing chambers of commerce. The proportion of Indians, including Indian Muslims, was high, one quarter of those appointed. It seems that there was great competition to serve the country as one of the sixteen. As the final date for making the appointments approached, the Prime Minister had already received 659 applications to be a Senator, and he expected the total number to reach a thousand.[40] But the large field of choice did not lead to appointments which were so perfect that they were immune from criticism. Dato Onn alleged that, in spite of what the Constitution said, many of the members had "not distinguished themselves in any way — except possibly in regard to their pockets." He also pointed to the fact that several of the Senators had recently been defeated in the federal

[38] *Straits Times,* December 6, 1962.
[39] Constitution, Article 45. The number of appointed members became 32 (instead of 22) in 1964.
[40] *Straits Times,* August 26, 1959.

and state elections.[41] This assertion is true, and the inference is also true that such Senators, including some appointed since, may not be very active politically after their appointment. But another development took place later. The Senate began to be used as a base for some very active politicians indeed who were concerned in running the Alliance Party machine. These have included, since 1959, T. H. Tan, the executive secretary of the Alliance, and, from 1963 to 1964, Khaw Kai Boh of the MCA, an important negotiator with the new pro-Malaysia parties in the Borneo territories. After the 1964 elections Mr. Khaw, who had run successfully for the House of Representatives, was made a member of the Cabinet.

From time to time it is proposed that the Senate should be directly elected, as was envisaged as a future possibility by the "Reid Commission."[42] But it is doubtful how much this reform would do to justify the continued existence of the Senate. Apart from the fact that it is normal for democratic countries to have two chambers, there is the special reason that, because Malaysia is a federation, a second chamber is especially desirable, since it represents the states and is an instrument for protecting states' rights. But a study of Senate debates shows that not even the Senators chosen by the state Assemblies actually perform this role. More generally, second chambers are supposed to prevent hasty and ill-considered legislation by providing an element of mature deliberation not attainable by first chambers. But the Malaysian Senate does not work this way; it rather acts as a rubber stamp for the House of Representatives. There is often not enough delay between a bill's passage in the House and its introduction in the Senate to allow proper consideration. On paper the Senate's powers are the same as those of the House, except that financial legislation cannot begin in the Senate and that such legislation cannot be debated in the same degree of detail as in the House. But in practice the Senate has shown little initiative. For instance, although it is empowered to originate nonfinancial legislation, it has not done so. An editorial assessment[43] was that the Senate debates have been brief and dull and that its liveliest session was one which was null and void, because it had no right to hold it.[44] The Senate might have become a forum for proposals to promote states' rights.

[41] *Sunday Times,* November 29, 1959. See also *Straits Times,* December 12, 1962. A similar criticism was voiced later by Dr. Tan Chee Khoon (*Straits Times,* July 10, 1964).

[42] *Report of the Federation of Malaya Constitutional Commission* (Kuala Lumpur: Government Press, 1957), para. 62. See also Constitution, Article 45 (4) (b).

[43] *Straits Times,* September 28, 1962.

[44] The debate was on the 1961 Supply Bill, and was contrary to Senate S.O. 53 (*Sunday Mail,* June 8, 1960).

It is conceivable that, if tensions arose between the governments of Sabah or Sarawak and the federal government, Senators from these states could use the Senate as a forum for this purpose. But, to date, the Senate has been of service mainly as a rubber stamp and as a source of genteel patronage for the party in power.

State Legislatures

The powers of the states are so limited that their role in the government of the country is comparatively small. Constitutionally, the legislature of each state bears the same relationship to the state executive as the federal Parliament bears to the federal executive: that is to say, the state executive is responsible to the state legislature and cannot remain in office without the legislature's support. In practice, harmony between the two bodies is secured by the fact that the state executive and the majority of the state legislature are members of the same political party.

In each state the legislature consists of a single chamber, the state Legislative Assembly. In the states of Malaya the membership ranges from twelve (Perlis) to forty (Perak). Procedure is modeled on that in the federal Parliament. Most state legislatures meet only four or five times a year, and these meetings are usually very short except for the budget debate. The most important state function, land, is the subject which is discussed at the greatest length. Three government officials — the State Secretary, the State Legal Adviser, and the State Financial Officer — may attend meetings of the state Legislative Assembly, but without the right to vote.

The Sarawak Council Negri (the state legislature) has now evolved into an entirely elected body except for three ex-officio and three nominated members. The State Secretary, the State Financial Secretary, and the State Attorney General are the ex-officio members. The three nominated members were apparently intended to provide for the representation of minorities, which would not be represented otherwise, but two of the nominations have in fact been used to give seats to two nonelected persons and so allow them to qualify as members of the Sarawak state executive, the Supreme Council. The number of elected members is now thirty-six, all indirectly elected via District Councils and Divisional Advisory Councils.

When Malaysia was formed the Legislative Assembly of Sabah contained eighteen members, indirectly elected through the District Councils and the Residency Advisory Councils, three ex-officio members (the State Secretary, State Attorney General, and State Financial Secretary) and five nominated members. In 1964 the number of indirectly elected members was raised to thirty-two. In the same year the ex-officio members were removed from the Assembly.

8

The Executive, Federal and State; The Conference of Rulers

The Yang di-Pertuan Agong

The Supreme Head of the Federation is the Yang di-Pertuan Agong ("He who is made Lord"). He is, constitutionally, the source of all authority, whether legislative, executive, or judicial. Bills passed by the two houses of Parliament become law only after he has assented to them. The Cabinet acts in his name and by his authority. He appoints the judges, and the law courts are "his" courts. The constitutional importance of the Yang di-Pertuan Agong (King) is indicated by the fact that he takes absolute precedence over everyone else in the Federation.

In practice, however, the King may not exercise these wide powers as he likes, any more than the British Queen can behave as an absolute monarch. The Constitution binds the King very strictly. In nearly every sphere he must act on the advice of his Ministers who form the Cabinet.[1] The Cabinet must have the support of the House of Representatives, which, in turn, is elected by the people. The King is therefore a "constitutional" monarch, and does not actually govern the country as an absolute monarch would do. On almost every point the King must accept the decisions of the Cabinet. He is consulted before these decisions are taken; he may give advice on them if he wants to, he is informed of what the decisions are. That is the limit

[1] Constitution, Article 40(1).

of his powers. On the death of the first King the Prime Minister paid tribute to him by saying that "never once had he tried to interfere with the running of the Government."[2]

On a few particular matters the King may exercise his discretion.[3] In the parliamentary system of government there are two vital points at which the constitutional mechanism may not be entirely self-sufficient and self-regulating. These concern the appointment of a Prime Minister (who after he is appointed will recommend to the King the appointment of the other Ministers in the Cabinet) and the granting of the refusal of a request for a dissolution of Parliament. The King must choose a Prime Minister, who in his judgment is "likely to command the confidence of the majority of the members" of the House of Representatives.[4] Obviously, if any single political party wins more than half the seats in the House of Representatives at a general election, then the King's task is easy. All he has to do is to send for the leader of that party, appoint him as Prime Minister, and ask him to form a Government. But if no single party wins an absolute majority, there may have to be a process of negotiation and trial and error before it is clear *which* party's leader, if any, can command a majority in the House. In these circumstances the King can help the mechanism to function and prevent a deadlock. The King also has a discretionary power over dissolution. The Constitution [Article 55(3)] lays down a maximum period of five years between elections, but the interval may be shorter than this. It is possible that a party might win a narrow majority at an election and its leader would be chosen Prime Minister by the King. The majority might disappear, however, through loss of by-elections or by members leaving the party and joining an Opposition party. The Prime Minister might then find it impossible to continue governing, and might request the King to dissolve the House and to authorize another election. The King might grant the request; but he might refuse it, in which case the Prime Minister, having lost the support of the House of Representatives, would have to resign. The King would then choose another party leader to form a Government which could obtain the support of the House. Factors which would influence the

---

[2] *Malay Mail,* April 2, 1960.

[3] Constitution, Article 40(2). The matters not elaborated on here include "the requisition of a meeting of the Conference of Rulers concerned solely with the privileges, position, honours and dignities of Their Highnesses, and any action at such a meeting" and other cases mentioned in the Constitution, including appointment of the members of the Public Services Commission and the Railway Service Commission.

[4] Constitution, Article 43(2).

King in granting or refusing a dissolution would include the length of time since the last election, and the prospects of any alternative Prime Minister being able to command a lasting majority.

The King has not had much opportunity to exercise these discretionary powers. But it does not follow that he is merely a figurehead. In the first place he can "exercise a vague yet powerful influence for good"[5] in advising the Cabinet, as described earlier, even although the Cabinet may not, and need not, follow his advice. The King also plays the important role of personifying the nation and in constituting a focus for loyalty.[6] This is a vital task in a multi-racial society like Malaysia. The King can, with persuasion and tact, do a good deal to encourage national unity, for instance, by meeting large numbers of his people, of many different racial origins, and by lending his support to the greater use of the national language. In playing this role, however, the King's influence is seriously weakened by two considerations. He is elected for only five years, too short a time to allow loyalty to each King to be firmly established and to produce maximum results. In point of fact the first two Kings did not live long enough to serve even five years; the first lasted for less than three years, the second for only half a year. The third served for the full term, 1960 to 1965. Because of these considerations, it has been suggested that the King should be elected for life.[7] On the other hand it has been argued that the very fact that the office rotates may ensure that the people of the several states "identify themselves more closely with the Federation."[8] In any case the Rulers themselves would probably not approve of the change, because it would greatly reduce any individual Ruler's chances of ever becoming King. The other factor weakening the institution of kingship is the existence of the Rulers of the states and the fact that they, as well as the King, can confer honors and titles.

The King is remarkable in being an *elected* monarch, although it is a very restricted kind of election. The electors are the nine

[5] R. H. Hickling, *An Introduction to the Federal Constitution* (Kuala Lumpur: Federation of Malaya Information Services, 1960), p. 32.

[6] Consequently, any criticism made of proposals to benefit the King may be construed as throwing a doubt on allegiance and loyalty. Tan Siew Sin took this line over Socialist Front criticisms of the golf course and swimming pool which were proposed for a new royal palace (*Straits Times*, January 12, 1962).

[7] R. H. Hickling, "The First Five Years of the Federation of Malaya Constitution," *Malaya Law Review*, IV, No. 2 (1962), 86.

[8] F. A. Trindade and S. Jayakumar, "The Supreme Head of the Malaysian Federation," *ibid.*, VI, No. 2 (1964), 281.

Rulers of the states and their choice is limited to one of their own number. The election[9] takes place in the Conference of Rulers, but for this purpose only the nine Rulers are included, not the four Governors. A custom has grown up that a Ruler need not attend in person; he may send a representative instead. Voting takes place on the candidacy of the Ruler next in precedence[10] after the previous King, unless this Ruler is a minor or has declined to offer himself for election. The voting takes the form of each Ruler declaring whether the Ruler who is being voted on is suitable or unsuitable to be King. A resolution that a Ruler is unsuitable is carried only if at least five members of the Conference have voted for it.[11] Presumably if, say, two Rulers were to abstain, a Ruler could be elected King even if the vote were four against him and three for him. The Rulers do not endorse automatically the most senior Ruler as King. When the first King was elected in August, 1957, the Ruler who was first in order of precedence, the eighty-four-year-old Sultan of Johore, withdrew his name. The next in order, the Sultan of Pahang, was voted unsuitable, so the third in precedence, the Ruler of Negri Sembilan was elected by eight votes to one.[12]

On appointment as King a Ruler ceases to rule his own state, and a Regent, or Council of Regency, is appointed to exercise the executive functions. The King, however, remains head of the Muslim religion in his state, and must also give his assent to any change in the state Constitution during the regency.[13]

There is also provision for a Deputy (Timbalan Yang di-Pertuan Agong), who may perform the King's functions if the King is unable to do so, for example because of illness or absence from the Federation. On such occasions the Deputy enjoys all the rights, prerogatives, and privileges of the King. He also acts between the death of a King and the election of his successor.[14] At the last three elections — in May, 1960, September, 1960, and September, 1965 — on each occasion the Deputy was elected King.

[9] Constitution Article 32(4) and Third Schedule. A parallel to the election is found in the choice of the Ruler of Negri Sembilan by the Undangs, or territorial chiefs (Sir Richard Winstedt, *The Malays: a Cultural History,* 6th ed. [London: Routledge and Kegan Paul, 1961], pp. 86–90.)

[10] Judged by the date of his accession to the throne in his state. For the method by which the "election list" is varied after an election and when there is a change in the Ruler of a state, see Constitution, Third Schedule, I, 4.

[11] *Ibid.,* I, 1(2).

[12] *Straits Times,* April 2 and 14, 1960.

[13] Constitution, Article 34.

[14] Constitution, Article 33.

The Cabinet

The actual government of the country is in the hands of the Cabinet, consisting of Ministers drawn from the majority party in Parliament. Thus, in contrast to the United States Cabinet, Cabinet members *must* be members of the legislature; in the United States they must not be members. Most of the members of the Cabinet come from the House of Representatives, but one or two may be taken from the Senate. However, Ministers (and also Assistant Ministers) may speak in either house.

Members of the Cabinet are appointed by the Yang di-Pertuan Agong on the advice of the Prime Minister. The Prime Minister has considerable discretion in choosing the Cabinet. However, he must pay attention to the claims of those members of his party who have shown political or administrative ability, or, who for various reasons, are powerful in the councils of the party. He must have an eye to the inclusion of a "fair" number of Chinese and Indians. There is also a Minister of Sarawak Affairs and a Minister of Sabah Affairs; in August, 1966, these posts were occupied by Temenggong Jugah and Tun Mustapha, respectively.

It is becoming established that the Minister of Finance and the Minister of Commerce and Industry should be Chinese. On the other hand, it is hardly conceivable that the Minister of Rural Development, the Minister of Education, the Minister of Agriculture or the Minister of Internal Security should be other than a Malay. After Malaysia Ministers were appointed for Sarawak and Sabah, respectively, each drawn from the territory concerned. The purpose of this arrangement is presumably to make sure that the problems of the Borneo territories may be kept properly in view by the Cabinet.

The total numbers in the Cabinet must not be too large; otherwise effective discussion of policy at Cabinet meetings would become impossible. Some Ministers are given more than one ministry. From 1964 the Prime Minister was also the political head of the Ministry of External Affairs and, for a time, of the new Ministry of Culture, Youth and Sports. Tun Razak, the Deputy Prime Minister, was Minister of National and Rural Development as well as Minister of Defence. On the other hand, occasionally Ministers without Portfolio are appointed, that is, Ministers who are not charged with the oversight of any particular ministry or ministries. The post of Minister without Portfolio seems to have been used for two distinct purposes. One has been to accommodate Cabinet members sent abroad as diplomatic representatives. Dato Suleiman bin Dato Haji Abdul Rahman and Dato Ong Yoke Lin remained members of the Cabinet when they were first appointed High Commissioner to Australia and High Commissioner to New Zealand (1961) and Ambassador to the United States and Permanent Representative to the U.N. (1962), respectively.[15] The other function which a Minister without Portfolio may be given is the management of party, as opposed to governmental, affairs. This is rather similar to the practice in the United States Cabinet by which in the past some Postmasters General have devoted much of their time to party business. Thus the newly appointed Senator Khaw Kai Boh was made Minister without Portfolio in April, 1963, and it was stated that his immediate task was to organize the Alliance campaign for the coming Malayan (local) elections and to consolidate the Grand Alliance in the Borneo territories.

The number of ministries may be increased or diminished. Functions may also be transferred from one ministry to another. The function of Social Welfare was transferred from the Ministry of Labour to the Ministry of Health in 1959, and moved back again in 1962. It was given to a separate ministry in 1964. Sometimes it is clear that changes may have been designed to meet political needs. In October, 1959, a new Ministry of Rural Development (since 1964 the Ministry of National and Rural Development) was formed, in the portfolio of the Prime Minister, but under the charge of the Deputy Prime Minister. It was announced that the new ministry would absorb the existing Ministry of Natural Resources, and would have general responsibility for community and *kampong* (village) development, adult education, the Rural and Industrial Development Authority and other departments. At the same time Information and Broadcasting were removed from the Ministry of Interior and made into a separate ministry under the Prime Minister. The Prime Minister was to have two Assistant Ministers, one for Rural Development and one for Information and Broadcasting, who were to link the people and himself. The Tengku explained these changes by saying, quite correctly, that the nation's prosperity depended on agriculture, and that it was necessary to have a special ministry which would look at the problems of the *kampong* areas as a whole.[16] But the changes could also be regarded as a *political* response to a political event, the 1959 elections. The elections demonstrated the importance of

---

[15] The previous Permanent Representative to the U.N., Tun Ismail, was also at the same time Minister without Portfolio. For Dato Onn's attack on this practice, see *Straits Times*, April 26, 1961.

[16] *Federal Government Press Statement,* October 6, 1959, and *Straits Times,* October 7, 1959; *Malaya Information Services Newsletter,* October, 1959.

the rural Malay vote and also showed, in the Kelantan and Treng-ganu results, that this vote could be captured by a party other than UMNO. Hence the need for rural development and for the voters, in these two states particularly, to be *informed* about what the Government was doing to promote development. It is also worth noting, with regard to the balance of power within the Cabinet, that the Ministry of Natural Resources was taken away from the Minister of Agriculture, Inche Abdul Aziz bin Ishak, whose differences with the rest of the Cabinet later led to his resignation. On the other hand, the important new Ministry of Rural Development, at first placed in the Tengku's portfolio but with Tun Razak in charge, was put entirely under Tun Razak in August, 1960.[17] The combined effect was to strengthen Tun Razak's influence in the rural areas, while decreasing the influence of Inche Aziz.

Assistant Ministers, Parliamentary Secretaries, and Political Secretaries

Some Assistant Ministers were already functioning between 1955 and 1959, but explicit provision for their existence was made in 1960. Assistant Ministers must be members of Parliament. They are not members of the Cabinet, but are subordinate to particular Ministers. "Assistant Ministers shall assist Ministers in the exercise of their powers and the performance of their duties";[18] more particularly, they assist Ministers in running of the ministries, speak on subjects within the scope of the ministries in Parliament, and sometimes act on behalf of Ministers who are out of the country. The job of Assistant Minister may also be used for training future Ministers.

By the Constitution Amendment Act of 1964 provision was made for Parliamentary Secretaries and Political Secretaries to be appointed.[19] "With the formation of Malaysia, the duties of Ministers and Assistant Ministers have multiplied; and it is desirable that Parliamentary Secretaries and Political Secretaries be appointed to assist them in the discharge of their duties and functions."[20] Parliamentary Secretaries must be drawn from members of either House of Parliament, but Political Secretaries need not be. The functions of the Secretaries are not laid down in detail. Parliamentary Secretaries

---

[17] *Straits Times,* August 19, 1960. At the same time a new Ministry of Internal Security was created, which took over Police from Tun Razak's Defence Ministry.

[18] Constitution, Article 43A.

[19] Articles 43A and 43B of the Constitution.

[20] *Explanatory Statement,* Dewan Ra'ayat No. 864 of 1964.

differ from Assistant Ministers in being lower in rank and in having only parliamentary, and not administrative, duties. In practice the Political Secretaries seem to have been given mainly public relations duties. When it was decided that the eight Alliance Mentri Besar and two Governors in Malaya should have Political Secretaries, an Alliance spokesman said: "Political secretaries have been found to be essential in the maintenance of close contact with the public. They will not only be the ears of the heads of state governments who are always hard-pressed for time but also will be able to help effectively in the work of putting across to the public the intentions behind any move by the state governments concerned."[21] For a country of only about nine million people, which also has a state level of government, these new additions to political hierarchy seem to be excessive. For a party with a large number of backbenchers, however, they are a useful means of providing employment. "At the rate the Alliance Government is creating jobs for M.P.'s, very soon there will not be any M.P. left without a job from the benevolent and paternalistic government."[22]

Another possible training ground for Ministers, and for Assistant Ministers, is the Alliance Party's "parliamentary groups" consisting of backbenchers, each group being led by one Assistant Minister or leading backbencher from the House or the Senate. The groups are advisory and intended to be a way of providing for liaison between each Ministry and a group of members of Parliament. In 1959, there were eleven such groups, each roughly corresponding in its area of interest to a Ministry.

Cabinet Procedure. The Prime Minister

The Cabinet usually meets once a week. The Prime Minister presides or, in his absence, the Deputy Prime Minister. The Permanent Secretary to the Prime Minister's department, as head of the Cabinet Secretariat, is responsible for summoning meetings of the Cabinet, arranging the agenda, keeping minutes, and passing on the decisions of the Cabinet to those government bodies which are required to implement these decisions. Records are not kept of the discussion; the Cabinet minutes are merely a statement of what has been decided and a direction to the Minister concerned and the civil service to implement the decision. Even the minutes are not made public. It follows that the information available about Cabinet proceedings is scanty. Even less is known about the operations of the Cabinet committees which have been set up for closer considera-

[21] *Straits Times,* May 6, 1964. See also *ibid.,* January 16, 1965.
[22] Dr. Tan Chee Khoon, *ibid.,* July 10, 1964.

tion of problems in particular fields than is possible in the full Cabinet. In August, 1959, however, it was revealed that the following committees had been appointed: Establishment, Malayanization, Defence, Internal Security, Economics, Social Services, Intelligence and Counter-Subversion.[23]

Obviously the Prime Minister holds a dominating position in the Cabinet. He has, in effect, the power to hire and fire Cabinet members; he presides at Cabinet meetings; he is the chief negotiator with representatives of foreign powers, a role which he would exercise even if he did not also happen to be Minister of External Affairs. If any program or project needs to be emphasized or conducted with special drive this can be attempted by bringing it within the Prime Minister's department. The creation of a Ministry of Rural Development, under the Prime Minister, in October, 1959, was explained by stating that, compared with any other Minister, the Prime Minister could obtain more cooperation from the states, more enthusiasm from government departments and the people, and more money from the Treasury.[24] However, too much stress should not be laid on the constitutional and institutional sources of the Tengku's power. Much of it derives from his position as party leader, and his strength in this position depends, in turn, on his personality and on the part he played in obtaining independence for Malaya. Indeed, the unimportance of the office of Prime Minister, as such, is shown by the fact that the Tengku gave it up for four months in 1959 in order to devote himself to working for the Alliance Party in the state and parliamentary elections. During this period, when Tun Razak was Prime Minister, there was, from the strictly constitutional point of view, a shift in the locus of power. But in practice, no such shift occurred, and it was generally accepted that, after the federal elections had been won, the Tengku would once again take over as Prime Minister.

The Prime Minister, according to the Constitution, must be a citizen by operation of law, not by registration or naturalization. He cannot be a Senator. The latter provision is based on British practice; though no legal prohibition exists, there has been no British Prime Minister from the House of Lords for over sixty years. When Lord Home became Prime Minister in 1963 he first had to take advantage of the new legislation to give up his peerage. The Constitution is silent on the ethnic origin of the Prime Minister, but it is most unlikely that in the near future Malaysia will have a non-Malay Prime Minister.

[23] *Ibid.*, August 26, 1959.
[24] *Ibid.*, October 7, 1959.

Tun Razak is often referred to as "Deputy Prime Minister," although this title is not mentioned in the Constitution. According to the Tengku, the Deputy "carries out the duties of the Prime Minister when the Prime Minister is away and helps him discharge his numerous duties." He has no extra powers apart from these.[25]

Collective Responsibility of the Cabinet

The Cabinet is collectively responsible to Parliament;[26] in practice this means that it is responsible to the House of Representatives. Each Cabinet member must support, and must be supported by, the expressed views of his colleagues. If any member is "out of step" with his colleagues, he is expected to resign.[27]

A case study, throwing light on the notion of collective responsibility, might be written about the resignation of one particular Minister, Inche Abdul Aziz bin Ishak, in 1962. In brief, the sequence of events was that the Prime Minister "reshuffled" several Cabinet posts, moving Inche Aziz from the Ministry of Agriculture and Co-operatives to the Ministry of Health; Inche Aziz tried to resist the move, but eventually he was forced to resign. Later he left UMNO, and founded a party of his own. In the course of the dispute between Inche Aziz and other Cabinet Ministers it was clear that there were several points of difference between him and his colleagues. Among other things he accused the Finance Minister of starving his projects by withholding funds; in turn, the Finance Minister alleged mismanagement on the part of Inche Aziz. Differences also existed over foreign policy; Inche Aziz thought that the Government was being too pro-British and hostile to Indonesia. And as early as May, 1961, Inche Aziz's views on a proposed urea factory which he favored were at variance with those of the rest of the Cabinet.

The Prime Minister first announced the changes in Cabinet posts in July, 1962. Inche Aziz, at a press conference, then said that he could not accept the Prime Minister's offer [sic] until he had seen him and asked him for the reasons.[28] When he was finally dismissed, he announced that he had been relieved of his appointment and was not

[25] *Ibid.*, February 23, 1960.

[26] Constitution, Article 43.

[27] The Constitution provides for a Minister's appointment being revoked by the King "on the advice of the Prime Minister . . . ." [43(5)].

[28] *Straits Times,* July 17, 1962. Later, in reply to a question in Parliament, the Tengku said that usually no explanation was given when a Minister was transferred from one portfolio to another (*ibid.*, August 15, 1963). On another occasion Tun Razak, who had never been particularly close to Inche Aziz, commented, "Macmillan sacked eleven Ministers without notice." (*Ibid.*, August 10, 1962.)

leaving office of his own accord, adding that he was happy to leave.[29] The Prime Minister seemed to be curiously slow in asserting his authority. His first reaction to Inche Aziz's resistance was to say that he could continue in his existing post until he (the Tengku) returned from London.[30] It was not until after the Prime Minister's return that his language became tougher. "The ball is at his feet. I have a right to tell a member of the Cabinet what he has to do. If he does not like it, he can lump it."[31] Two weeks later he stated the constitutional position on collective responsibility in more measured terms. The Cabinet should work together, and all actions of an individual Minister should be in accord with Cabinet policy. But, if a Minister continued to go his own way, sought publicity for himself and blamed his colleagues, the Cabinet could not function.[32] Even then the actual announcement of Inche Aziz's dismissal was not made until October, and he was then sent on three months' leave "prior to relinquishing his appointment."[33]

The Prime Minister's delay in asserting unambiguously the doctrine of collective responsibility may be partly explained by his preoccupation with the formation of Malaysia and his absence in London at the end of July. Moreover, Inche Aziz was believed to have some popular support, especially among some fishermen and *padi* (rice) planters, and had been Minister of Agriculture since independence. In the circumstances the Tengku was in a stronger position to take a tough line successfully after his return from London where he just concluded a successful agreement on Malaysia with the British.

It is suggestive that there was a very short interval between Inche Aziz's forced resignation from the Cabinet and his voluntary resignation from UMNO. Party differences inside the ruling party had been reflected inside the Cabinet and had led to a breakdown of collective responsibility.

Government Departments and Other Governmental Bodies

The number of government departments in existence is a matter of convenience. There is usually more than one department in each ministry. Sometimes a new department may be set up to meet a need which has just arisen; thus a new department was set up early in 1964 to direct the manpower call-up necessitated by Indonesian Con-

[29] *Ibid.*, October 11, 1962.
[30] *Sunday Times,* July 26, 1962.
[31] *Straits Times,* August 10, 1962.
[32] *Malay Mail,* August 23, 1962.
[33] *Straits Times,* October 2, 1962.

frontation. Usually a department will deal with subjects which are related to each other. But, whatever the division of responsibilities, the need for coordination between departments (as well as *inside* departments) remains. The need is particularly evident in field operations, where cooperation and coordination are called for between different departments and also with agencies of state and local governments. "In the past there were so many departments, each not knowing what the other was doing. As a result a school would be built in one place, a health centre in another and something else somewhere else. . . ."[34] To overcome lack of coordination of this kind a system of seventy district rural development committees has been set up in Malaya, each headed by the District Officer: above them are eleven *state* rural development committees.

Other governmental bodies exist, which are not departments, such as the Central Bank (Bank Negara Tanah Melayu), the Central Electricity Board and the Federal Land Development Authority. Control of the general policy of such organizations is exercised by the government through a Minister, but they are given a discretion in their day-to-day administration which is not permitted to a government department.

The Rulers and Governors

The Rulers and Governors are the heads of the executive in each state. The Rulers of the nine states of Malaya (excluding the former Straits Settlements of Penang and Malacca) are chosen by a variety of methods, laid down in each state constitution.[35] In most states the Ruler succeeds by primogeniture, but there are some exceptions. The Governor of Malacca, the Governor of Penang, the Governor of Sarawak, and the Yang di-Pertuan Negara of Sabah (collectively known as "Governors") are chosen by the Yang di-Pertuan Agong, the Head of State of the whole Federation of Malaysia, acting in his discretion, but after consultation with the Chief Minister of the state concerned. They need not be Muslims, although at the beginning of 1965 all of them were. Their appointment is normally for four years at a time, although a Governor may be reappointed; the nine Rulers hold office for life, unless they become unfit.

The Heads of all thirteen states are obliged to rule "constitutionally." They are bound to act on most matters in accordance with the advice of their Executive Councils, just as the Yang di-Pertuan Agong must act on the advice of his Cabinet. However, each of them also

[34] Tun Razak, *ibid.,* November 14, 1963.
[35] See *Malayan Constitutional Documents,* 2nd ed., Vol. 2 (Kuala Lumpur: Government Press, 1962).

has a sphere in which he may act "in his discretion," which to some extent corresponds to the discretionary sphere of the King: the appointment of a Mentri Besar or Chief Minister; the withholding of consent to a request for the dissolution of the Legislative Assembly. The nine Rulers have a wider field of discretion, arising from their more permanent nature and from the fact that each is head of the Muslim religion in his state. Each may also act without ministerial advice on the following: the making of a request for a meeting of the Conference of Rulers concerned solely with the position of the Rulers or with religious acts, etc.; performing any function as head of the Muslim religion or relating to the custom of the Malays; appointing heirs, a consort, Regent or Council of Regency; appointments to Malay titles and honors, etc.; the regulation of royal courts and palaces.[36]

It is hard to pierce the constitutional shell which surrounds the Rulers and make an accurate evaluation of their social and political role. Clearly they retain influence over many Malays through tradition and because of their religious authority. Little has been published on the Rulers of today, except adulatory material on who married whose cousin, or who wore what ceremonial dress, when, where. Without exception the Rulers are Western-educated, and several attended the Malay College at Kuala Kangsar. Many are also "Western," for example, as judged by their interest in Western sports. It is expensive to maintain the Rulers, largely because of the need to keep up a number of residences and to provide for members of the royal family or the royal household. In the larger states the cost may amount to a million Malayan dollars a year. In the small state of Perlis the cost is much less, but may constitute about a quarter of the revenue raised by the state (excluding federal grants).[37] The fact that the Rulers continue to confer titles and honors[38] strengthens their positions inside their states, but detracts from the influence of the King and weakens his role as a unifying force. However, it may be argued that to the Malays, who have been exposed to severe shocks and threats, the Rulers are a necessary part of the social fabric. Their existence may tend to reassure Malays of their political supremacy. Even conspicuous consumption on the part of the Rulers may give vicarious pleasure to poorer Malays, who may not in the foreseeable

---

[36] Constitution, Eighth Schedule.

[37] Willard A. Hanna, "Perlis: A Malay State in Miniature," *American Universities Field Staff Reports Service, Southeast Asia Series* (Malaya), VIII, No. 12 (1960), p. 3.

[38] For instance on his sixty-second birthday (August 9, 1959), the Sultan of Kelantan conferred 10 titles, 17 orders of chivalry, 11 decorations and 46 medals. *Kelantan Government Press Statement*).

future be able to derive pleasure from their own consumption. More broadly, as the Minister of Finance (a Chinese) argued when introducing a trust fund to make loans to the Rulers, a stable and constitutional monarchy is a guarantee of political stability.[39]

The difficulty of judging the "value" of a Ruler is shown by a frank article on a senior Ruler who has been passed over in the choice of a King.[40] According to the article, the Ruler rides, dances, and plays golf and tennis; has been married half a dozen times or so, twice to dance hall girls (but not to more than four wives at once); has 22 polo ponies and 24 children. At his Silver Jubilee celebrations in 1957 60 Malays pounded tuba roots for hours, and 15 *piculs* (200 pounds) of pulverized root were dumped in the Pahang River so that the fish might be more easily speared in a giant fish drive. Yet, if this suggests the picture of a playboy, it should be added that the Sultan was active against the Japanese in World War II and against the Communists in the Emergency. He travels tirelessly throughout the state to promote rural development, and in some of the more remote areas the population look to him, rather than to the state government, to deal with such problems as the leaking roof of the village school. On many of these trips instruction is combined with entertainment. He is accompanied by mobile film vans from the (federal) Information Department and also by a troupe of *joget*[41] girls from Kuala Lumpur. The Sultan leads the dancing but makes sure that the villagers join in. It is arguable that, while a more conventional personality would be suitable in a King, the Sultan is just the kind of dynamic ruler who is most needed at state level. Without considerable research, however, some questions must remain unanswered. To what degree do the Rulers command the allegiance of younger, as opposed to older, Malays? What are the attitudes of members of other races towards the Rulers? In their present form do the Rulers help in the process of economic and social development, or do they act as a drag on progress?

On one or two occasions since 1957 the political role of the Rulers has come into prominence. In 1961 several members of the Trengganu state Assembly changed parties, and the PMIP Government had no longer a majority. The (PMIP) Mentri Besar requested a dissolution, which the Sultan refused. The Mentri Besar then tendered the resignation of his Executive Council to the Sultan, who asked the leader of the Alliance Party in the Assembly to form a

[39] *Straits Times,* May 31, 1963.
[40] Barry Conn, "The Peripatetic Sultan of Pahang," *Asia Magazine,* October 6, 1963.
[41] A Malay dance.

government, which he succeeded in doing. The fact that, as a result of the switch between parties, the Alliance was immediately able to form a government, strengthens the case for believing that the Sultan acted constitutionally. He claimed that he had no intention of taking sides. "I will not be fair if I do not give a majority group which came into being in the State Legislative Assembly an opportunity to form another government before I take steps to dissolve the Assembly." However, the Sultan also observed, "I took this decision after careful consideration of the past government and also of the restlessness of the people of Trengganu for change and progress."[42] This remark might conceivably be construed as "taking sides."

Two incidents concerning the Rulers and politics occurred in the single month of May, 1963. The Sultan of Perak, in an address, criticized some representatives in the state Legislative Assembly for not carrying out their responsibilities.[43] A few weeks later the Sultan of Selangor launched a triple attack on the state government: it had placed unreasonable restrictions on the use of ten acres of land which it had sold to him; it was a "weak" government; the royal town of Klang was filthy.[44] At one time it was possible that these disputes would reach grave proportions. The Tengku told the Rulers that they were symbols and must steer clear of politics. "As things stand now the Rulers can be assured of their future forever."[45] He left them to draw the inference. Another federal Minister said that the Malays would not have had one Ruler left, if it had been for UMNO's victory over the Malayan Union proposals of 1946.[46] However, both disputes were settled peaceably, aided by the Tengku's having referred them to the Conference of Rulers. There was considerable publicity about a dispute between the Ruler of Negri Sembilan and the state Mentri Besar in December, 1964.[47] Among the points at issue were the allowance to be paid to the wives of the Undangs (chiefs) and minor chiefs in the state and the constitutional position of the Ruler and the Undangs in regard to Malay customs. There were also other questions involved, because the Ruler complained to the Tengku on ten different topics. The dispute ended as suddenly as it began without any public announcement of a settlement.

In December, 1964, there was some discussion of the "political" role of the Yang di-Pertuan Negara of Sabah, Tun Datu Mustapha bin

[42] *Straits Times,* November 10, 1961.
[43] *Ibid.,* May 13, 1963.
[44] *Sunday Times,* May 26, 1963.
[45] *Ibid.,* May 12, 1963, also *Sunday Mail,* May 12, 1963.
[46] Inche Mohamed Khir bin Johari, *Sunday Times,* May 19, 1963.
[47] *Straits Times,* December 22, 23, 25, and 28, 1964; *Sunday Times,* December 27, 1964, and January 3, 1965.

Datu Harun. In the dispute between two Alliance parties, the UPKO and the USNO, the Chief Minister, Dato Donald Stephens, alleged that Tun Mustapha had unduly delayed his assent to a nomination for the post of State Secretary. The Constitution of Sabah lays down that appointments to this office "shall be made by the Yang di Pertuan Negara acting in accordance with the advice of the Chief Minister. . . ."[48] The Tengku replied to a suggestion that this delay by Tun Mustapha amounted to a breach of the Constitution by saying that, when Tun Mustapha's appointment was made, he had been a prominent party man (leader of the USNO). "It was agreed between all parties that the Governor enjoys not only constitutional status, but also should be a party man. It should, therefore, be understood that the Chief Minister should consult the Governor on all matters affecting the party." This interpretation was denied by Dato Stephens. "I would not have accepted the Chief Ministership had it been agreed that the Yang di-Pertuan Negara should be allowed to continue taking an active part in politics after taking office." He had indeed consulted Tun Mustapha, but "consultation" did not mean "approval."[49] In 1965 Tun Mustapha resigned as Yang di-Pertuan Negara and devoted himself to party politics as president of the USNO. He became Minister for Sabah Affairs in the federal Cabinet in July, 1966.

State Executive Bodies

On most issues the Ruler or Governor of each state is obliged to act on the advice of the State Executive Council. In Sarawak this body is called the Supreme Council; in Sabah it is known as the Cabinet. The chairman of the Executive Council is the Mentri Besar ("Chief Minister" in the states which do not have a Ruler). The Executive Council is responsible to the people, because it must command a majority in the Legislative Assembly of the state. When it loses that majority it must either resign and be replaced by another Executive Council which can obtain a majority (as in Trengganu in 1961), or the Ruler or Governor must dissolve the Assembly and cause fresh elections to be held. In June, 1966, the Governor of Sarawak replaced the Chief Minister, Dato Ningkan, by Penghulu Tawi Sli on the ground that Ningkan was no longer supported by the majority of the Alliance councillors who formed the majority in the Council Negri. This action was taken without Ningkan having been actually defeated by a vote of the Council Negri. Ningkan was restored to office by a Court decision, September, 1966. But a constitutional

[48] Article 11(1).
[49] *Straits Times,* December 14 and 16, 1964.

amendment was passed enabling the Governor to call a meeting of the Council Negri, which he did. The Ningkan government was defeated there and was dismissed by the Governor. Tawi Sli again became Chief Minister (September 24).

The Conference of Rulers

The Conference of Rulers is a modification of the previous "Durbar of Rulers" and of the "Council of Rulers" (1948–1957). Unlike these two bodies, however, the Conference includes not only the hereditary Rulers of the nine states but also the Governors of Penang, Malacca, and (since 1963) Sabah, and Sarawak. An important function of the Conference, which has already been described, is to elect the Yang di-Pertuan Agong and his Deputy, and for this particular purpose, and some others, only the nine Rulers are included. But the Conference also has the more general function of acting in some respects as a "third chamber" of Parliament. The Conference's powers under this heading are laid down in the Constitution (Article 38 and Fifth Schedule). In some fields the members of the Conference "may act in their discretion," that is, without following the advice of ministers. These fields include: legislation affecting the position of the Rulers; agreeing or disagreeing to the extension of any (Muslim) religious acts, observances or ceremonies to the Federation as a whole (except to Sabah and Sarawak); election or removal from office of the Yang di-Pertuan Agong or the election of a Deputy;[50] advising on appointments which under the Constitution require the consent of the Conference or consultation with it (for example, the Auditor-General, judges of the Supreme Court, members of the Election Commission and of the Public Services Commission); and legislation altering the boundaries of a state.

On some subjects on which the Conference deliberates, however, the Rulers must take the advice of persons who are responsible to the people through democratic processes. So, when the Conference of Rulers considers "matters of national policy" the King is accompanied by the Prime Minister and the other members by their respective Mentri Besar or Chief Minister.

The Constitution specifically provides [38(5)] that the Conference should be consulted before any change in policy is made affecting administrative action under Article 153, which deals with the special position of the Malays.

Many of the meetings of the Conference seem to be of a routine nature. From the reports available, a good deal of attention seems

[50] In the exercise of all the powers so far listed in this sentence the Governors are not members of the Conference.

to have been given to religion: conditions for divorce and polygamy for Muslims; Ministry of Rural Development proposals to conduct religious classes for adults; the banning of Kitab, a religious publication advocating that it was forbidden (*haram*) for a Muslim to support non-Muslim political parties; whether or not money derived from the Social and Welfare Services Lottery could properly be used for religious purposes, such as mosques and religious schools. On this last point a Religious Standing Committee of the Conference had previously decided that the lottery was a form of gambling contrary to the teachings of Islam. With great ingenuity, however, a "purification ceremony" was devised. Parliament passed an act to allow the net proceeds from the lottery to be transferred to the government's *general* revenue, so becoming no longer identifiable. The Conference of Rulers immediately decided that, because of this, it need take no decision on the issue.[51]

The Conference has also been useful as a place in which the federal government can brief the Rulers, and their Ministers, on important political developments, such as the formation of Malaysia and "Confrontation" by Indonesia. It was also used in 1963 to settle, and announce the settlement of, the disputes between the Sultans of Perak and Selangor and their respective state governments. The disputes were discussed at the Conference and a statement was issued, which concluded, "The Conference notes with regret the misunderstandings which have arisen between the Rulers and the party in power and is happy to note that these incidents are now closed. The Conference therefore resolves to express its confidence in the present Government and to re-affirm its faith in the party in power."

[51] *Malay Mail,* May 3, 1962; *Straits Times,* May 4, 1962.

9

The Civil Service

Malaya: Origins and Structure

The pattern of administration in Malaya was complex even before the formation of Malaysia. In it could be seen three successive stages: the traditional, the colonial, and the responsible-democratic. But the later stages had not totally replaced the first; they had been superimposed on it. So the traditional structure of Malay government, from the Ruler down to the *Penghulu* (headman) remained, although it was fitted into a modern democratic-bureaucratic frame of government. The colonial "layer" was "Malayanized" in the sense that practically all British civil servants were replaced by Malayans. The colonial *structure* remained, and the districts (70) and the District Officers, patterned after the system in British India, persisted. But the civil service became responsible, not to colonial rulers but to a government formed as the result of democratic elections. At the same time an attempt was made to extend the scope of elected local government authorities, although, in practice, the functioning of these bodies was often dependent on the assistance and cooperation of the District Officer. This has been the general trend, but the precise sequence of events during the extension of British rule was more intricate, because of differences in the rate of British penetration and the existence of various types of indirect rule. Hence the need to make distinctions between the Straits Settlements, the Federated States, and the Unfederated States, although since 1948 there has been a tendency in the former Unfederated States to follow gradually the general pattern obtaining in the former Federated States as regards general orders and schemes of service.

It is impossible therefore, to give any brief and complete account of the development of administration in Malaya. However, for purposes of comparison, descriptions are available of administration under the traditional type of Malay Ruler in the Unfederated States before they came under effective British control. In Trengganu, before 1909, Malay rule was still unaffected by the presence of the British, even in an "indirect" form. Government was almost completely lacking. There were no written laws, no courts and no police, and crime flourished unchecked. The Ruler's powers were largely in the hands of his relatives, and so were his revenues.[1] Less well-known, but worthy of record, was the style of administration of the Sultan of Johore, who did not appoint a British "General Adviser" until 1910, but who introduced many reforms on his own initiative. When the Sultan came to the throne the salaries of government officers in Johore were irregularly paid, and their attendance at their work was equally irregular. The Sultan put an end to this, cut government holidays to a minimum, and prohibited any government employee from receiving presents or other compensation apart from his official pay. In a sense this was "modernization," but it was *personalized* modernization, dependent on the Sultan's own views, or whims. Some of the roads he ordered to be built, it was suspected, were those which would open up for himself the most desirable new hunting opportunities. At this diamond jubilee banquet in 1955 the Sultan publicly regretted the glory which had departed. "In the days gone by I issued orders and things were done. I wanted the railway, and it was built according to my wishes. But nowadays things are different."[2]

However, the bulk of this section is concerned with the existing civil service, which has evolved from the British colonial civil service. Originally the British bureaucracy in Malaya consisted of the servants of the British East India Company. In 1858 responsibility passed to the British Crown, and in 1867 the dependence on India ended and the Straits Settlements were transferred from the India Office to the Colonial Office. On result of this was the creation of a distinct Malayan Civil Service (MCS), corresponding to the Indian Civil Service, from which it sprang. It also resembled, in its responsibility

---

[1] Rupert Emerson, *Malaysia: A Study in Direct and Indirect Rule* (New York: Macmillan, 1937), p. 255. Government in Kelantan, as described by Emerson, was equally chaotic. The privilege of minting money belonged to a local company, comprised of the Ruler and his uncles — "the wicked uncles." See also, for a general description of traditional Malay rule, J. M. Gullick, *Indigenous Political Systems of Western Malaya* (London: Athlone Press, 1958); Sir Frank Swettenham, *British Malaya,* rev. ed. (London: Allen and Unwin, 1948), pp. 141–143 (on Perak).

[2] *Straits Times,* September 19, 1955. See also the *Souvenir* commemorating the Diamond Jubilee of the Sultan, issued by the *Free Press,* September, 1955.

for top policy-making, the British institution now known as the "Administrative Class." But, unlike the Administrative Class, one important function of both the MCS and the ICS was to provide officers to serve "in the field" as District Officers. Later in the century entry to the MCS, as in Britain and in India, was by competitive examinations. However, in 1932 these were abolished and replaced by qualifying examinations to conform to the system currently used by the Colonial Office for other territories, apart from Malaya and Hong Kong. The Colonial Secretary believed that this system was impartial and that it produced a sufficient standard of intellectual ability. An "official" view was that the new method would probably recruit some cadets rather older than in the past, which would be an advantage, but that care would have to be taken in selecting staff for the legal and secretarial branches.[3]

The present structure of the civil service dates from after the Second World War. From one point of view the service is grouped "functionally," each government department employing mostly persons carrying out related functions, although there are also "common-user" services, largely clerical and administrative, of which the MCS is the most obvious example. Between the administrative and clerical classes, since 1957, there has also been an executive class. But there is a second type of division, corresponding to the level within the whole service. This takes the form of four "divisions," based on degrees of education, experience, and responsibility. For instance, selection for first appointment to Division I "is normally made from candidates who have acquired the appropriate academic or professional qualifications. Such candidates may be in competition with serving officers who are eligible for promotion to the service concerned."[4] The shape of the four-divisional structure is pyramidal, with smaller numbers in the higher divisions. Only about 300 are in Division I.

A few years ago the question of the "Malayanization" of the public service provided much material for controversy. From the political and nationalist points of view it was desirable that Malayanization should take place as quickly as possible after the attainment of independence in 1957. But, as has occurred in other ex-colonies, political developments had resulted in independence coming before sufficient Malayans had been adequately trained to take over all the jobs held by the British "expatriates." A program was therefore worked out, laying down targets for Malayanization over a period

[3] *Straits Times,* February 9 and March 11, 1932.
[4] *Service in the Government of the Federation of Malaya* (Kuala Lumpur: Government Printer, 1957), p. 5.

of several years and also determining the compensation to be paid to particular groups of expatriates.[5] In November, 1965, there were only a hundred and fifty, most of whom were on contract. Very few were in administrative jobs; only three were in the MCS.

Apart from expatriates, there are differences in the distribution of personnel by ethnic origin inside the various sections of the service. In some sections the Malays are preponderant, either because a section is restricted to Malays (as in the Malay Administrative Service), or partly because there is a quota of Malays to non-Malays (as in the Malayan Civil Service). In 1962, according to Tilman,[6] there was a slight preponderance of Chinese over Malays among all Division I personnel. In 1962 Tilman made the generalization that in services requiring a general educational background the Malays were in the majority, while in technical and professional services requiring a scientific, medical, or mathematical background, the Chinese predominated and there was also, in proportion to their numbers in the population, a high percentage of Indians. Indians are particularly strongly represented in the railways, in public works and in telecommunications. Racial relations inside the public service are potentially a delicate subject. It would be an extremely serious thing if favoritism on a racial basis were to exist, or were widely believed to exist. So far the Public Services Commission seems to have handled this danger adequately. In 1957, however, a Minister alleged that some government officials were trying to get people of their own race into jobs in their departments.[7]

The control of the public service is shared between the Federal Establishment Office and the Public Services Commission.[8] The former is responsible for schemes and conditions of service, scales of salaries, training courses and for supplying information to the Public

[5] See *Reports* of the Committee on Malayanization of the Public Service (Kuala Lumpur: Government Printer, 1954 and 1956); Robert O. Tilman, "The Nationalization of the Colonial Services in Malaya," *South Atlantic Quarterly,* LXI, No. 2 (1962), 183–196; T.E. Smith, "The Effect of Recent Constitutional Changes on the Public Service in the Federation of Malaya and Singapore," *Public Administration* (London), XXXVII, No. 3 (1959), 267–273.

[6] Robert O. Tilman, *Bureaucratic Transition in Malaya* (Durham, N. C.: Duke University Press, 1964), p. 70.

[7] Inche Mohamed Khir Johari, *Malay Mail,* November 18, 1957.

[8] For the origins of these two bodies and for the relations between them see Tilman, *The Public Services of the Federation of Malaya* (Durham, N. C.: Duke University, 1961 [microfilm]. See also the *Annual Reports* of the Public Services Commission. There are three other commissions with functions similar to the Public Services Commission but in different spheres: police; railways; judicial and legal service.

Services Commission. The latter is concerned with appointments. Formerly it had powers over promotions and discipline, but in 1966 a constitutional amendment authorized the transfer of these powers to departments.

Until recently there was a lack of long-term training courses for civil servants. Training courses for periods of several weeks have been in existence for some time, and a new Staff Training Centre, built with Colombo Plan funds from New Zealand, began operations in 1964 in Petaling Jaya, a suburb of Kuala Lumpur. Some public servants are also sent abroad for training courses. But until 1966 there was nothing approaching the longer training courses given, for instance, in India, Pakistan, or the Philippines. Early in 1966, how-ever, a post-entry training scheme was announced which would be carried on in cooperation with the University of Malaya.

The Malayan Civil Service

The whole tone and temper of the civil service is fashioned by the Malayan Civil Service, so it is worth while looking more closely at this small group of about three hundred officers. The MCS provides practically all the senior administrative officials of the federal govern-ment. It also provides many of the top civil servants in the states under the system by which important posts in the state governments are filled by officers seconded from the federal government.

The MCS was originally composed entirely of British officials, al-though some Malays were admitted between the two world wars and, from 1953 onwards, a few Malayans were appointed who were not Malays. It was then that the "four-to-one ratio" was introduced for the MCS,[9] i.e., for every four new Malay entrants there was one vacancy for a non-Malay. The proportion of Malays in the very top MCS posts is high; in 1962, 50 out of the top 53 were Malays.[10] The members of the MCS are generalists, as are the members of the British Administrative Class and the Indian Administrative Service, that is, they are not selected on the basis of any special professional or technical qualifications. There are, however, various avenues of recruitment. One, by possession of an honors degree and competition through interview, is direct from the universities, mostly the Univer-sity of Singapore and University of Malaya. Another is from the Malay Administrative Service (MAS), discussed below. A few are

[9] Other ratios exist in some other branches of the public service.

[10] Robert O. Tilman, "Policy Formulation, Policy Execution, and the Political Elite Structure of Contemporary Malaya," in *Malaysia: a Survey,* Wang Gungwu, ed. (New York: Praeger, 1964), p. 352.

recruited direct from the state services of the former Unfederated States. The channel of recruitment through the MAS is well established. The MAS was created in 1910 to open up subordinate administrative positions to Malays. At first nominees could enter only from the Malay College at Kuala Kangsar, itself originally restricted to entrants of princely blood, but later entry to the MAS was opened to others. Promotions could take place from the MAS to the MCS, and so, on Malayanization, the MAS was the main source for making good shortages of manpower in the MCS which resulted from the departure of expatriates. Consequently in the present MCS most of the senior positions are held by former MAS members, many of whom do not have university degrees. But almost half of the junior MCS posts are held by direct entrants from universities, all of whom hold an honors degree. Because of the large numbers of appointments to top positions made just a few years ago during Malayanization, the promotion of the second group to the top will be blocked for some time. Now that direct entry to the MCS is possible, the former function of the MAS as a channel for entry to the MCS, no longer seems to be so important, although it is still useful as an avenue to the MCS for holders of pass, as opposed to honors, degrees after they have had MAS experience. By 1961 MAS numbers had fallen to fewer than 75.[11]

The MCS has incurred some criticism on the ground that it is an "élite." Of course, by élite may be meant only that its members fill most of the highest positions in the civil service. It would seem, however, that the statement may be made with one or more of the following implications: that the MCS is drawn from restricted sources; that the MCS behaves with an unwarranted assumption of superiority towards other civil servants; that the MCS behaves with an unwarranted assumption of superiority towards the public. There has been no detailed research on the social origins of the MCS. Certainly the *racial* sources of recruitment have been limited, at first only to the British, then only to British and Malays, now predominantly to Malays. Racially, the MCS has always been an élite in this sense. Originally, also, only well-born Malays were recruited to the MCS. Nowadays, however, the basis of recruitment has been broadened as access to educational opportunities has been extended. On the second point, the president of a civil service union has complained

[11] Tilman, *The Public Services of the Federation of Malaya,* p. 177. Even by 1954 the standards of entry to the MAS had been lowered, because of the difficulty of getting recruits (*Report* of the Committee on Malayanisation of the Public Service [1954], p. 15).

that it was time that top government officials discarded their colonial attitudes and treated their subordinates as friends.[12] In reply the president of the MCS Association said that here *had* been a change of this kind in MCS attitudes since independence.[13] The relation of the MCS towards professional and technical officers is also relevant. In the past there had been some dispute about comparative rates of pay between administrative and specialist officers, but in 1954 it had been agreed that both groups should be placed on similar pay-scales.[14] The argument has now shifted to the arrangements for promotion inside these scales and to the competence in administrative posts of generalists and specialists, respectively. Recently, for instance, professional officers protested against the appointment of an MCS officer to the new post of permanent secretary in the Ministry of Health, on the ground that powers were thus being transferred to this officer, who had had a legal training and away from the medically qualified Director of Medical Services.[15] If it is assumed that the equivalent of an "administrative class," like the MCS, is unjustified, then its claims to give instructions to professional and technical officers may be interpreted as symptoms of an élite attitude. The MCS may sometimes appear to act as if it were superior to members of the public. The appearance, however, may simply result from "reserve" on the part of the MCS towards the public, to protect themselves from the belief that they can be easily influenced by their contacts and from any suspicion of corruption. Perhaps it may be a reflection of the powerful role of government in a society which still retains many traditional values. What is not always appreciated is that the assumption of superiority by the MCS may be a necessary accompaniment to the self-respect of MCS members, and a necessary guarantee for their adherence to high standards of integrity and responsibility.[16]

In 1966 it was decided that the MCS should become more specialized. Within the MCS there will be several "professional career patterns," in the fields of, for instance, economics, state and district government, and administrative management.

[12] *Sunday Times*, April 8, 1962.
[13] *Straits Times*, April 11, 1962.
[14] Tilman, *The Public Services of the Federation of Malaya*, pp. 124–126.
[15] *Straits Times*, July 20, 1963. There was a similar dispute later about the appointment of an MCS officer to be Controller of Immigration (*Sunday Mail*, December 20, 1964). In a few "nonintegrated" departments, e.g., transport, the top technical officer is to some degree "independent" of the generalist permanent secretary.
[16] See R. Braibanti, "Reflections on Bureaucratic Reform in India," in *Administration and Economic Development in India*, R. Braibanti and J. J. Spengler, eds., (Durham, N. C.: Duke University, 1963).

Another, related, contention is that there has been a drop in civil service performance and efficiency since Malayanization, which is attributable mainly to deficiencies in the MCS. One accusation pointed to "delays, disinterestedness [*sic*], dishonesty, and discourtesy," and said that leadership in some instances had been thrust on young shoulders or on old men who rose from the colonial ranks but were too dazed or too fossilised to meet the challenges of modern national administration.[17] Incidentally, this allegation came from a not completely impartial source, but from an association of professional officers, somewhat resentful of the "generalist" MCS. A more penetrating criticism has been made by Tilman.[18] He maintains that, during Malayanization, some men may have been promoted beyond their capabilities.[19] He points, too, to the dislocation caused by the process of replacing top personnel during Malayanization, and to the fact that some of the replacements in technical jobs were less well technically qualified than their predecessors. He also argues that the promoted men in the MCS have been reluctant to make decisions and have stuck too closely and too literally to rules and regulations.[20] The rules were framed during the colonial era. However the colonial MCS was master of the rules, in the sense that it was sufficiently confident to use its discretion in interpreting them; the present MCS, it is said, are, in effect, slaves to the rules.

An official view is that there has been no lowering of standards since Malayanization. "Experts in the technical and professional services are still here because we know that we are still shaky in these spheres."[21] Another view is that, largely because of the dislocation of Malayanization, the level of performance has fallen in technical and professional fields, but not in the sphere of administration. An expatriate observer thought that the civil service functioned as well as, if not better than, before Malayanization as far as general administration is concerned.[22] On the question of whether or not there is a tendency to stick too closely to the rules, a highly placed official has

[17] *Sunday Times,* July 21, 1963, quoting the latest *Newsletter* of the Senior Government Officers' Association.

[18] *Bureaucratic Transition in Malaya,* pp. 77–81.

[19] There may also have been too much emphasis placed (as in many countries) on seniority as a factor in promotions, *ibid.,* p. 95.

[20] Cf. Lucian W. Pye, "Southeast Asia," in *The Politics of the Developing Areas;* Gabriel A. Almond and James S. Coleman, eds. (Princeton: Princeton University Press, 1960), pp. 144–145.

[21] Interview with the permanent secretary to the Prime Minister's Department, *Straits Times,* May 5, 1963.

[22] R. H. Hickling, "The First Five Years of the Federation of Malaya Constitution," *Malayan Law Review,* IV, No. 2 (1962), 196.

said in conversation that this may be attributable to a change in expectations; the actions and procedures of government are not actually any slower than they were, but since independence expectations that government will act swiftly have been greater in some spheres, for instance in rural development.

Characteristics

There are several features which distinguish the working of the civil service in Malaya from its operation in some adjacent countries. There is no desperate competition for the better-paid civil service jobs; there is comparatively little corruption; in spite of the allegation referred to earlier about "sticking to the rules," bureaucratic processes are not excessively slow or legalistic; the relation between politicians and higher civil servants conforms to the "Western constitutional" pattern.

The first of these features results from the comparatively small output of university graduates. The output, if only English-educated graduates are considered (that is, excluding Nanyang University), is low, only several hundred a year. These are readily absorbed in teaching, in the civil service, in the professions, and, increasingly, in the private business enterprises set up under the government's policy of industrialization. In particular, there has been no surplus of law graduates whose main hope of employment has been in government service. The first law graduates trained in local universities qualified only in 1961, and until now they have been absorbed mainly by the legal profession. Malaya has so far avoided having a university-educated élite, discontented and unemployed, with job expectations greatly in excess of their job opportunities. The general official opinion is that, provided industrialization continues, such a situation will not arise in Malaya for about the next fifteen years and, with good management, need not occur even then.

Corruption is not completely absent. An official enquiry concluded that it existed in some government departments,[23] and it may also occur in other departments; but by the very nature of corruption it is always difficult to prove its existence. There is an Anti-Corruption Agency, which from time to time conducts "drives" by calling on heads of departments to take special anticorruption measures. But there are few allegations of widespread civil service corruption, and it is probably rare compared with most neighboring countries. Per-

[23] *Report* of a commission to enquire into matters affecting the Integrity of the Public Services (Kuala Lumpur: Government Printer, 1955). The government, in a statement attached to the *Report,* disputed some of the commission's findings.

haps this may be attributed partly to the relatively high level of civil service pay in Malaya, which is made possible by the relatively large national income. The salaries of top civil servants are particularly high, because they are the same as those of the British they replaced with the exception of various "expatriation" allowances.

The comparative absence of legalism might be partly a reflection of the generalist nature of the MCS. Few of its members have law degrees. Another factor may also be present. The argument will be presented later that Malay's success, indeed its continued existence, depends on its efficiency, on its ability to "deliver the goods." This alone can compensate for its lack of widespread consensus and national consciousness. If there is anything in this argument, then it is necessary for Malaya's survival that its administrative processes be efficient and that administrative business should not be unduly hampered by red tape and devotion to routine procedures. The previous point — that there is no general shortage of jobs for the English university-educated — is also relevant. There is not the same pressure, perhaps unconscious, to "create" work in the civil service as there might be if a shortage of jobs existed.

The "Western" view of democracy is that the politicians who constitute the government have been chosen by the people and that civil servants, who have not been so chosen, are in a clearly subordinate position. However, in some developing countries which claim to be generally democratic in the Western sense this relationship may not hold. It may not always be obvious exactly who is a politician and who is a civil servant, and, insofar as it is discernible, it may not always be the "politician" who is in control. In Malaya, it is true, many of the top Malay politicians and the top civil servants at present are still drawn from what appears to be a rather narrow social circle. But this does not indicate the absence of a "Western-type" relationship between the two. In late nineteenth-century Britain the Secretaries of State for Foreign Affairs and the top officials of the Foreign Office both came overwhelmingly from a restricted social group, but the constitutional relation between them was "Western-democratic" in the sense that the latter deferred to the constitutional superiority of the former. A special feature in Malaya is that the Prime Minister and the Deputy Prime Minister have both been civil servants, and so are able, from inside knowledge, to hold the civil service in check. The Deputy Prime Minister, in his capacity as Minister of Rural Development, has, for instance, played back tapes of the oral progress reports made by civil servants with interesting results.[24] In 1962 he travelled 43,000 miles throughout the country-

[24] Hickling, 196.

side and attended 118 district rural development committee brief-ings.[25] Finally, in some of the states at least, in pre-colonial times there was no centralized rule through a powerful civil service. Unlike some other developing countries, a centralized bureaucracy did not exist before the adoption of democratic government. Both are recent importations and the former is not more solidly rooted than the latter.

The Civil Service in the States of Malaya

All the eleven states of the former Federation of Malaya have their own state clerical services. This means that there is a large number of different schemes of service for clerical personnel all over the area. But only the five former Unfederated States and Penang and Malacca, have state civil services which fill posts above clerical level. A proposal to integrate these separate services, launched soon after independence, failed, partly because Johore and Kedah feared that, if it came into effect, they might lose some of their best men.[26] Under an "Establishment Agreement," originally concluded in 1934 but amended since, the Federation may, at the request of a state, second any member of the public service to the service of that state; and a state may, at the request of the Federation or of another state, second any member of its own public service to the service of the Federation or, as the case may be, of that other state. A person so seconded shall remain a member of the service to which he belongs, but shall be paid by the organization (state or federation) to which he is seconded.[27] In practice this provision has been used, *inter alia*, to second MCS men to key positions in some states, for instance to state secretaryships, or as Commissioners of Lands and Mines or as District Officers.

The Civil Service in Sarawak and Sabah

In 1884 a French writer and explorer wrote of Sarawak: "In reality thirty Englishmen, no more, govern and administer econom-ically the country, and that with only a few hundred native soldiers and policemen, and almost without written laws. A handful of men of a strange race is blindly obeyed by 300,000 Asiatics!"[28] This

[25] Peter Palomka, "Razak: Rural drive — the Men in the Witness Box," *Straits Times*, November 14, 1963.

[26] Malay Mail, October 31, 1958; *Standard,* November 2, 1958; *Straits Times,* January 5, 1959.

[27] Constitution, Article 134; Tilman, *Bureaucratic Transition in Malaya,* pp. 82–83, 102–104.

[28] Quoted in S. Baring-Gould and C. A. Bampfylde, *A History of Sara-wak under its Two White Rajahs, 1839–1908* (London: Sotheran, 1909), p. 409.

statement ignores the fact that the Brookes had to face several re-
bellions, but it brings out their dependence on the already-existing
local chiefs. On top of this was imposed a structure of "divisions"
(eventually five) each under a "Resident": the divisions in turn were
composed of districts, each under a District Officer. Under the
second Rajah a minimum of records was kept, and many decisions
were made by word of mouth.[29] The personal wishes of the Rajah
led him to intervene in administration as well as policy. "We find
him himself ordering music from Messrs. Hawkes for the Municipal
Band, and dismissing the conductor when he thought the performance
was inadequate."[30]

Although the Brookes' personal rule was replaced by colonial rule
in 1946, the chief posts in the administration were filled by the British.
However, in 1959, a committee was set up to consider the replacement of public servants recruited outside Sarawak by persons recruited locally. But in Sarawak and North Borneo, this was a more
difficult problem than it had been in Malaya. The slow movement
towards self-government had been matched by a slow pace of advance
in education. This was not a fatal barrier to the emergence of local
politicians. Community leaders existed who could be trained by being
given the opportunity to acquire experience through service on legislative or executive bodies. But the inadequate educational system
impeded the growth of a locally staffed civil service. There were
insufficient local people with the necessary general education to
qualify for the higher levels of administration or the necessary specialist training for top technical posts. There was an additional racial
facet to the problem. The 1959 committee had touched on a delicate
matter when it said, ". . . it must be clear to all that it would not be
in the best interests of Sarawak, or of the provision of racial harmony,
if the service came to consist predominantly of representatives of any
one race."[31] The fact was that at this time about 85 per cent of the
enrollment in the secondary schools was Chinese. In 1958 only one
native was eligible to apply for a degree course: in 1959, two; in
1960, five; in 1961, fourteen.[32] Compared with Malaya, where for
years Malays had been trained for posts with some responsibility, the
advantage of the Chinese over the rest in being educationally prepared for high civil service jobs was overwhelming. The conclusion
was that, from the point of view of the natives, the pace at which

[29] Steven Runciman, *The White Rajahs* (Cambridge, England: Cambridge
University Press, 1960), pp. 204–205.
[30] *Ibid.,* p. 218.
[31] *Straits Times,* August 15, 1960.
[32] Jeffrey Francis, "Why Borneanisation Is Slow in Sarawak," *Sunday
Mail,* September 30, 1962.

expatriates were replaced must be dependent on the pace at which native successors could be trained. Otherwise a disproportionate number of Chinese would be appointed to the higher posts.

Seven months before Malaysia was formed the slow pace of Borneanization was deplored by the President of the Sarawak Government Asian Officers Union. He stated that in Division I of the Sarawak Civil Service there was only one local man out of thirty; in Division II approximately thirty out of a hundred posts were held by local men. The Union was particularly dissatisfied with the slowness of Borneanization on the administrative side, where it claimed that there was no shortage of local administrators to take up Division I and Division II jobs.[33] In the short run the natives were given constitutional protection. In the new Sarawak Constitution the Governor was given the power to safeguard the special position of the natives by giving directions to the Sarawak Public Services Commission to reserve offices in the public service for them, although actual numerical quotas have not been laid down, as for some parts of the civil service in Malaya.[34] At the same time the government initiated a long-term solution for stepping up native education as a whole, selecting particular natives to go for degree, and shorter courses, abroad. Less ambitious, but valuable, training was carried out at the Inservice Training Centre in Kuching. The effect of these measures in reducing the proportion of expatriates in the higher levels of the state civil service was estimated by Dato Stephen Kalong Ningkan, then Chief Minister of Sarawak, in 1964. In that year out of the twenty-seven posts corresponding to head or deputy head of a department twenty-two were held by expatriates. In 1966, he estimated, the number would fall to thirteen, and in 1967 to nine.[35]

The additional complication introduced by Malaysia was that the natives, in seeking to replace a high proportion of the expatriates in the civil service, must now face potential competition, not only from Chinese inside Sarawak, but also from officials who might be appointed to posts in Sarawak from Malaya. Some of the reasons for opposition to "Malayanization" were based purely on the economic advantages of promotion. In 1964 the Chief Minister said: "I wish to emphasise that the Sarawak Government intends to see that the terms of the inter-governmental committee report are strictly observed

[33] *Straits Times,* February 8, 1963. Many of these Division II posts were equivalent to Division I posts in Malaya.

[34] Article 39. As for Sabah, there is reference to scholarships and educational or training privileges.

[35] *Straits Times,* September 25, 1964. In 1966 Dato Ningkan announced that, on the Tengku's suggestion, a committee on the "Borneanisation" of the Civil Service would be set up (*ibid.,* March 30, 1966).

as regards Borneanisation and that Malayanisation will be resisted. As a result of this policy the opportunities for Sarawakian officers in terms of promotion are immense."[36] Apart from the prospects of opportunities for promotion, distaste for the previous Malay rule of Brunei still lingered, it was alleged, and the recent secondment of some Malay officers to Brunei had been marked by incidents and had resulted in unfavorable publicity. The issue became charged with political significance during 1964, when it formed one strand of the tangled argument between Inche Abdul Rahman bin Yaakub, then an Assistant Federal Minister, and the Chief Minister and others on the expatriate question. Significantly, after the change of government in June, 1966, the departure of some top expatriate officials was accelerated.

In North Borneo the government, like the Brooke Rajahs, economized in European manpower. Fifty or sixty British officers were sufficient, aided by a system of native administration which made use of headmen and chiefs.[37] "Residencies," of which eventually there were four, corresponded to the divisions in Sarawak: under them, as in Sarawak, were districts. In North Borneo, the Borneanization question was also widely discussed. At the end of 1962 there were 357 key posts in the civil service, most of them in Divisions I or II, and only sixty-five of them were held by local officers.[38] The expected rate of Borneanization varied from department to department. In 1963 it was said that the estimates of how long expatriates can stay "vary from indefinitely in the case of some postings where there is no hope of getting local officers for many years to periods of two or three years. Most departments have asked expatriates to stay on for from five to ten years."[39] Here again, the long-term solution was a vast expansion in the number of highly educated natives. It was only 1964 that the first group of students, sent abroad to qualify with degrees and then enter the civil service, returned, and there were

---

[36] *Ibid.*, January 13, 1964. See the *Malaysia Report of the Inter-Governmental Committee* (Kuala Lumpur: Government Printer, 1963) ("Lansdowne Report"), Annex B, paras. 8–9 and 30. It had previously been pointed out that for vacant federal posts Borneanisation would be a priority, but it could not be guaranteed that a Malayan would not be appointed to any particular vacancy. Vacant state posts were being filled by local promotion or by expatriates, employed on temporary terms (*Sarawak by the Week*, 37/63, September 8–14, 1963, p. 6, quoting a statement in the Council Negri.)

[37] Tregonning, *Under Chartered Company Rule* (*North Borneo 1881–1946*), (Singapore: University of Malaya Press, 1958), ch. 6. On the postwar system see *North Borneo Annual Report, 1962* (Jesselton: Information Office, 1960), p. 237.

[38] *Straits Times,* March 15, 1963.

[39] *Ibid.*, October 11, 1963.

only half a dozen of them. In the Constitution of Sabah the Yang di-Pertuan Negara must "ensure such degree of participation by natives as he may deem reasonable in the public service of the State . . .,"[40] and specific mention is made of scholarships and educational or training privileges in this connection. The Chief Minister, however, pointed out in 1964 that the Constitution did not provide for any special *promotion* preferences for natives. He quoted figures showing that in the year or so after Malaysia out of eleven Sabahans promoted to Division I, five were natives, and of eighty-one promoted to Division II, forty-three were natives.[41] These numbers are low compared with the proportion of natives in the population, but high considering how far behind the natives have been until now, educationally, in relation to the Chinese. Generally, the pattern has been that the expatriates employed on administrative jobs have left quickest. It has been possible to replace them largely by natives, sometimes by temporary measures such as lowering the entry qualification to Division I from an honors degree to a pass degree. As the expatriates leave, the picture will probably come to resemble that in Malaya: administrative posts will contain a relatively high proportion of natives, while a relatively high percentage of Chinese will be found in professional and technical posts. In the meantime, some posts are being filled by expatriates on short-term contracts.

As in Sarawak, there has been some local feeling that, if the posts vacated by expatriates were filled by men appointed from Malaya, these officers would be hard to move and would block the promotion of local men when they were ready to take over.[42] In 1964 this led to a bitter debate in the press on the conduct of Malayan officials serving in Sabah and also on the conduct of expatriates.[43] The issue of the appointment of the Sabah State Secretary was also closely related to the development of the party system in Sabah.[44]

After Malaysia, when the federal government assumed some functions previously undertaken by the state governments of Sarawak and Sabah, some of the state government departments became federal;

[40] Article 41.

[41] *Straits Times*, September 24, 1964.

[42] Dato Donald Stephens, *Malayan Times*, December 13, 1963.

[43] E.g., *Straits Times*, April 7 and July 15, 1964. The expatriate issue came up again after Singapore left Malaysia. In September, 1965, Tun Razak warned senior expatriate officers not to involve themselves in Sabah's internal politics. (*Ibid.*, September 15, 1965) Presumably his remarks referred to the USNO-UPKO controversy over renegotiation of the terms of Sabah's remaining in Malaysia after Singapore's departure. The warning was repeated by the USNO leader, Tun Datu Mustapha bin Datu Harun (*ibid.*, December 11, 1965).

[44] See p. 105.

the civil servants in these departments consequently became federal toc. Instead of coming under the state Public Services Commission, they came under the federal Public Services Commission. It was provided, however, that, in both states, the federal officers serving in the territory would be dealt with by a branch of the Public Services Commission, set up in the territory, which would include, ex officio, the members of the *state* Public Services Commission.[45] The civil servants who had become federal were also made subject to the Federal Establishment Office.

A Federal Secretary for the Borneo states was therefore appointed,[46] as well as subordinate officers, to take charge of establishment matters in the territories. The Deputy Federal Secretary in Sabah at this time, Yeap Kee Aik, found it difficult to keep out of the expatriate controversy previously mentioned. One of the most pressing problems will be to carry out successfully the proposed scheme of exchanging officers, so that new federal officers from the Borneo territories gain experience in Malaya, while a selected number of high-level officers from Kuala Lumpur gain some first-hand knowledge of conditions in Sarawak and Sabah.

SUGGESTED READINGS

Tilman, Robert O. *Bureaucratic Transition in Malaya.* Durham, N.C.: Duke University Press, 1964. Apart from the same author's unpublished Ph.D. thesis, the only recent comprehensive account of the civil service in Malaya.

Tilman, Robert O. "The Bureaucratic Legacy of Modern Malaya," *Indian Journal of Public Administration,* IX, No. 2 (1963), 162–173.

Reports of the Committee on Malayanization of the Public Service. Kuala Lumpur: Government Printer, 1954 and 1956. These state the policy on Malayanization and also contain much additional material.

---

[45] Constitution, Article 146B.
[46] For his functions see *Sarawak by the Week,* 39/63, September 22–28, 1963, pp. 14–15.

10

Local Government;
The Judiciary

Introduction: The District Officer

The details of local government in Malaya are complex, but the broad outlines may be grasped if three points are borne in mind. First, only a small portion of the whole area of Malaya (although a high percentage of the population) is covered by local authorities, that is, separately constituted bodies set up to deal with a number of functions in a particular area; the part covered is mostly urban. Most of the area of Malaya is administered, not by officials who are responsible to some local government authority, but by federal or state government officials.[1] Second, the system of local government was largely imposed from above, and did not arise as a spontaneous expression of grass-roots feeling. It did not evolve directly from a native system of government; it was superimposed on a native system which had already been overlaid with alien features of administration such as the District Officer. Even today inside local government there is a curious and intricate mixture of elected and appointed persons. Third, the pattern resembles local government in Britain, at least outwardly. But there are significant differences which reduce the extent of autonomy of local authorities as compared with Britain. Prominent among these is the small degree of financial autonomy (even among those which are described as being "financially autonomous") and the large part still played by officials, notably District Officers, in the operation of local government.

---

[1] W. C. Taylor, *Local Government in Malaya* (Alor Star: Kedah Government Printer, 1949), p. 63.

164

The system of District Officers (seventy in number) introduced by the British from India, still remains. In the past the District Officers' primary responsibility was land administration. They still have the powers and duties of magistrates, although they seldom act in a judicial capacity. Under them are Assistant District Officers, each in charge of a subdistrict, who, as well as assisting District Officers generally, have each specific responsibility for supervising a land office. The traditional *Penghulu*, or headman, in charge of one of the 1,100 or so *mukims* (districts) in the Federation of Malaya, has been "bureaucratized" by being appointed as a state government official.[2] Below him is the traditional unpaid headman of each village, the *Ketua Kampong*. Before independence the District Officer was a key figure. "To many a peasant the District Officer is the embodiment of the government to whom he can and does make his appeal directly."[3] Nowadays, under a democratic system of government, it might seem that he is becoming an anachronism. Nevertheless the District Officer is still an important figure in rural areas. Since the drive for rural development started, the District Officer has acquired a new role. Each of the district rural development committees is headed by a District Officer.[4] In 1960 the Assistant Minister for Rural Development stressed the importance of this aspect of the District Officer's work. If any officer was found to lack initiative in implementing the development plan, the government would have to transfer him from his district and get a new man to take over.[5]

Local Government Authorities

Before 1945 the prevailing type of authority was the Town Board (previously named Sanitary Board), although the Settlements of Penang and Malacca each contained a municipality and several Rural Boards. The Town Boards were essentially organs of the state gov-

[2] Stanley M. Middlebrook and A. W. Pinnick, *How Malaya Is Governed* (London: Longmans Green, 1940), pp. 45–50; *The Penghulu's Handbook* (Johore Bahru: Government Printer, 1951); William H. Newell, *Treacherous River* (Kuala Lumpur: University of Malaya Press, 1962), pp. 29–32. In Kelantan the equivalent of a *Penghulu* is a *Penggawa* [Tjoa Soei Hock, *Institutional Background to Modern Economic and Social Development in Malaya (with special reference to the East Coast)* (Kuala Lumpur: Liu and Liu, 1963), p. 272].

[3] Taylor, p. 11. On the District Officer's difficulties in coordinating the work of technical departments in his district as early as the 1920's, see Rupert Emerson, *Malaysia, A Study in Direct and Indirect Rule* (New York: Macmillan, 1937), pp. 158–159.

[4] Peter Polomka, "Razak: Rural Drive — the Men in the Witness Box," *Straits Times,* November 14, 1963.

[5] *Ibid.,* May 4, 1960.

ernment, created to deal with local affairs. The chairmen of the authorities were appointed; in the Town Boards the District Officer was normally chairman. Government officers, for instance engineers or health officers, were also appointed ex officio. They often had a dual capacity as members of the Board and as technical officers of the Board. At the same time there was a degree of local representation through the nomination of some unofficial persons to the Boards. After the Second World War two main lines of development were followed simultaneously. One was the introduction of elected representation and some decease in the number of appointed officials. The other was the granting of a measure of financial autonomy. Much of the complexity of the system arose from the fact that these two developments have not proceeded at an equal pace for all local authorities, but that either one of them has sometimes outstripped the other. The *ultimate* aim was that *all* local authorities should become relatively independent, with all members elected and with "financial autonomy."

The chief postwar enactment on local elections was the Local Authorities Election Ordinance of 1950. It provided, among other things, that municipalities should have an elected majority of members. *All* members of the Council could be elected, and the president of the Council could be elected from among the members. Town Boards could also have a majority of elected members. When this stage was reached the Board was to be renamed a "Town Council." Town Councils may have elected presidents.

"Financial autonomy" was provided for by the Town Board (Amendment) Ordinance of 1954. By this ordinance Town Boards or Town Councils may become separate statutory bodies and be permitted to have a separate fund instead of having their revenue and expenditure managed by the state, and figuring only as items in the state budget. Any surplus in the fund at the end of a year may be carried forward, and will not be claimed by the state government.

A confusing term, "Local Council," was used for a new type of local authority provided for by the Local Councils Ordinance of 1952. It was confusing because existing local authorities already were run by "councils," for example, as is obvious from the name, Town Councils. However, although the name of the new authorities was not distinctive, the authorities themselves were. New Villages had been set up over large areas of the country to resettle persons removed from their existing homes during the Emergency.[6] It was considered important that as many as possible of these villages should

---

[6] See pp. 32–33, above.

be given a measure of local self-government. This was essentially a political decision, taken as part of the fight against the Communist insurrection. By 1965 about 60 per cent of them had fully elected Councils with an elected chairman, and they also enjoyed "financial autonomy." Their functions relate mainly to public health and the development of communications and water supply. They are dependent on the District Officer and other government officials for advice and assistance. Those New Villages which do not have elected councillors have informal committees, which exist to advise the District Officer.

The intricacy of the system can be seen from the range of types of local authorities now in existence:[7]

Cities[8]	1
Municipalities (including Kuala Lumpur)	3
Town Councils (financially autonomous)	25
Town Councils (not financially autonomous)	11
Town Boards (financially autonomous)	5
Town Boards (not financially autonomous)	32
Rural District Councils[9] (financially autonomous)	4
Rural District Councils[9] (not financially autonomous)	3
Local Councils[10]	296
New Village Committees[10]	181

Constitutionally every local authority (except that for Kuala Lumpur, the federal capital) is subordinate to a state government.[11] Officials still sit on most local authorities: the District Officer is often president or chairman of the Council or Board, and the District Health Officer and the District Engineer are usually members. The extent of their dependence on the states may be judged from the fact that even those which are "financially autonomous" and have separate budgets of their own must submit these budgets to the state government for prior approval. Another reason for dependence is the large extent to which all authorities, except the very largest (for instance, the municipalities) must lean on the states for professional

[7] Figures as of April 7, 1965 (obtained from the Commissioner of Local Government, Kuala Lumpur).

[8] The legal powers are the same as those of municipalities, but the status and prestige are higher.

[9] These exist only in Penang and Malacca.

[10] These exist only in New Villages.

[11] The federal Constitution lists local government, outside the federal capital, as a state function (Article 74 (2), Ninth Schedule, Second List).

and technical advice, because of their financial weakness. In these ways the subordinate legal status of local authorities is underlined and confirmed.

Only the government of the federal capital, Kuala Lumpur, is not subordinate to a state. Since 1961 its government has been in the hands of a federal commissioner, appointed by the Yang di-Pertuan Agong, who is directly responsible to the Minister of the Interior. The commissioner is advised by an Advisory Board consisting of six official members, mostly the civil service heads of various government departments, and five unofficial members who are prominent citizens of various communities in the capital. The government explained the change from an elective to a nonelective system in Kuala Lumpur by saying that the importance of the national capital had so increased that its further progress had become the concern of the nation as a whole.

Local authorities derive their current revenue from a number of sources. An important source is the general assessment rate, arrived at by estimating the value of immovable property and then fixing a percentage "rate" of that value. Property belonging to the federal or state government is not actually assessed, but these governments pay a roughly equivalent sum "in aid of rates." Other revenue comes from licenses, for instance for eating houses, places of entertainment, and the licensing of non-motor vehicles. Apart from the municipalities, most other local authorities are also subsidized, in effect, by receiving free or cheap services, for example the technical advice given by the federal or state governments. Both the nonfinancially autonomous local authorities and the Local Councils also receive annual general grants from the states.

The possible range of functions of local authorities is very wide. Some local Councils have only simple functions, usually in the field of public health and communications. On the other hand, an authority such as George Town, Penang, may have a great number of activities. The City Council is responsible for the welfare of over a quarter of a million people. It is run by fifteen elected Councillors who choose their own Mayor and Deputy Mayor. The council's numerous functions are indicated by the names of its ten standing committees: Health, Water and Veterinary; Town Planning and Building; Transport, Vehicles and Fire Brigade; Public Works; Traffic; Electricity Supply; Establishment and Disciplinary; General Purposes; Finance; Assessment Appeals. In 1962 the council held 25 ordinary and 6 special meetings. The standing committees held 168 meetings, and there were also 36 meetings of special committees and subcommittees. The annual revenue of the three "trading" departments — Water, Electricity Supply, and Transport — totalled about $15 million. The corresponding figure for the non-trading departments was about $10 million. The staff employed in the Electricity Supply Department alone was over 700.[12]

George Town is not typical, either in the wide scope of its activities or in the freedom of its elected members from domination by officials. In these respects it approximates roughly to the English model. But perhaps, in time, the larger local authorities may come to resemble it.

State-Local Government Relations — Coordination of Local Government

Party solidarity is a good basis for satisfactory state-local government relations, just as it is a good basis for satisfactory federal-state relations. Friction is likely to occur when an important local authority is governed by a majority party which is different from the party controlling the state government. It is perhaps significant that in recent instances of a major breakdown of local government, the parties in control of the local authority were different from the parties which controlled the state. In July, 1965, the Seremban Town Council (controlled by a UDP, Labour-Independent and Socialist Front coalition) was suspended by the (Alliance-controlled) state government, pending an enquiry into charges of maladministration against the Council.[13] During the suspension the state government took over the Council's functions. Other examples of friction (not necessarily in connection with maladministration) have been between George Town (Socialist Front) and Penang (Alliance); Ipoh (PPP) and Perak (Alliance); Malacca (Socialist Front) and the State of Malacca (Alliance); Kota Bharu (Alliance) and Kelantan (PMIP). The immediate points of dispute have varied: the appointment of a municipal secretary (Malacca); the conditions for state loans for municipal housing (George Town and Ipoh); municipal reluctance to provide flags and illuminations to celebrate the end of the Emergency or the founding of Malaysia (George Town); state insistence that an amusement park should be closed down (Kota Bharu). An especially interesting case occurs when the federal government is drawn into a dispute between a local authority and a state government. In Treng-

[12] Data from the *Annual Report* of the George Town City Council. See footnote 13, below.

[13] *Straits Times,* July 24 and December 15, 1965. In March, 1966, the Penang state government ordered an enquiry on the George Town City Council's management of affairs (*ibid.,* March 18, 1966), which began in July, 1966, when the state government took over the Council's functions. The Malacca Town Council also had its powers taken over, by the Malacca state government, in 1966.

ganu in 1960 an Alliance-dominated local government Council (Kemaman) was able to obtain financial help from the federal (Alliance) government, instead of obtaining it through the normal channels of the PMIP-controlled state government. The state government had cut down two road schemes put forward by the Council. The Council appealed direct to the federal government informally, obtained $67,000, and completed work on the roads well in advance of many of the corresponding projects of the PMIP-controlled Councils in Trengganu.[14]

The pattern of local government is so extremely varied and is changing so rapidly that there is clearly need for some coordination. To some extent this is provided by the office of the Commissioner of Local Government and Housing. The Commissioner has an office in the Ministry of the Interior, and, under the direction of the Minister, is responsible for framing and implementing local government development policy. He maintains contact with state governments and local authorities, partly by means of visits. Generally he is available for advice and tries to realize one part of the aim suggested by John Stuart Mill in *Representative Government:* "Power may be localised, but knowledge, to be most useful, must be centralised. . . ."[15]

The original Constitution provided that the federal government could give advice and technical assistance to the government of any state,[16] and this could have been used to secure some coordination of local government. But no provision was made for setting up any formal body in which consultation could take place. In 1960 an Amendment[17] to the Constitution provided for a National Council for Local Government. Its purpose was to formulate a national policy for the promotion, development and control of local government and for the administration of any relevant laws. In particular, any projected legislation on local government can be examined with a view to securing uniformity. Both federal and state[18] governments are bound to implement any policy decided on in the Council.

An instance of the Council's work was that it drafted, and approved for submission to Parliament, a bill for a "Local Government Service" for employees in all financially autonomous local authorities. Many of the officers who work for these authorities are seconded from other posts, which makes it desirable to have some uniformity in conditions of service. Drafting the bill was made difficult by the great

---

[14] *Ibid.,* December 5 and 6, 1960; *Malay Mail,* December 23, 1961.
[15] *Utilitarianism, Liberty and Representative Government* (London: Everyman's Library Ed., 1910), p. 357.
[16] Article 94 (1).
[17] Article 95A. See also p. 78, above.
[18] But not the Borneo states.

differences in the financial resources of the authorities and by the problems of transferring officers from one service to another without loss of pension. There are many other fields where uniformity is desirable. In England, through long experience, the respective roles of elected members and appointed officials have become quite clearly defined. But in Malaya this is not so. In some Town Councils, for instance, there is an elected president, who corresponds roughly to an English mayor, and an official, often legally qualified, called the "secretary," who resembles the English town clerk. But in Malaya the division of duties between these two persons differs radically from one local authority to another. In some, for example, the president himself will make decisions on the issue of licenses to particular persons. In other authorities he will not. Uniformity in fields like this might be hastened through the work of the National Council for Local Government.

Opinions on the work of the Council probably depend on the view which is taken of federal-state relations generally. The Council could be regarded as one more example of the federal government's domination over the states. Alternatively, it could be held that, since the Constitution assigns a preponderance of power to the federal government, it is only logical that this power should extend to the securing of some uniformity in local government. Incidentally, the process by which the Council would enforce a decision on a recalcitrant state, or states, remains to be seen. So far there is no known example of a state which has been outvoted in the Council and then compelled to implement the policy it had opposed.

Another, informal, body exists which attempts to standardize the practices of the city and the municipalities and to allow them to exchange views on matters of common interest, the Consultative Committee of Municipal Corporations. It has been suggested that the membership of this body should be expanded, and that an Association of Local Authorities should be set up. It has been argued that the case for such an association has recently been strengthened by the amalgamation of civil service unions, which calls for some corresponding uniformity of approach on the employers' side.

Local Elections

How successful has the introduction of democratic elections been in local government? The most recent system of local elections in the Federation came into operation in 1951, although in the Straits Settlements of Penang and Malacca there had been elections on a limited franchise in the second half of the nineteenth century and at the beginning of the twentieth. Two important administrative changes were made by the Local Government Elections Act of 1960, which provided that the organization and supervision of all local elections should be transferred from the state authorities to the "independent" election commission. It was also laid down that all members of a local authority would retire at the same time, every three years. Previously one-third of the members had retired every year. This system had ensured continuous sensitivity to public opinion, but it was administratively inconvenient, and sometimes produced too frequent changes in control in these councils where the parties were evenly balanced.

Politically it has become plain that national party politics largely dominate local elections. It is units of the *national* parties that organize for local elections. Election issues are partly national and partly local. It would seem that the acute shortage of water and the cholera epidemic (both local factors) were partly responsible for the Alliance Party's loss of control over the Malacca Town Council in 1963. Conversely, the Tengku claimed that the 1963 local election results, in which the Alliance won about 70 per cent of the seats, were evidence that the electors favored the Alliance's policy on the formation of Malaysia.

Local elections perform some useful functions for the parties. They keep the party machinery in use and prevent it from getting rusty between national (and state) elections. They also provide pointers to the parties' prospects at the next national and state elections and so help them to shape their strategies for these elections. Local elecions also provide an opportunity for rewarding party members by nominating them as candidates.

There has not been much grass-roots enthusiasm for local elections. On several occasions motions have been passed at UMNO party meetings to abolish them. When a bill to provide that Kuala Lumpur should no longer be governed by an elected Council but by a Federal Commissioner was being discussed in Parliament in 1960 protests came from Socialist Front leaders (whose party was strong in Kuala Lumpur) but not conspicuously from the grass roots.[19] In 1965 and 1966 it was announced that, in view of the emergency which had been proclaimed because of Indonesian Confrontation, the local elections due to be held these years would be suspended.[20] Later in 1965 it was announced that a Royal Commission on local government was being appointed to consider, among other things, whether or not elective local authorities should continue to exist. The enquiry was attacked by D. R. Seenivasagam of the PPP and by representatives of

[19] *Straits Times,* September 13 and 14, 1960.
[20] *Ibid.,* March 2, 1965.

other opposition parties. Mr. Seenivasagam said that the UMNO and the MCA, which had failed to capture several most important Councils, such as Penang, Ipoh, and Seremban, by democratic elections, were now trying to gain control by "dictatorial methods by doing away with elections."[21] Whatever the reason for setting up the Royal Commission, it is certainly true that non-Malay communal parties have controlled many of these important authorities, and that there have been many instances of friction between them and Alliance-controlled state governments.

One reason for the general lack of enthusiasm for local government authorities has been disinclination to pay the local rates levied by the authorities. In many areas rates are notoriously hard to collect, and it is not politically attractive for local authorities to become really tough with those who do not pay them promptly. In 1965 it was announced that the increasing expenditure on education in Malaya would make it necessary to impose a new rate for education in 1966.[22] In areas covered by local authorities the rate is to be collected by the authorities; in other areas it is to be imposed directly on landowners and collected by state governments. Once again, unless procedures are improved, the collection of this rate will present a problem.

Local Government in Sarawak and Sabah

Local bodies in Sarawak date from 1921, when the Kuching Sanitary Board was set up. But although there were some further developments before the war, it was not until after the war that significant changes took place. The greatest advances were made in Kuching, where by 1953 there was a Kuching Municipal Council with a measure of autonomy and responsibility for the conduct of municipal affairs. But the unofficial membership of the Council was mainly on a communal basis, Councillors being nominated by the various community associations. By a 1957 ordinance, however, the Council acquired more powers and became fully elected on an adult franchise. Outside Kuching the emphasis was at first on setting up local bodies consisting entirely of natives. But the first racially mixed local authority was tried at Limbang in 1948. Gradually it became the government's aim to increase the number of racially mixed authorities as a conscious instrument of policy. By 1957 nearly all Sarawak was covered by local government bodies, and in 1959 elections were for District Councils throughout Sarawak on an adult franchise. There

[21] *Sunday Times,* August 1, 1965.
[22] *Straits Times,* September 15, 1965. The necessary legislation, enacted in March, 1966, vested the authority to impose the education rate in the central government (*ibid.,* March 26, 1966).

is now a Municipal Council in Kuching, and twenty-three District Councils, including two for urban districts, Miri and Sibu.

Compared with Malaya, there are two big differences in the system of local government. Every part of Sarawak is inside the area of an elected local authority, while some areas in Malaya are outside any local authority. Also, until there are direct elections to the Sarawak legislature, the Council Negri, and for the Sarawak representatives in the federal Parliament, the District Councils and the Municipal Council will continue to form the lowest tier of a system of indirect elections, which, via the Divisional Advisory Councils, provides members for these bodies. Otherwise, local government has gone through some of the same stages and faced some of the same problems as in Malaya. Among the main functions are the provision of primary education and maternity and child health. The Councils rely partly on rates for the collection of revenue, but also receive income and capital assistance from the state government. State government control has been confined to major policy principles, and the approval of annual revenue and expenditure estimates, by-laws and senior staff appointments.[23]

Many of the weaknesses found in local government elsewhere exist in Sarawak. In the Kuching Rural District Council, the "attendance rate at meetings continued to be reasonable to good. There was at times a tendency to discuss at full meetings what should have been or had been discussed at committee meetings, and unfortunately some of the Councillors seemed to have an eye more on publicity or slogans than on formulating a constructive, if sometimes unpopular, policy for the future. The Council once again desired to raise its capital and recurrent expenditure rate in its estimates for 1963, and once again refused to increase its rates, but reckoned on using up the savings made by previous councils to finance its projects. . . . The Council has got very behind hand in collecting its rates and its arrears to an embarrassing amount. The criticism in my last report . . . that Councillors of all races are very bad at touring their wards and at making efforts to establish contact with people of races other than their own, is still unfortunately fully valid."[24] Against this, however, should be set the conviction of one Resident, in the Fourth Division, who in 1949, when the idea of local government was first being introduced, doubted whether the people would take any real interest. But in

[23] *Sarawak Annual Report, 1962* (Kuching: Government Printing Office, 1963), p. 327.
[24] "Excerpts from the Annual Reports of the Administrative Officers for the Year 1962," *Sarawak Gazette*, May 31, 1963, p. 110.

1962, seeing the progress that had been made, he admitted that he had been unduly pessimistic.[25]

In North Borneo effective local government authorities were set up even later than in Sarawak. In 1952 a District Council in Kota Belud[26] was formed under the presidency of the District Officer. Further District Councils were established in Sipitang and Papar. Also, from 1954 onward, a number of "district teams" were formed, consisting of local representatives of government departments and prominent unofficials, under the District Officer, some of which evolved into District Councils, which were given wider functions and more finance by the Local Government Ordinance of 1961. Town Boards were established in 1954 and 1955 in the four urban centers of Jesselton, Sandakan, Tawau, and Labuan. The first elections, which were on an adult franchise, were held in the four Town Boards and some of the District Councils in December, 1962; elections in the others, covering nearly all the rest of Sabah, were held in 1963 and 1964. As in Sarawak, for the present these elections to the lowest tier of government in Sabah *indirectly* choose representatives for the higher tiers. Not all the members of the local authorities in Sabah are elected (although only the elected ones take part in the elections for the higher tiers): some are still nominated, but it is expected that these will disappear by the time the next elections for District Councils take place.[27]

The Judiciary

The present system of courts followed the spread of British influence in Malaya; it extended from Penang to Malacca and Singapore, to the Federated States, then to the Unfederated States. The 1957 Constitution continued the judicial system already in existence by providing that there should be a Supreme Court and such inferior courts as might be determined by federal law. There were two divisions of the Supreme Court — the High Court, constituted by a single judge, and the Court of Appeal, constituted by three or more judges. Additionally, there could be appeal, beyond the Supreme Court, to the Judicial Committee of the Privy Council in London, which con-

[25] *Straits Times,* October 24, 1962.

[26] K. G. Tregonning, *North Borneo* (London: H.M.S.O., 1960), pp. 58–62; and, on local government in Papar, see pp. 107–109. On the prewar experiments, see M. H. Baker, *North Borneo, the First Ten Years* (Singapore: Malaya Publishing House, 1962), pp. 49–50.

[27] *Sabah Times,* March 26, 1964, quoting the Minister of Local Government.

sists of members of the Queen's Privy Council who have held high judicial office in the British Commonwealth. "Inferior courts," established by federal law, include Sessions Courts, Magistrates' Courts, and Penghulus'[28] Courts which exercise a limited and local jurisdiction. There are also Muslim religious courts, which enforce religious observance and regulate the domestic, and in particular the matrimonial, life of Muslims. These are established by the state legislatures, and form a separate system of courts. There is no state judicial system with general functions.

On the creation of Malaysia it was necessary to integrate the machinery with that in existence in Singapore and the Borneo territories, not too difficult a task in view of the fact that these areas also had a British-type judicial system. The new Federal Court of Malaysia has six judges, including the Lord President. It is the highest judicial authority in Malaysia, and has jurisdiction to interpret the Constitution and decide disputes between states and between any state and the federal government. It is also the Court of Appeal for the whole of Malaysia. Under it are three High Courts, in Malaya, Borneo, and Singapore respectively. These courts have original jurisdiction in their areas; appeal from each of them lies in the Federal Court. The only permanent member of the new Federal Court will be the Lord President, who is its chairman. The other members will include the Chief Justices of the High Courts and two other judges.[29]

In interpreting the Constitution it is the function of the judges to protect the citizen against possible abuses of power by agents of the government and to act as arbiters in disputes between state governments or between federal and state governments.[30] It is therefore vital that the independence of the judges should be preserved. The Constitution therefore provides that judges shall hold office until the age of sixty-five and that their remuneration shall be charged upon the "Consolidated Fund," a method of protecting them from motions in Parliament aimed at reducing their salaries. A judge can be re-

[28] See p. 165, above.

[29] Constitution, Article 122. A 1966 constitutional amendment provided that, with a minor qualification, a judge of the High Court appointed to the Federal Court would cease to be a member of the High Court. On the separation of Singapore from Malaysia in 1965 it was announced that, until the Singapore Legislative Assembly provided otherwise, the arrangements described in the text would continue.

[30] On the action brought by the government of the state of Kelantan against the federal government to seek a declaration that the Malaysia Act was null and void or not binding, on Kelantan, see H. E. Groves, *The Constitution of Malaysia* (Singapore: Malaysia Publications, 1964), p. 132.

moved from office on the ground of misbehavior or inability to discharge his judicial functions properly. But the procedure for removal is made cumbersome in order to safeguard judicial independence. The Yang di-Pertuan Agong, acting on the recommendation of the Prime Minister, or of the Lord President after consulting the Prime Minister, must set up a tribunal, consisting of not less than five judges or ex-judges. On the recommendation of the tribunal the Yang di-Pertuan Agong may then remove the judge from office.[31] One previously existing provision on the appointment of judges was abolished in 1960.[32] By the 1957 Constitution judges could be appointed only on the recommendation of the Judicial and Legal Service Commission. But since 1960 the Yang di-Pertuan Agong must act on the advice of the Prime Minister, after consulting the Conference of Rulers. In the case of judges other than the Lord President of the Federal Court, the Lord President (and for some appointments also certain other judges) must be consulted. One commentator has written that "the risk of political influence over judicial action has, since 1960, arisen on the horizon, a cloud no bigger than a litigant's hand: no such influence has, happily, been apparent so far. . . ."[33]

The Prime Minister has vigorously repudiated fears expressed in Parliament of political interference with the judiciary. "I do not think any Prime Minister in his right senses would interfere. Once that happens there will be no more law and order and there will be no more respect for the law."[34] An apparent example of the absence of effective political interference occurred in 1964, when an Alliance Minister lost a libel case in which one of the defendants was an opposition member of Parliament.[35]

---

[31] Constitution, Article 125, (3)–(5).

[32] By the Constitution (Amendment) Act, which abolished the Judicial and Legal Service Commission. The Commission was later re-established but without the function of recommending on judicial appointments.

[33] R. H. Hickling, "The First Five Years of the Federation of Malaya Constitution," *Malaya Law Review,* IV, No. 2 (1962), 194.

[34] *Dewan Ra'ayat Debates,* V, No. 12, August 19, 1963, cols. 1297–1298. See also *Sunday Times,* December 26, 1964. For allegations, and denials that the appointment of the Chief Justice of Singapore was "political" see *Straits Times* June 13 and 14, 1963.

[35] *Sunday Times,* December 6, 1964.

❦

SUGGESTED READINGS

Bedale, Harold. *Establishment, Organization, and Supervision of Local Authorities in the Federation of Malaya.* Kuala Lumpur: Government Press, 1953. Report by a British Town Clerk.

Groves, Harry E. *The Constitution of Malaysia.* Singapore: Malaysia Publications, 1964. Chapter VIII refers to the Judiciary.

Selected Papers from a Local Government Course held at the British Council Centre, Kuala Lumpur. Kuala Lumpur: Khee Meng Press, 1958. Useful for background, especially on the relationship between the British and the Malayan systems.

Taylor, William Cecil. *Local Government in Malaya.* Alor Star: Kedah Government Printer, 1949. Describes local government in the period when most members of local bodies were nominated.

11

Foreign Policy and Defense

Foreign Policy

Although Malaya gained her independence in 1957 and was there-fore then able to formulate her own foreign policy, her freedom of maneuver was in fact limited by a number of considerations. Because independence was gained at a time when the fight against the Communist terrorists was still continuing, her foreign policy has been resolutely anti-Communist. To that extent it has been "pro-Western." According to the Tengku, "where there has been a conflict between the two ideologies — Western and Eastern ideologies — then I have made myself quite clear before that we side with the Western ideology, or the Western understanding of democracy." The Tengku contrasted Western democracy, which included belief in freedom of thought and freedom of speech, with "Eastern democracy," where "they think for you and talk for you," and "guided democracy," where "you don't know which way you are going to be guided."[1] The existing pro-Western orientation, however, is only part of the basis of Malaya's foreign policy. Policy has also been influenced by membership of the British Commonwealth, by a growing identification with the "Afro-Asian group," by the desire to create a grouping of states in Southeast Asia, and by external "ethnic" pulls, mostly from China and from Indonesia. Some opposition parties, particularly the Socialist Front, have denounced the alignment with the West and the continued presence of British troops and bases; seeing this policy as inevitably involving Malaya in a conflict between the two big power blocs, they would prefer a policy of neutrality by which Malaya would be a member of an Afro-Asian "third force."[2]

[1] *Straits Times,* December 15, 1962.
[2] *Ibid.,* October 11, 1962, and *Sunday Times,* June 30, 1963.

Malayan activities in the United Nations reflect some of the cross-pressures mentioned earlier. Some of the targets she chose to attack there were obvious ones for an "Afro-Asian" country: Portuguese colonies in Africa, the South African Government's brutality and *apartheid* policy, French policy in Algeria. The Tengku was one of the toughest opponents of *apartheid* at the Commonwealth Prime Minister's Conference of 1960, which ended with South Africa's leaving the Commonwealth. But other objects of denunciation by Malaya were not "colonial," at least, not in the old sense of the word. Among them were Russian repression in Hungary and the Chinese attack on Tibet. As the Malayan representative said, when attacking Communism in the U.N. General Assembly, "while considerable progress has been achieved in the struggle against the old traditional form of European colonialism, in Asia and Africa, we have become increasingly aware of a new and more devilish and sinister form of colonialism."[3]

Malaya also showed its loyalty to the United Nations by providing over a thousand troops for the U.N. force in the Congo, from 1960 to 1963.

In spite of its anti-Communist stand, Malaya has not become a member of the Southeast Asia Treaty Organization. From the military point of view, membership would presumably not confer any appreciable benefits over and above the existing defense arrangements with the British. Even if adequate British military help were not forthcoming, because of British weakness or extensive commitments elsewhere, presumably United States help might be available if there were a real threat of a Communist Chinese invasion through Thailand. Another consideration is the unpopularity of SEATO, not only with the Communist Chinese but also with India and Indonesia. Indeed, unpopularity with the last two countries was explicitly given as a reason for Malaya's not having joined SEATO by the Tengku, when interviewed in Canberra in 1954.[4] Even Indonesia's policy of Confrontation did not result in any overt change in Malaya's (or Malaysia's) policy on SEATO.

The regional group which interested the Malayan government most was an association of Southeast Asian states. As early as 1959 the

[3] *Ibid.*, October 13, 1959.
[4] *Free Press*, November 10, 1959. But in voting on East-West "cold war" issues in the United Nations, 1957–1962, Malaya's voting closely paralleled that of SEATO members (R. O. Tilman, "Malaysian Foreign Policy: the Dilemmas of a Committed Neutral," paper presented at the Asia Society and Association for Asian Studies Conference on the Foreign Policies of the Southeast Asian States, May, 1965, pp. 41–43).

Tengku was saying in public that one day the defense and other pacts with the British might end, and that it was therefore essential for Malaya to be a participant in a Southeast Asian Friendship and Economic Treaty.[5] This proposal aroused some suspicions, on the ground that Britain and the United States were behind it and that it was merely an imperfectly disguised extension of SEATO.[6] The Tengku was also aware that some other countries in the area might be "touchy" because newly independent Malaya was leading the way in such a venture.[7] Indonesia, certainly, was not attracted by the proposal. However, by 1960, Malaya, the Philippines, and Thailand had agreed to set up an association which would be non-political and which would not be identified with any ideological bloc. The association took the name "The Association of Southeast Asia" (ASA), and the first meeting of ASA Foreign Ministers was held in Bangkok in July and August, 1961.[8] Arrangements were made for future meetings, and for the setting up of national secretariats. Officials from the three countries also started work on tourism, the formation of an ASA airline, an ASA shipping line and other transport schemes, international trade, cultural exchanges, and research. Another meeting of Foreign Ministers was held in Manila in April, 1963. The severance of diplomatic relations between Malaysia and the Philippines later in 1963 put an end, temporarily, to further work on these projects, but ASA meetings began again in 1966. A long list of ASA projects was announced in August, 1966.

The end of the Emergency in 1960 resulted in a new policy on the admission of Communist China to the United Nations. Malaya's original view had been that Communist China should not be admitted to the U.N., while Malaya was still fighting internally against the Communists.[9] But in 1960 the Tengku said that Malaya would support Communist China's admission to the U.N. Apart from the fact that the Emergency had ended, the Tengku had been persuaded that no general disarmament program could be effective without the participation of the mainland Chinese.[10] But, at the same time, Malaya would have no diplomatic relations with Peking. "We have to build our own nation. We have plenty of Chinese"; the implication was that recognition of either Communist China or Nationalist China

---

[5] *Free Press,* November 10 and 17, 1959; *Straits Times,* November 18, 1959.

[6] *Sunday Times,* May 28, 1961; *Straits Times,* January 12, 1962.

[7] *Malay Mail,* June 16, 1960.

[8] ASA, *Report of the First Meeting of Foreign Ministers* (Kuala Lumpur: Government Press, 1961).

[9] *Free Press,* January 20, 1960.

[10] *Straits Times,* December 7, 1960.

would hamper the effort of building a Malayan nation.[11] In 1961 Malaya stated in the United Nations General Assembly that she would support the admission of mainland China to the United Nations "in principle," but only if Formosa (Taiwan) were allowed to maintain its own separate political identity.[12] Malaya consequently voted against admission in 1961, but abstained on a similar motion in 1962 on the ground that it was ambiguous. From 1963 onward she has voted against, her attitude having hardened in 1963, largely as a result of Chinese "unprovoked armed aggression" on India.[13] Speaking in New Delhi, the Tengku had previously given three reasons for supporting India. There was emotional support for India, because of her peaceful emergence from British rule, faith in democracy, and membership in the Commonwealth. There was sympathetic identification, because, in the Emergency, Malaya had had a taste of what India was then suffering. From a realistic viewpoint, if China were successful against India, she might then attack Malaya. Malaya pledged all-out support to India in case of open war,[14] and a "Save Democracy Fund" was opened, sponsored by a committee with the Tengku as chairman. According to the government, the fund was indeed intended to preserve democracy, and it was believed to be obvious that the money raised would go to help the Indian refugees.[15] The opposition, however, alleged that the money might be spent on arms. More important was the objection that the fund was being used by politicians to divide the people of Malaya.[16] No doubt the fund was not intended for that purpose, but it could have had some such effect. One of the few subjects on which the Nationalist and Communist Chinese were agreed was that the Chinese claim to some of the border territory occupied by India was justified. Significantly, in the published list of subscribers to the fund there was a high incidence of Indian names and a correspondingly low proportion of Chinese names.[17]

[11] *Ibid.,* June 16, 1960. A Nationalist Chinese consulate, for trade purposes only, was set up in Kuala, Lumpur, unaccompanied by recognition, in November, 1964.

[12] United Nations General Assembly 16th Session, *Official Records,* 1077 Plenary Meeting, December 13, 1961, p. 1019.

[13] *Ibid.,* 18th Session, 1243 Plenary Meeting, October 16, 1963, p. 16.

[14] *Ibid.,* October 29 and November 2, 1962.

[15] *Ibid.,* December 5, 1962.

[16] *Ibid.,* December 4, 1962; *Sunday Times,* December 2, 1962.

[17] In October, 1965, Pakistan broke off diplomatic relations with Malaysia. Ostensibly, the reason for the break was that the Malaysian permanent delegate to the United Nations had made anti-Pakistani remarks in the debates on the India-Pakistan conflict. But a deeper reason was the close relations between India and Malaysia, on the one hand, and "a sinister

The timing of Malaya's independence may have had something to do with the intensity with which she has expressed support for South Viet Nam and has openly stated the view that "the Communists" were the aggressors. Believing that both Malaya and South Viet Nam were the subject of attacks by Chinese Communist-inspired guerrillas, she identified South Viet Nam's troubles with her own. The Tengku's first official foreign visit after independence was to South Viet Nam. Support for South Viet Nam, even though it invited charges of being favorable to colonialism, persisted after the end of the Emergency in Malaya, the fall of Diem and increasing United States involvement in the war. Malaya showed similar sympathy for South Korea.

When independence was won, Malaya had to evolve not only a foreign policy but also the machinery with which to implement it. The Tengku had placed himself at the head of the External Affairs Ministry as early as 1957, with an interruption of one-and-a-half years from 1959 to 1960. An entirely new department of government had to be created, and one that, by its nature, had to be completely Malayanised.[18] The officials to staff it had to be trained at the same time as new diplomatic missions were being opened up. There was a total of twenty missions early in 1966.

Many of the heads of missions are "amateurs" rather than professional diplomats. Several have been related to high political figures in Malaya and/or to Malay Rulers.[19] This has raised the question of possible nepotism, although perhaps the explanation is to be found rather in the small size of the political élite in a developing country and the fact that there are not enough men to fill the jobs available without using members of the political élite, or "quasi-élite," who often happen to be related to each other. However, some few appointments are perhaps best explained as rewards to individuals to whom political obligations exist, rather than as "merit" appointments.

On attaining independence Malaya might constitutionally have insisted on being responsible for her own defense, without any aid

---

pattern of collusion" between Pakistan, China, and Indonesia, on the other ["Statement by the Government of Malaysia on the severance of relations, 7th October," *Press Release* (New York, Permanent Mission of Malaysia to the United Nations, October 12, 1965)]. With the end of Confrontation, in August, 1966, it became likely that relations would soon be restored between Malaysia and Pakistan.

[18] Radio talk by the Tengku, quoted in *Government Press Release*, October 6, 1961. In 1966 the title of the department was changed from "External Affairs" to "Foreign Affairs." In the same year the separate "foreign service" was merged with the MCS.

[19] "Malaya's Foreign Relations," *Far Eastern Economic Review*, XLI, September 12, 1963, p. 686.

from Britain. But in fact it was unthinkable that this should occur because in 1957 British (and Australian and New Zealand) troops were still engaged in fighting the Communist rebels in Malaya. So a defense agreement was concluded, providing for such British assistance "as the Government of the Federation of Malaya may require for the external defence of its territory,"[20] in exchange for which the Federation allowed Britain to maintain troops and use bases and facilities in its territory.[21] No time limit was specified for the agreement, but it was recognized that each party would retain the right to suggest its review. Even when the Emergency ended in 1960, there was no move to end or alter the agreement. The British government wanted to supplement the troops it could keep in politically volatile Singapore, so that it would be equipped to deal with limited wars in the area. Malaya was aware that, if British troops left, she would have to spend more on defense and therefore less on other things, especially rural development.[22]

Malaysia

However, the creation of Malaysia made it necessary to revise the agreement, because in its original form it did not apply to Singapore, Sabah, or Sarawak.[23] But the extension of the agreement to Singapore raised a problem. Malaysia, like Malaya, would not be a member of SEATO. The 1957 agreement had provided for cooperation between the two governments in the event of armed attack, or the threat of armed attack, on Malaya or on any British territories or protectorates in the Far East.[24] But the British (and other Commonwealth) troops in Malaya could not be sent directly on a SEATO mission, for instance to Thailand,[25] without the prior agreement of the government of Malaya. The British had retained control over Singapore's defense, and claimed that, under the new agreement, British troops in Singapore could continue to be deployed elsewhere without restriction; the agreement stated that they could be used for "the preservation of peace in South-East Asia,"[26] which, presumably, could include SEATO missions. This interpretation was denied by the Tengku, who main-

---

[20] *Proposed Agreement on External Defence and Mutual Assistance* (London: H.M.S.O., 1957, reprinted 1959) (Cmnd. 263), Article I.

[21] *Ibid.*, Articles III and IV.

[22] The Tengku and Tun Razak, as quoted in *Straits Times*, December 1, 1959.

[23] London *Times*, November 25, 1961.

[24] *Proposed Agreement*, Articles VI and VII.

[25] Tengku Abdul Rahman, *Sunday Mail*, May 20, 1962.

[26] London *Times*, November 23 and 25, 1961; Article VI of the Malaysia Agreement; T. H. Silcock, "Development of a Malayan Foreign Policy," *Australian Outlook*, 17, No. 3 (1963), 51.

tained that Britain would now no longer be entitled to use the Singapore base as she pleased, but would have to obtain the consent of the Malaysian government. In fact no difficulties arose during the time when Singapore was part of Malaysia. But when Singapore became independent in August, 1965, she indicated that, although the British base could remain, she would insist on some restrictions being placed on its use.[27]

Indonesian Hostility

When the defense agreement was being negotiated there were no signs that Britain would have a substantially greater defense commitment in the area than before. Previously she had been directly responsible for defending the Borneo territories; now she was to be indirectly responsible, via the agreement with Malaysia. In fact, however, defense soon became a crucial issue, because of the hostility of Indonesia. At first this hostility was not evident, except on the part of the Indonesian Communist Party. On November 13, 1961, Dr. Subandrio, the Indonesian Foreign Minister, wrote, "As an example of our honesty and lack of expansionist intent, one-fourth of the island of Kalimantan [Borneo] consisting of the three Crown Colonies [sic] of Great Britain is now becoming the target of the Malayan Government for a merger. Of course, the people there are ethnologically and geographically very close to the others living in the Indonesian territory. Still, we do not show any objection toward this Malayan policy of merger. On the contrary, we wish the Malayan Government well if it can succeed with this plan."[28] This assurance was repeated by Dr. Subandrio one week later, when speaking to the General Assembly of the United Nations, with the proviso that such a merger should be "based upon the will for freedom of the peoples concerned."[29] Not until the "Azahari revolt" of 1962 did Indonesian Government opposition to Malaysia come clearly into the open. A. M. Azahari,[30] leader of the Brunei Party Rakyat, opposed Malaysia and put forward plans for the creation of an independent state under the Sultan of Brunei, consisting of Brunei, North Borneo, and Sarawak. This would have restored the boundaries of Brunei roughly to what they had been over a hundred years earlier, before Sarawak

[27] See p. 223, below.

[28] *Malaya-Indonesia Relations* (Kuala Lumpur: Government Press, 1963) p. 11, quoting a letter to the *New York Times*.

[29] *Ibid.*, p. 12.

[30] Gordon Means, "Malaysia — A New Federation in Southeast Asia," *Pacific Affairs*, XXXVI, No. 2 (1963), 150 ff.; *Straits Times*, December 14, 1962; "The Azahari Rebellion"; *Sunday Mail*, December 16, 1962; *Straits Times*, January 18 and 19, 1962 (interviews by Alex. Josey with Nicasio Osmeña and A. M. Azahari).

and North Borneo had come into existence. But the Sultan did not favor this proposal, and the members of the Brunei legislature appointed by him exceeded the elected members, who all supported Azahari. Azahari then resorted to extraconstitutional methods, namely a revolt, although he himself was not present to lead it. When fighting broke out in December, 1962, in Brunei and adjacent territory, he was in Manila, and afterwards in Indonesia. The revolt caught the British by surprise. They had ignored intelligence reports of impending trouble on the tenuous ground that *previous* intelligence reports of an uprising had proved to be unfounded.[31] But, although the revolt achieved some initial success, its direction was incompetent, and it failed in its most essential objective, the capture of the Sultan. If he had been taken prisoner, the rebels could have issued proclamations in his name which could not have been authoritatively contradicted. As it was, British troops were flown in, and the revolt was quickly suppressed.

The importance of Azahari's rebellion lay not so much in its effects inside Brunei, or in the other Borneo territories, as in its triggering open Indonesian hostility. Various Indonesian leaders quickly declared their support for Azahari, from President Sukarno down. The timing of this declaration of opposition could be variously interpreted. The Indonesians may have thought that, since opponents of Malaysia had proved themselves strong enough to stage a revolt, they deserved to be encouraged. Alternatively, they may have calculated that the rebels were being rather easily defeated and that the prospects of Malaysia's being formed according to plan were so favorable that they had to be disrupted. Whatever the reasons, it is not hard to see the underlying grounds for Indonesian enmity. Indonesian leaders regarded Malaya, and Malaysia, as neo-colonialist and neo-imperialist. In the light of their own history as a colony, they found it difficult to believe that the Malayan government freely chose to have a defense agreement permitting British troops to remain on Malayan soil. They also alleged that British troops in Malaysia, especially in Sarawak and Sabah,[32] constituted a threat to Indonesia. Also, because of Indonesia's size as compared with Malaya, or Malaysia, the Indonesians tended to think of Malaya/Malaysia as merely a small part of a potential *Indonesia Raya* — Greater Indonesia.[33] The Indonesian leaders

[31] Duncan Sandys, *House of Commons Debates,* Vol. 669, Col. 33, December 10, 1962.

[32] It is worth noting that there were practically no British troops in these two territories before Indonesian Confrontation.

[33] For the attitude of Indonesian leaders, including President Sukarno, on this point in July, 1945, see B. K. Gordon, "The Potential for Indonesian Expansionism," *Pacific Affairs,* XXXVI, No. 4 (1963–1964), 378–393.

saw development in terms of national culture first and economic progress second. "The most frequently encountered Indonesian criticism of Malaya can be stated simply: Malaya is a 'backward' nation because she has not undergone a revolution."[34] The proposition, based on Indonesia's interpretation of her own experience, was that a colony could become truly independent only after a long armed struggle with the colonial power; Malaya had had no such struggle — she was therefore not truly independent. More specifically, the Indonesians had not forgiven the aid to Indonesian rebels in 1958 from sources in Malaya and Singapore or the political asylum given some of them by the Malayan government.[35] They also remembered, with distaste, the Tengku's attempted mediation in the West Irian dispute.

The Philippine Claim to Sabah

The situation has been complicated by the Philippine claim to North Borneo, revived early in 1962. It was based on several contentions: that the Sultan of Sulu had merely "leased," not "ceded,"[36] the territory in 1878 to the predecessors of the British North Borneo Company, from which it had passed to the British Crown; that, in any case, sovereignty could be transferred only to sovereigns, and the Company's predecessors were not sovereigns; that the Philippine government was the heir of the Sultan.[37] The legal claim is partly irrelevant in a world where the wishes of the inhabitants of a territory, as opposed to documents dating from a colonial past, are increasingly being considered as decisive in determining who shall govern it.[38] This consideration is pertinent to the Malaysian government's reluctance to accept a ruling on the claim by the International Court of

[34] *Ibid.,* p. 387.
[35] *Malaya-Indonesian Relations,* pp. 4–6.
[36] In the Malay version the English meaning of the word is unclear. It has sometimes been said that the British have an original version in English, but this has never been produced.
[37] Martin Meadows, "The Philippine Claim to North Borneo," *Political Science Quarterly,* LXXVII, No. 3 (1962), 321–335; Emmanuel Pelaez (Vice-President and Secretary of Foreign Affairs), *Statement at the Opening Meeting of the Anglo-Philippine Talks,* [London, January 28, 1963 (reproduced by the Philippines government)]; K. G. Tregonning, "The Claim for North Borneo by the Philippines," *Australian Outlook,* XVI, No. 3 (1962) 283–291; Pacifico A. Ortiz, "Legal Aspects of the North Borneo Question," *Philippines Studies,* II, No. 1 (1963), 18–64.
[38] However, Vice-President Pelaez referred to a referendum to be held in North Borneo "within a reasonable period after its restoration to the Philippines." President Macapagal also spoke of a referendum held "at an appropriate time" and preferably under U.N. supervision ["State of the Nation Address," Appx. IV of *Malaya-Philippine Relations* (Kuala Lumpur: Government Press, 1963)].

Justice. The revival of the claim may be attributed to several factors. President Macapagal, elected in November, 1961, had a special interest in the claim, because in 1948, as a Foreign Affairs official, he had been present when the Turtle Islands, a British territory near North Borneo, had been handed over to the Philippines. In 1950 as a congressman, he had co-sponsored a resolution favoring the North Borneo claim in the Philippine House of Representatives. A newspaper campaign, led by *The Free Press*, a journal with a hard-hitting reputation, was also behind the revival. Further support came from Nicasio Osmeña, a backer of Azahari, whose motives were as clearly financial as President Macapagal's were patriotic. Additional Philippine arguments were that Malaysia had been conceived as an anti-Indonesian scheme and that North Borneo could be better protected against Chinese communism as part of the Philippines than as part of Malaysia. Behind these arguments may have been the feeling that, in the face of Indonesian aggressiveness against the Western nations and their allies, the Filipinos, whose own revolution had occurred so long before (1898), should determinedly and dramatically "prove" their nationalism and their freedom from colonial domination. To have and to cherish a territorial claim of one's own was one way of doing this.[39]

Unfortunately Britain and Malaya were perhaps not scrupulous enough in going through procedures to indicate that they took the Philippine claim seriously, and this lack of *delicadeza* led to a hardening of Filipino attitudes. There are no truly fundamental antagonisms between Malaysia and the Philippines. Both governments are "pro-free enterprise" and "pro-Western"; neither is rabidly nationalist. Provided that the North Borneo claim can be settled, either by international arbitration or by financial concessions to the Philippines, or both, no animosities should remain. As it is, in the triangular maneuvers in which the countries have participated in the last few years, the Philippines has sometimes played an anti-Malaysian role, while at other times she has played the party of mediator.

Confrontation

From early 1963 Indonesia pursued a policy of "Confrontation"[40] toward Malaysia, although there were several *détentes* in which threats alternated with expressions of brotherly love. Confrontation stopped short of full-scale war, but included aggressive patrolling by Indo-

[39] See R. S. Milne, "The Uniqueness of Philippine Nationalism," *Journal of Southeast Asian Studies*, IV, No. 1 (1963), 75–87.

[40] *Straits Times*, January 21, 1963, quoting the Indonesian Foreign Minister, Dr. Subandrio.

nesian vessels between Sumatra and Malaya which seriously interfered with Malayan fishermen, using members of the *Tentera Nasional Kalimantan Utara* (North Borneo National Army) to provoke a long series of incidents on the borders of the North Borneo states and Indonesia, and, from 1964 onwards, dropping or landing troops on the coasts of Malaya. The Indonesians made use of almost any kind of manpower for these operations — small numbers of defectors from Malaysia, Indonesian regulars, and Indonesian "volunteers." Indonesian intervention encouraged the already existing threat of Communist Chinese subversion in Sarawak,[41] and in April, 1963, it was necessary to call in all arms and ammunition from "non-natives," that is in effect Chinese, in Sarawak.

A temporary lull in Confrontation accompanied a series of meetings of representatives of Malaysia, Indonesia and the Philippines, April–June, 1963, which culminated in a "Tripartite Summit Meeting" in Manila, in July and August, 1963. Before this summit meeting, however, Confrontation had been resumed. Dr. Sukarno resented the fact that the Malaysia Agreement had been signed in London (July 9, 1963) before the summit meeting took place. He also asked that the wishes of the Borneo peoples be ascertained by a referendum.[42]

At the summit conference it was decided that a new organization, Maphilindo, should be formed. This was not to be a federation but "a grouping of the three nations of Malay origin working together in closest harmony but without surrendering any portion of their sovereignty."[43] The purpose of Maphilindo was obscure. The "Declaration" announcing it had a strong Indonesian flavor, containing references favorable to the U.N. Charter and the Bandung Declaration and hostile to colonialism and imperialism.[44] To some extent the impulse was cultural and emotional. Potentially, it seemed to be aimed at Communist China, and yet that country was working closely with Indonesia. Chinese in Malaya feared that it might have been directed against them, and the Tengku and the MCA were quick to deny this possibility. In any case Confrontation was immediately renewed, so that it was never necessary to work out exactly what the scope of Maphilindo would have been, if it had been implemented. At the

[41] *The Danger Within* (Kuching: Sarawak Information Service, 1963).
[42] *Straits Times,* July 12, 1963.
[43] *Malaya-Philippine Relations,* Appx. X (*Manila Accord*), para. 6. Note that on July 27, 1962, President Macapagal had proposed a confederation consisting of Malaya, Singapore, the Borneo territories and the Philippines (*ibid.,* p. 4).
[44] It included a statement that foreign military bases in the area were "temporary" (*Malaya-Philippine Relations,* Appx. IX, "Manila Declaration").

summit meeting both Indonesia and Malaya made concessions on the issue of ascertaining the wishes of the inhabitants of the Borneo territories on Malaysia. The Indonesians no longer insisted on a referendum. Malaya acknowledged that, if the original date for the formation of Malaysia were adhered to, a United Nations team would not have enough time to find out the wishes of the inhabitants. The original date for Malaysia, August 31, 1963, was postponed — until September 16 — in order to give enough time (but only just) for the publication of the U.N. Secretary-General's report due to appear on September 14.[45] The report found that Malaysia had indeed been a major issue at the recent elections in North Borneo and Sarawak, and that the elections had been "free" and had indicated the approval of a large majority of the people for Malaysia.[46] Indonesia, however, did not accept the conclusions of the report, claiming that the U.N. team's procedures differed from those which had been agreed on by the three countries. The situation worsened, to the point of undeclared but open war. Malaysia broke off diplomatic relations with Indonesia, when Indonesia did not recognize her, a step which she regarded as "tantamount to the severance of diplomatic relations" with herself.[47] Confrontation was stepped up by more and more serious Borneo border incidents, and, from 1964, by armed attack on the coasts of Malaya. "Economic confrontation" accompanied political confrontation. Indonesia cut off trade with Malaysia; in particular, she no longer sent rubber for processing or tin for smelting.

Attempts to promote mediation were numerous. To name only the most prominent, Senator Robert Kennedy made a visit to Southeast Asia in January, 1964, and his mediation led to a temporary cease-fire in Borneo. A ministerial meeting between Malaysia, Indonesia, and the Philippines followed in Bangkok in February, 1964. A further summit meeting was held between the three countries in Tokyo (June, 1964), but no agreement was reached, a critical point of difference being the presence of some two hundred Indonesian guerrillas in Sarawak. Malaysia insisted that the guerrillas be with-

---

45 In *United Nations Malaysia Mission Report* (Kuala Lumpur: reproduced by Department of Information, Malaysia, 1963), pp. i–ii, the Secretary-General deplored the fact that the date, September 16, was fixed before his conclusions were reached and made known. The timing also caused resentment on the part of Indonesia. The Tengku was under pressure from the Borneo states and Singapore to proclaim Malaysia. The postponement represented a concession to Indonesia, but he insisted that the formation of the new federation was not dependent on the U.N. assessment (*Straits Times,* August 26 and 30 and September 4, 1963).

46 *U.N. Report,* especially, para. 245.

47 *Straits Times,* September 18, 1963.

drawn as a precondition for any settlement. The Indonesians insisted equally fiercely that a settlement must come first; they also once more advocated that a referendum be held in North Borneo and Sarawak.

The battle between Indonesia and Malaysia was continued in a wider arena. Malaysia won a moral victory in the United Nations Security Council on September 17, 1964. A draft resolution, regretting and deploring the incidents which had occurred and requesting that the parties concerned try to prevent a recurrence and also "to refrain from all threat or use of force and to respect the territorial integrity and political independence of each other" received nine votes and only two were cast against.[48] However, one of the opposing votes came from the U.S.S.R.; so this constituted a veto. Malaysia's election to the Security Council for 1965[49] was followed within a few days by the withdrawal of Indonesia from the United Nations.

At the same time as Malaysia's diplomatic rupture with Indonesia the Philippines had said that they were not prepared to "recognise Malaysia for the time being," and had proposed that in the meantime the embassies in both countries should be replaced by consulates.[50] This was unacceptable to the Malaysian government, and it therefore broke off diplomatic relations with the Philippines. Some Filipino spokesmen claimed that this step took them by surprise and that they had not intended a complete severance of diplomatic ties. Consular offices were re-established in Manila and Kuala Lumpur in May, 1964. Early in 1966, after Marcos replaced Macapagal as President of the Philippines, the resumption of diplomatic relations was discussed, and in June, 1966, their restoration was announced.

Indonesia's policy of Confrontation was not abandoned immediately after the failure of the pro-Communist coup of September and October, 1965. Before the attempted coup the army's freedom of maneuver was restricted. If the conflict grew, there was a danger that the Communists might be given arms, and, if the pace of Confrontation was increased and there were military setbacks, some of the high-ranking generals might be dismissed.[51] The Army therefore had to "compete" with the Communists in opposition to Malaysia, but had to limit the

---

[48] *Malaysia's case in the United Nations Security Council, documents reproduced from the official record of the Security Council proceedings* (Kuala Lumpur: Government Press, 1964), p. 80. Bolivia, Brazil, Republic of China, France, Ivory Coast, Morocco, Norway, Britain, and the U.S.A. were in favor; the U.S.S.R. and Czechoslovakia were against.

[49] *Straits Times,* December 31, 1964.

[50] *Ibid.,* September 18, 1963.

[51] Arnold C. Brackman, *Southeast Asia's Second Front: The Power Struggle for the Malay Archipelago* (New York: Frederick A. Praeger, 1966), p. 207.

scale of its activities. The shift in the balance of power in Indonesia, towards the Army and away from the Communists, changed the situation. Nationalism, in the form of opposition to neo-colonialism, is general in Indonesia: it exists in the Army as well as in the Communist Party. But the suppression of the Communist leadership removed the pressure on the Army to be competitively anti-colonialist. The new Indonesian government was apparently anxious to improve the state of the economy, and it was Indonesia, not Malaysia, which had suffered seriously from the severance of trade relations. If Confrontation ended, it was also more likely that substantial Western foreign aid might be forthcoming.

Consequently, the new Indonesian government made approaches to both Singapore and Malaysia. It decided to recognize Singapore, and early in June, 1966, representatives of the Indonesian and Malaysian governments met in Bangkok and agreed to submit proposals to their governments to end their dispute. The proposals covered the ending of military Confrontation, the establishment of diplomatic relations, and the old question of the feelings of the inhabitants of Sabah and Sarawak on Malaysia. The talks included a wider issue than any of these — the foundation of a new regional association, comprising, to begin with, Indonesia, Malaysia, the Philippines and Thailand, resembling a wider version of Maphilindo, or ASA. In such an association Indonesia, by virtue of her population and resources, would necessarily play a predominant rôle. If the new association is to succeed, the governments concerned must decide in concrete terms exactly what the scope of their operations is to be, politically, economically, culturally, militarily. As with Maphilindo, there may be fears among the Chinese in Malaysia that the less favorable treatment given the Chinese in the other member countries would be extended to Malaysia. Singapore could play a quite outstanding rôle in the proposed association. The association will have the effect, in the short run at least, of making Singapore an even more important trading center for the entire area.

On August 12, 1966, an accord was signed between Indonesia and Malaysia. Hostilities were to cease and diplomatic relations were to be restored. Elections were to be held in which Sabah and Sarawak would be given an opportunity to reaffirm their position in the Malaysian Federation. Mr. Malik, the Indonesian foreign minister, said Indonesia was waiting for a suitable chance to rejoin the U.N.

If Indonesia had embarked on a full-scale attack, Malaysia would have been quite unable to resist it without outside help. The Borneo border with Indonesia is almost a thousand miles long, even though hills and swamps offer obstacles to penetration. When Confrontation began, early in 1963, Malaya had an army of about 10,000 regulars and 5,000 reserves (compared with an Indonesian army of over twenty times that size), an air force of about thirty planes and a navy of ten old vessels.[52] Even in December, 1962, after the Brunei revolt, the defense estimates for the coming year amounted to just M$94 million, only a 4 per cent increase on the previous year and less than 10 per cent of the budget. It was not until May, 1963, that an extra $75 million was voted for defense, and it was stated that defense expenditure would approximately double over a five-year period.[53]

By the beginning of 1965 it was estimated that the armed forces included 30,000 men plus 15,000 territorials and some naval reserves.[54] Other measures included the raising of a new defense force, the Border Scouts, in Sarawak and the raising of a local defense corps in Malaya and Singapore. In March, 1964, it was announced that all males in Malaysia between the ages of twenty-one and twenty-eight would be required to register for national service. In spite of these measures Malaysia's armed forces were inadequate to meet even the limited war which was the product of Confrontation. Her population is only about a tenth of Indonesia's, and she has deliberately chosen, until now, to allocate only a small proportion of her budget to defense and a larger share to welfare measures, such as rural development. Obviously this policy depends on the existence of the defense agreement with Britain and on an understanding, but not a formal treaty, with Australia and New Zealand that they will come to her help in case of need. Early in 1965 there were 50,000 British troops (not all of them fighting troops) and seventy British warships in the Malaysia area,[55] as well as troops from Australia and New Zealand. Included in the "British" troops were Gurkhas from Nepal, who were particularly successful in the border fighting. The importance of the British and Commonwealth troops was greater than the figures suggest because of their experience compared with some of the Malayan troops, and because of their role in training. Military equipment has been given by Canada and a loan to purchase equipment has been granted by the United States.

The United States provided some help to Malaysia by diplomatic intervention, for instance through Robert Kennedy's talks with Presi-

---

[52] *Straits Times,* February 15, 1963. Indonesia's navy and air force were well-equipped, mainly from Soviet sources.

[53] *Ibid.,* December 14, 1962 and May 30, 1963. The defense estimates for 1966 were M$237.6 million (Tun Razak, *ibid.,* December 3, 1965).

[54] *Ibid.,* January 9, 1965.

[55] *Malay Mail,* January 14, 1965.

dent Sukarno in January, 1964. In the general scheme of United States foreign policy, however, Indonesia necessarily has a greater significance than Malaysia. In any search for possible barriers against future Chinese Communist expansion in Southeast Asia, Indonesia, because of her large population and her geographical situation, is an obvious choice. The Indonesians have not failed to make this point plain to the United States. The war in Viet Nam complicates the situation. Malaysia, while sympathetic to South Viet Nam to the extent that it is engaged in an anti-Communist struggle, wishes it to be clearly understood that her own problems are quite different. Viet Nam is a country which is internally divided. With the exception of a comparatively small number of internal rebels, Malaysia's problem is one of meeting external aggression.

On its limited scale Confrontation was tolerable; it was an irritant rather than a cancer. Its military effect was negligible. Psychologically, in spite of Indonesian radio programs beamed at Malaysia, it probably had limited impact in Malaya. The 1964 general election results in Malaya indicated that Confrontation had increased anti-Indonesian feeling and had strengthened the people's determination to resist. The Pan-Malayan Islamic Party has an emotional link with Indonesia, but it is doubtful if many of its members would have sided with President Sukarno against Malaysia, unless they were convinced that the Chinese in Malaya had become so powerful that they were about to "take over" the country. It also happens that the PMIP strength is greatest on the east coast of Malaya, where communications with Indonesia are more difficult than on the west coast. On the west coast many Malays, or their immediate ancestors, originally came from Sumatra or other parts of Indonesia. What information they have about conditions of life in Indonesia did not make them enthusiastic about the prospects of living under the Sukarno regime. In spite of the arrests of a number of Indonesian sympathizers, particularly to top PMIP and Socialist Front politicians, early in 1965,[56] and a number of bomb explosions, subversion seems to have been comparatively unsuccessful. However, from the beginning of 1965 the Malaysian and Thai governments have been increasingly concerned about subversive activity in the border region between the two countries. In August, 1966, the Communists stepped up their military operations.

In Sarawak, although not in Sabah, the situation was very different. Subversion in some Chinese schools, in some trade unions and inside

[56] *Indonesian Intentions Towards Malaysia* (Kuala Lumpur: Government Printing Office, 1964); *A Plot Exposed* (Kuala Lumpur: Government Printing Office, 1965).

the Sarawak United People's Party, meant that quite large sections of the population could not be relied upon to resist Indonesian attacks made in the name of "anticolonialism." In July and August, 1965, and January, 1966, the government found it necessary to relocate several thousand inhabitants of a border area which had been exposed to subversion. The persons, who were mostly Chinese, were settled in New Villages similar to those set up during the Emergency in Malaya.[57] With the end of Confrontation in sight, in July, 1966, the government launched an appeal to those rebels who had taken up arms to persuade them to surrender.

Economically, Confrontation did not hit Malaysia as hard as had been generally expected. However, because Confrontation caused resources to be diverted from development to military purposes, the adverse impact could have been considerable in the long run.

The military situation was manageable during Confrontation, but only because of the presence of British troops under the defense agreement. The existence of these troops, however, made it possible for the Indonesians to invoke the bogey of "neo-colonialism." It did not matter that the defense agreement was freely negotiated; nor were the Indonesians troubled by the inconsistency of objecting to British troops in Malaysia, while remaining officially silent about the existence of United States bases in the Philippines. The fact remains that nowadays any allegation of neo-colonialism falls on fertile ground among the new nations in Asia and Africa. Malaysia worked hard to explain the situation and to gain international support, for instance at the Commonwealth Parliamentary Conference in Kuala Lumpur in 1963 and through tours of African countries by Tun Razak and others. But it was only too easy for pro-Communist elements to gain acceptance for their version of events, as in the Afro-Asian Solidarity Conference held in Tanganyika, February, 1963, where the Malayan-Singapore delegation did not even succeed in being seated.[58]

On the international scene Malaysia perhaps paid a penalty for being, and having been seen to be, too obviously pro-Western. She indeed spoke out, and struck out, against many forms of colonialism. But Indonesian attacks on her as "colonial," which cited the presence of British troops as proof of colonialism, placed her in a dilemma. If the troops left while Confrontation continued, what guarantee would there have been against Indonesian *armed* attack? A new Malaysian approach to the problem was revealed during the visit of the Deputy Prime Minister, Tun Razak, to a number of African countries in April, 1965. The purpose of the visit was not limited to

[57] *Straits Times,* July 7 and August 9, 1965, and January 6, 1966.
[58] Means, 156.

putting the case for Malaysia, planning to set up Malaysian diplomatic missions in Africa and securing support for Malaysia's admission to future Afro-Asian Conferences. In addition it was said that Malaysia expected to make a formal request to the Afro-Asian members of the British Commonwealth that they should contribute help towards her defense.[59] There was no intention that British troops should be totally withdrawn, at least in the short run. A scheme of this kind would have been a useful counter to the often-heard Indonesian demand that her dispute with Malaysia should be settled only by Afro-Asians, a proposal which favored Indonesia, the most powerful Afro-Asian country in the immediate area. However, nothing came of this scheme before the end of Confrontation was announced in June, 1966. About this time Malaysia's relations with Britain became strained. It was arranged that Malaysian troops would replace British troops in Sarawak and Sabah. But Britain did not grant Malaysia the economic aid, both military and non-military, which Malaysia requested. The British justified their refusal by pointing to the weakness of their economy. The Malaysian government, however, believed that the British were reluctant to grant such aid, partly because they wanted to press Malaysia to conclude a defense treaty with Singapore. But the Malaysian government is not anxious to conclude a defense treaty, since it believes that Singapore would insist, as a precondition, on forming a common market, on terms unfavorable to Malaysia.

In the summer of 1965 there were signs of a change of emphasis in Malaysia's foreign policy, perhaps because it had become evident during the search for allies against Confrontation that her previous policy had lacked flexibility. The chairman of the Malaysian Afro-Asian People's Solidarity Organization, Dr. Mahathir bin Mohamed, an UMNO member of Parliament, urged the government to initiate moves for an honorable settlement with Indonesia.[60] The government did not welcome his advice, but a few days before, the Alliance Parliamentary Group on Foreign Affairs, a more representative group consisting of over one-quarter of the Alliance members of Parliament, did urge that Malaysia establish the "widest diplomatic representation possible with countries, irrespective of their ideologies."[61] The chairman of the group, in making the above recommendation, referred to "the present independent and nonaligned policy of the Alliance Government," a description which, if correct, could indicate that some shift in policy was advocated. A few days later the Cabinet discussed the possibility of establishing friendly relations, but not diplo-

---

[59] *Straits Times,* April 9, 1965.
[60] *Ibid.,* August 17, 1965.
[61] *Sunday Times,* August 9, 1965.

matic relations, with the U.S.S.R.[62] There were also reports that increased trade was being considered with the U.S.S.R. and with mainland China.

This alteration in emphasis does not imply any fundamental change in policy towards mainland China. China is a threat, both because of her possible expansionist ambitions and also because of her influence over the overseas Chinese. Trade relations with the U.S.S.R. might lead to the establishment of diplomatic relations later, but, where China is concerned, establishing diplomatic relations would open up too many possibilities of subversion in Malaysia. Consequently the evolution in Malaysian foreign policy which seems to have begun recently is least evident towards China and towards those areas of Southeast Asia, such as Viet Nam, where Chinese expansionist pressures are strongest. Indeed it is possible to view the agreement to end Confrontation, arrived at between Indonesia and Malaysia on August 12, 1966, as the prelude to a regional bloc against Chinese expansion in Southeast Asia. If the proposed association, consisting of these two countries, the Philippines, Thailand and others, took a military form, the arguments for stationing troops from Western nations in the area would be weakened. The case for quickly scaling down, and later eliminating, the British base in Singapore would be strengthened.

SUGGESTED READINGS

Brackman, Arnold C. *Southeast Asia's Second Front: The Power Struggle in the Malay Archipelago*. New York: Frederick A. Praeger, 1966. An account of the relations among Malaysia, Indonesia and the Philippines and the role played by the great powers in the area.

Fifield, Russell Hunt. *Southeast Asia in United States Policy*. New York: Frederick A. Praeger, 1963. A standard work.

Gordon, Bernard K. *Dimensions of Conflict in Southeast Asia*. Englewood Cliffs, N.J.: Prentice-Hall, 1966. Contains valuable chapters on the dispute with Indonesia, the Philippines' claim to Sabah, and ASA.

Gordon, Bernard K. "The Potential for Indonesian Expansionism," *Pacific Affairs*, XXXVI, No. 4 (1963–1964), 378–393. Among other things considers the implications for Confrontation and Malaysia.

[62] *Straits Times*, August 26, 1965.

Kahin, George McT. "Malaysia and Indonesia," *Pacific Affairs,* XXXVII, No. 3 (1964), 253–270. A sophisticated statement of the Indonesian case which is nevertheless fair to Malaysia.

Malaya-Indonesian Relations. Kuala Lumpur: Government Press, 1963. Background information and reproductions of documents assembled by the Department of External Affairs.

Malaya-Philippines Relations. Kuala Lumpur: Government Press, 1963. A similar collection with reference to the Philippines.

Rose, Saul. *Britain and South-East Asia.* Baltimore: The Johns Hopkins University Press, 1962. Contains sections on Malaya, Singapore and Borneo.

Silcock, T. H. "Development of a Malayan Foreign Policy," *Australian Outlook,* 17, No. 3 (1963), 42–53. The most comprehensive general interpretation.

12

Singapore, In and Out of Malaysia

Singapore Parties: The 1962 Referendum and the 1963 Election

Until the 1963 election in Singapore each successive party elected to form a government was more radical than the last. It appeared that the electorate was behaving as if there were indeed "no enemies on the left." Among the reasons for this behavior were the increasingly large numbers of Chinese-educated electors who voted at successive elections, and the ease with which a largely rootless urban population could be made to applaud anticolonial and pro-socialist slogans. After the Barisan Sosialis split off from the PAP government in 1961, it was the task of the government to try to stop this trend to the left. Its tactics were based on emphasizing the Malaysia issue. It was essential for the PAP that Malaysia should be brought about and also that the Singapore electors should be convinced that it was desirable. The government decided to hold a referendum on merger with Malaya, in September, 1962, although there was no legal obligation to do this.

The voters were not given the opportunity to vote against merger with Malaya; the PAP claimed that all the Singapore parties, even at one time the Barisan, had gone on record as supporting merger in principle.[1] So the voters could choose only which type of merger they preferred, or disliked least. They could choose: type A, based on the PAP government's negotiations with Malaya as set out in a

[1] But the Barisan wanted "genuine merger," with all Singapore citizens automatically becoming federal citizens on merger (S. T. Bani, *Singapore Legislative Assembly Debates*, XIX, No. 1, July 11, 1962, col. 276.)

White Paper;[2] type B, on the same terms as Penang and Malacca; type C, on terms no less favorable than those on which the Borneo territories would be admitted. Voting is compulsory in Singapore, so the only way of indicating disapproval of all three types of merger was to cast a blank vote. The Barisan accordingly asked opponents of merger on any of these terms to express their opposition by casting blank votes. All the government's propaganda resources, including slogans and songs on the radio and illuminated signs on the streets, were used to promote the idea of Malaysia. Of the votes cast 71 per cent were for type A, while 25 per cent were blank. The blank vote figure gave the government valuable information. Probably not all the Barisan supporters followed the confused dispute between the government and the Barisan about blank votes, and some may have treated Malaysia as a non-party issue. So the blank vote total probably represented the *minimum* Barisan support at a future election. Moreover, the government had access to, although it did not publish, the distribution of referendum votes in the various areas of Singapore. The blank vote proportion was greatest in the rural areas (it was as high as 45 per cent in some constituencies), which led to the government's stepping up its program for providing community centers and other benefits for these areas.[3]

It had originally been the PAP's intention to hold an election in 1963 for the fifteen seats allocated to Singapore in the Malaysian federal Parliament, and later to hold an election for the fifty-one seats in the Singapore Legislative Assembly. But it lacked the majority to pass through the Singapore Legislative Assembly its Election Bill to create fifteen parliamentary seats.[4] So it was decided to hold the elections for the fifty-one Assembly seats first, in September, 1963, and then to choose the fifteen federal representatives from Singapore indirectly, the members from each party to be proportional to the members in the Singapore Legislative Assembly. At the September, 1963, election the PAP had many advantages. It benefited from the enthusiasm which had accompanied the formation of Malaysia only a few days before. The election campaign period was very short, and opposition parties did not obtain permission to hold some rallies before nomination day. Some Barisan leaders, including Lim Chin Siong, the strong man of the party, and party workers had been removed from political activity in the arrests of February, 1963. The

[2] See p. 65, above, fn. 29.

[3] Lee Kuan Yew, reported in *Straits Times,* October 7, 1962; *The Plebeian* (Barisan newspaper), January 23, 1963.

[4] The voting on the motion was 23–23 (*Singapore Legislative Assembly Debates,* XXI, No. 1, July 25, 1963, cols. 181–182).

Prime Minister, Lee Kuan Yew, on the other hand, undertook an extensive program on constituency tours for months before the election.

The PAP made full use of radio and television, although in strictly party political programs the opposition was given a reasonable share of the time. The Barisan had the largest attendance at its mass meetings. The PAP also used, as an ultimate deterrent, the argument that, even if the Barisan won, the federal government would not allow them to take over power in Singapore. The main danger to the PAP was that the right-wing Singapore Alliance coalition would split the vote, but in fact the previous right-wing vote rallied to the PAP.

Table 3

Singapore elections: Percentage of total vote by Party, 1959 and 1963

	1959	1963
Singapore People's Alliance (SPA)	20	—
Liberal-Socialists	8	—
UMNO-MCA	6	—
Singapore Alliance	—	8
PAP	53	47
Barisan Sosialis (including its ally, Party Ra'ayat)	—	33
United People's Party[5]	—	8
Others	13	4
Totals	100	100

It is doubtful how the UPP vote would have gone, if the party had not existed; probably most of it would have been cast for the Barisan. Because of changes in the composition of the electorate, no exact comparisons can be made. But, if it is assumed that in 1963 the Barisan votes and the bulk of the UPP votes, say just under 40 per cent of the total vote, came from the PAP's 1959 vote, then most of the 1963 PAP vote must have come from right-wing electors, most of whom had previously voted SPA, Liberal-Socialist, or UMNO-MCA. It is significant that all the seats lost by the PAP in 1959 were won by it in 1963. Conversely, the seats lost by the PAP to the

[5] The UPP was led by Ong Eng Guan, a previous mayor of Singapore, who had been expelled from the PAP a few years before. It ceased to exist in 1965 after Ong resigned his seat in the Assembly.

Barisan in 1963 (most of them in rural areas) had all been won by it in 1959. The PAP, having lost its left-wing support, had succeeded in persuading most of the other voters that it, not the Alliance, was the best defense against a pro-Communist government in Singapore.

The PAP won 37 seats, the Barisan 13, and the UPP 1 (Ong Eng Guan himself). Of the 15 seats in the federal Parliament, 12 were allocated to the PAP and 3 to the Barisan.

The PAP ideology is "socialist" in so far as one of the party's long-term constitutional aims is to abolish unjust inequalities of wealth and opportunity. But Singapore's dependence on entrepôt trade and its economic benefits from the existence of the British defense base set a limit to some of the steps towards socialism which have been attempted in some other countries, such as government ownership of business. The PAP's "socialism" has taken the form of welfare measures, notably in health, education, housing, and the promotion of favorable conditions for labor. It is hoped that the relatively high standard of living will make a peaceful transition to a socialist industrialist society possible. The PAP has been resolutely opposed to both communalism and Communism. One reason for its desire that independence should take the form of merger with Malaya was the belief that an independent Singapore would succumb to Chinese chauvinism.[6] This was why the PAP worked so hard to encourge a national *Malayan* consciousness in Singapore — to reassure the government of Malaya that the Chinese would be "ready, willing and able to be absorbed as one Malayan people, all able to speak Malay, and willing to work together for the economic betterment and upliftment of the Malays as equals of the other races."[7] On the other hand, because the Chinese-educated constitute a high proportion of Singapore voters, the PAP has had to go to great lengths to make a clear distinction between the Communists and the non-Communists among them; the PAP believes that the Lim Yew Hock government failed to do this.[8] The desire to show the Chinese-educated that the PAP was *their* government explains the PAP's early voluntary labor schemes to beautify the Singapore sea front and also its original toughness with English-educated civil servants, described later in this chapter.

Economic prosperity and a more equal distribution of wealth are the PAP's long-term weapons against communism. But, in the short

[6] Lee Kuan Yew, *The Battle for Merger* (Singapore: Government Printing Office, 1961), Appx. 6, pp. 169–170, quoting a PAP policy statement of 1960.

[7] *PAP 4th Anniversary Celebration Souvenir* (Singapore: *Petir* Editorial Board, 1958), p. 3.

[8] Lee Kuan Yew, pp. 57–58.

term, it has had to work directly against Communists and pro-Communists, both by fighting them at the 1962 referendum and the 1963 election, and also by trying to prevent them from dominating politically important organizations. Most important, the non-Communist leadership has had to fight to retain control over the PAP organization itself. Control was lost temporarily in 1957, and when the Barisan split off in 1961, capturing about thirty-seven out of the fifty-one branches. The need to keep Communist elements from capturing the leadership accounts for the PAP's extreme concern with its choice of "cadres," activists with a special standing in the party, including the power to elect the central executive committee.[9]

The other Singapore parties also had their weak points and schisms. The UPP was essentially a one-man party. The Singapore Alliance, consisting of the Singapore UMNO, MCA, and MIC and the Singapore People's Alliance, was founded in 1963 after long negotiations. But there were tensions between the partners, and also at one time, between the Singapore MCA and the Federation MCA. After the Alliance defeat in the 1963 election, the leader of the SPA, Tun Lim Yew Hock, who did not himself contest a seat at the election, resigned. None of the constituent parties in the Alliance, with the possible exception of the Singapore UMNO, had so far developed an organization which functions effectively between elections. The Barisan, weakened by its election defeat and by further arrests, split temporarily in May, 1964. The split was not the result of ideological differences, but of divergence in the strategy to be followed by the party when manpower registration for defense was introduced. The chairman, Dr. Lee Siew Choh, himself almost certainly not a Communist, wished to oppose registration openly. A group consisting mainly of young Nanyang University intellectuals thought that a showdown would not command popular support and would merely result in further arrests of key party members over an issue which was not vital. Dr. Lee and a small number of others then resigned, leaving the Barisan under the control of extremists who had temporarily adopted a "soft," non-extremist line. Nine months later Dr. Lee and his companions returned to the party, following an "admission of mistakes by the then party leadership."[10] Early in 1966 Dr. Lee's leadership of the party was again challenged, partly on the ground

[9] See "On the Question of the Selection of Cadres" and "Statement by the Central Executive Committee of the PAP in reply to the 16 Resolutions raised by Mr. Ong Eng Guan," *Petir* (PAP newspaper), July 14, 1960; Lee Kuan Yew, pp. 20–22.

[10] *Straits Times,* May 6, 1964; *Sunday Times,* May 10, 1964; *Straits Times,* March 9, 1965; *Statement by Dr. Lee Siew Choh and Others on Return to the Barisan Sosialis* (March 9, 1965).

that his strategy was ineffective, partly because he was allegedly placing his own men in various party positions. There were important defections from the party and friction with the trade unions which had previously supported it.

Interest Groups

In Singapore the role of groups in the political process has been dominated by the struggle between Communist and non-Communist groups for control. The most obvious battleground has been the trade unions. The PAP leaders who were released when the PAP came into office in 1959 were mostly trade union leaders, although, both chronologically and ideologically, they were politicians first and union leaders second. When the Barisan split came in 1961 the majority of these leaders identified themselves with the Barisan. The PAP therefore had to meet the industrial challenge made by the Barisan-controlled unions, in particular by means of the attempted mass strike of October, 1963. At the same time it had to try to break the hold of the pro-Barisan Singapore Association of Trade Unions (SATU) by inducing unions to leave it and join the rival National Trades Union Congress (NTUC) under Devan Nair.[11] Weapons used by the government included the arrest of pro-Barisan trade union leaders, notably in February, 1963, soon after the Azahari revolt in Brunei, and by government refusal to register SATU (November, 1963) on the grounds that it was being used for unlawful purposes.

An obvious problem of the leaders of the non-Communist unions has been to prevent themselves from being identified as "stooges" of the PAP government. When Singapore was part of Malaysia, Devan Nair, himself the PAP member for a Kuala Lumpur constituency of the federal Parliament, attempted to do this on occasion by attacking Singapore government officials.[12] The NTUC, however, was happy to join the Singapore government in protesting against the Malaysian federal government. In order to demonstrate against the 1964 federal budget taxes, the NTUC wished to hold a rally in Singapore. The police authorities refused permission, a decision which apparently originated in Kuala Lumpur. So the protest took the form of an indoor meeting.[13] In revenge, the PAP tried to gain support in trade unions in Malaya and to forge links between the MTUC and the NTUC.

[11] Milton E. Osborne, *Singapore and Malaysia* (Ithaca: Cornell University Press, 1964), pp. 4–5 and 72; *Straits Times,* October 9 and 11, 1963; *The Plebeian,* October 15, 1962.

[12] *Sunday Times,* March 29, 1964; *Straits Times,* November 13, 1964.

[13] *Sunday Times,* December 13, 1964; *Straits Times,* December 15, 1964.

The PAP has tried to eradicate Communist influence in other organizations, including Chinese Middle Schools and Nanyang University. Nanyang was opened in 1956, and the teaching in it was largely in Chinese. It therefore attracted Chinese-educated students, and soon had the same problem as the Chinese Middle Schools of how to deal with an appreciable number of left-wing students who were thought to have been Communist-infiltrated. It also came under the control of Tan Lark Sye, the chairman of its University Council, a millionaire who heavily backed the Barisan to win the Singapore elections of 1963. Because the PAP government disliked Tan's influence and knew the left-wing inclinations of the student body, it was unwilling to support the university financially without being assured of having control over it. And without adequate financial support standards of instruction in some subjects were low. After the 1963 elections the government attempted to reorganize Nanyang. Mr. Tan was deprived of his Singapore citizenship, and left-wing students were arrested and detained in September, 1963, and June, 1964. Reorganization was agreed upon between the university authorities and the Singapore government. In September, 1965, a Nanyang University "curriculum review committee" recommended, among other things, that the students should no longer come overwhelmingly from Chinese-medium schools; that all students should be at least bilingual, if not trilingual; that a new department of Malay studies should be established; that new salary scales should be introduced to attract and retain good staff.[14] In spite of opposition from left-wing students, implementation of these reforms was begun.

After the Barisan split away from it the PAP government also had to fight to retain control of the "People's Association," an authority for promoting community recreation, which it had previously set up. The 1963 Singapore election showed that the Barisan was strong in the rural areas of Singapore, and in October, 1963, two rural associations (the Singapore Rural Residents Association and the Singapore Country Residents Association) were dissolved on the ground that they had become political organizations operating on behalf of the Communists. As a positive measure of community development it was announced in January, 1964, that the Singapore government would set up "grass roots committees" throughout the state, which would be anti-Communist but not identified with any political party. In the same year the Singapore government began a massive program to train youth leaders, aimed at meeting the temptations to youth to join secret societies or support disloyal causes. A more limited project had been in existence since 1960, when a "Work Brigade" was

[14] *Straits Times,* September 13, 1965.

set up, with a planned strength of 5,000, to harness the energy of young unemployed persons to the cause of national construction.

While Singapore was a part of Malaysia the Chinese Chamber of Commerce in Singapore was clearly subject to political cross-pressures. Some of its members' dealings with "government" were with the PAP government in Singapore, but others were with the Alliance federal government. In supporting the formation of Malaysia there was no problem, because the Alliance and the PAP were ranged on the same side. But, later, on other issues they were opposed. When the Singapore Chinese Chamber of Commerce opposed the turnover and payroll taxes imposed in the federal budget of 1964, it found itself protesting to the federal government in company with the Singapore government.

In the course of its fight to deny control of interest groups in Singapore to pro-Communist elements, the PAP has been led into a situation where it tends to try to control the groups themselves. In February, 1965, Tan Siew Sin charged the PAP with turning Singapore into a one-party state. Without commenting on the correctness of the charge, this was really only one aspect of the growing quarrel between the federal government and the Singapore government, which forms a main theme of this chapter.

The Formal Structure of Government

In its broad outlines the structure of government in Singapore resembles that of government in Malaya (or Malaysia), except that it is not federal. Some constitutional changes were made after the separation of Singapore from Malaysia in 1965. The Head of State was to be known as President instead of Yang di-Pertuan Negara, and was to be elected by the legislature, and not appointed, as previously. A Constitutional Commission was set up to draft a new Constitution. The active executive, the Cabinet, is responsible to the unicameral legislature, the Singapore Legislative Assembly, which has a longer tradition of popular election than the federal Parliament in Kuala Lumpur. Its debates have combined sophistication with acrimony. They were of exceptional interest during the period when the PAP government's majority was minimal, 1961–1963. Since the 1963 elections the Assembly has been much more tame. The principal opposition party, the Barisan, won only thirteen seats to the PAP's thirty-seven, and some of its members have been absent from Assembly meetings because they were under arrest or in hiding. The Barisan boycotted the session of the Assembly which began in December, 1965.

The Cabinet is headed by a "Prime Minister," since 1959 Lee Kuan Yew. The Cabinet members are the political heads of various ministries. Assisting them, but not actually in the Cabinet, are other members of the Assembly who have been appointed Ministers or Parliamentary Secretaries. Most of the left-wing detainees who were released when the PAP came into power in 1959 were made "Political Secretaries," a way of keeping them employed without giving them responsibility. Even after they left the party in 1961 when the Barisan was formed, the device of using Political Secretaries was continued.

There is no separate local government body in Singapore. The People's Action Party won control of the Singapore City Council two years before it gained a majority in the Singapore Legislative Assembly. However, on coming to power after their victory at the Assembly elections in 1959, they abolished the City Council. Some of the Council's functions, such as providing gas, water, and electricity, were given to a Public Utilities Board and others were given to ministries of the state government. At one time there were three Rural District Councils in Singapore island, but these have also been abolished. Consequently, no elected local government authorities remain in Singapore.

The Civil Service

The civil service in Singapore is worth examining, because it illustrates an important aspect of the PAP government's political style. The PAP is an "ideological" party, which has certain explicitly formulated beliefs which guide its actions. As was seen in the section on Singapore interest groups, it is unwilling to tolerate any important groups in Singapore coming under the control of a rival party or ideology. When the PAP first came to power it was particularly concerned to eradicate "the colonial mentality" among Singapore's higher civil servants.

In some respects, particularly in structure and remuneration, the civil service in Singapore strongly resembles that of Malaya. This is not surprising, considering that Singapore was one of the Straits Settlements, and it was not until 1954 that the civil services of Malaya and Singapore were separated. Like the federal civil service in Malaysia, the Singapore civil service has four divisions; it has the equivalent of an MCS, the Singapore Administrative Service; it was even earlier than Malaya in introducing an executive service (1954). There was also a Malayanization program in Singapore, which envisaged "rather more drastic steps" than its counterpart in Malaya. For instance, all the posts of permanent secretary of a ministry were filled by local officers by early in 1957.[15] On the other hand, there are certain differences which follow from the preponderance of Chinese in the population of Singapore. There is no Malay Administrative Service and there is no "quota" for particular ethnic groups in any part of the civil service.

The Singapore civil service is efficient and relatively free from procedural delays. To some extent, as in Malaya, this could be attributed to a *need* to be efficient in order to prosper or even to survive. Singapore's success as a free port depended partly on the services she provided, including governmental services. The civil service under the PAP has the reputation of being notoriously incorrupt, although it has been alleged that, when city government existed in Singapore, the former mayor, Ong Eng Guan, appointed friends to jobs for which they were unqualified.

There is an unemployment problem of a particular kind in Singapore, which hardly exists in Malaya. It is relatively easy for graduates from both English-speaking universities, the University of Malaya (Kuala Lumpur) and the University of Singapore, to find employment. But this is not so where Nanyang University is concerned. Quite apart from Nanyang's previous standards of academic achievement, or previous standards of subversion, there is a language problem, which affects employment prospects for Nanyang graduates. Most of the instruction in Nanyang has been in Chinese, and few of its graduates know sufficient English to be easily placed in the Singapore public service, which operates mainly in that language. The Singapore government was alert to the dangers of the volcanic eruptions which would come from a Chinese-educated élite which had been denied a share of power. The Singapore Prime Minister, speaking of the necessity of attracting talent into the civil service, said that, if the Chinese-educated were not absorbed, "then I say you are going to build up an élite that will challenge you."[16] The Singapore government promised that it would absorb about seventy of the first four hundred or more students to graduate early in 1960; about fifty would be absorbed in the education service and twenty in the other departments of the public service.[17]

The Singapore government's whole policy towards the civil service, and especially toward top civil servants, has been calculated and so-

[15] T. E. Smith, *The Background to Malaysia* (London: Oxford University Press, 1963), p. 269. See also *Malayanization Commission, Interim Report* (Singapore: Government Press, 1956).

[16] *Straits Times*, November 22, 1962.

[17] *Ibid.*, October 29, 1959.

phisticated. Before it came to power in 1959 the People's Action Party was regarded as belonging to the left. In turn, it regarded the top civil service as having been conditioned to work in colonial ways and at a colonial tempo. As the Finance Minister said in 1962, as a result of past training and the traditions of the British system, particularly the colonial systems, "the local civil service, through no fault of their own, have not been made aware of the importance of their keeping in touch with the masses, to understand their attitudes, hopes and aspirations. Civil servants, however, have not been equipped with an understanding of the political movements and the philosophies which inspire these movements. The present government believes that the civil service, although it must maintain its political neutrality, must be able to judge and assess any problem in the context of the political consequences of their actions. Only by being able to see their actions in the political context of our society will civil servants be able to implement government's policy properly."[18]

The point was put a little more forcefully in the Government party's newspaper. Some local officials who had benefited by Malayanization "saw themselves as the new privileged caste entitled to all the favours and courtesies enjoyed by their white superiors." Unless local officers "prepare themselves psychologically for the new demands that are likely to be made on them they may find the future full of frustrations and conflicts."[19] However, according to the Prime Minister, after the 1959 election the political leaders had an alternative to blaming the administrators every time something went wrong and so causing the morale of the civil service to suffer — namely to make the civil service understand the government's difficulties and ask it to work harder and root out corruption and slackness. To bring this about, the government set up a Political Study Centre, directed by an able expatriate already in government service, which has attempted "to telescope into a study course the main elements of the political forces which caused the post-war revolutions in Asia."[20] The courses, which have lasted for several days, have included such topics as: the civil service in the new Singapore, economic problems of Singapore, political movements in Malaya, the basic ideas of democracy, the challenge of communism, the Indian national movement, the Chinese national movement, and communism in China.

At the same time — the reason being given as economy — the variable allowances of civil servants were cut by the government. This

[18] *Ibid.*, July 29, 1959.
[19] "A Democratic Civil Service" by "a PAP Member," *Petir*, April, 1959.
[20] *Singapore Government Press Statement*, 1959.

meant a drop of M$400 a month for the highest paid civil servants. Opposition critics alleged that this measure was designed to demonstrate the government's intention to keep the civil service firmly under control, or that it was designed to show Chinese-educated voters that the government was capable of "getting tough" with the English-educated. The Prime Minister pointed out that the ministers had reduced their own salaries by a larger figure than the cut in the top civil servants' salaries. The pay cuts were restored, in stages, during 1961. After the 1963 general election, when the government party was returned to power, an "*ex-gratia*" payment was made to civil servants "in appreciation of the integrity and loyalty which they had displayed during the past four years under the PAP Government."[21]

The question of civil service "neutrality" has obviously been more delicate in Singapore than in Malaya (or Malaysia) where the federal government has not yet changed, and where it has not seemed likely to change. In Singapore the morale of higher civil servants was affected, temporarily, by the coming to power of the PAP, which had a much more radical program than the government it replaced. By 1963 they no longer feared the PAP. However, after the left-wing Barisan Sosialis split from the PAP government in 1961, civil servants were warned by a member of the new party that the PAP would not be in power forever, a warning, which, according to the Minister of Culture, amounted to an attempt to frighten civil servants.

Because it believed that it had radically different policy from its predecessors, the PAP government was desirous of finding able men, either inside or outside the existing civil service, who sufficiently shared its ideals to work well in the top ranks of the service, along with Ministers. The government has not in fact brought in any such people from outside (except, from 1965 onwards, into its new diplomatic service), but has been able to promote rapidly some people who have been judged exceptionally meritorious from the lower ranks of the service to higher positions. It should be remarked that Ministers in Singapore do not confine themselves to policy questions, but often go into the details of administration. This may be a consequence of their desire to ensure that the civil service, which it originally thought had been "colonially" conditioned, would really carry out their policy. It may result partly from the smallness of Singapore, which encourages Ministers to believe that it is feasible to concern themselves with some individual cases. Whatever the reason, it places a premium on the government's finding higher civil servants who are committed to its own broad values.

[21] *Singapore Government Press Statement,* September 25, 1963.

Frictions between Singapore and the
Federal Government inside Malaysia

While Singapore was in Malaysia, from September, 1963, until August, 1965, many points of friction developed between the Singapore state government and the federal government in Kuala Lumpur. These points of friction interacted, and in the end make it impossible for Singapore to remain inside Malaysia without violence erupting. However, for the purpose of analysis, it is possible to classify the contentious issues under four headings: constitutional, party, racial, and personal.

Many of the constitutional points were on economic and financial issues. Singapore is the biggest port in Southeast Asia, and in the past profited greatly by being a "free port," where customs duties did not apply. Tourists also profited by buying watches, cameras, and other equipment at bargain prices. But, although the revenues from this source have been considerable, even before Malaysia was proposed the Singapore government had decided that they were not enough to support Singapore's increasing population and growing economic expectations. So the decision was made before 1963, to industrialize Singapore, even though the need to protect some of the new local products by tariffs would injure Singapore's revenue from trade. With the formation of Malaysia the problem became more complex. Malaya had also started to industrialize, notably in the area of Petaling Jaya, a suburb of Kuala Lumpur. Most of the products to be manufactured in Malaya or Singapore were intended for internal consumption, not for export. It was desirable, therefore, to take advantage of the economies offered by the *whole* internal market in Malaya, Singapore, Sarawak, and Sabah and not have wasteful competition between factories in Singapore and Malaya which produced almost identical products.[22] This implied that industrial expansion in Singapore and Malaya had to be coordinated. At the same time the free port status of Singapore, and of other free ports in Malaysia, Penang and Labuan, could not be ended too abruptly, or dislocation and suffering would result. However, after Malaysia was formed little progress was made in setting up a common market.

By the Malaysia Agreement, until December, 1968 the federal government had to obtain the consent of the Singapore government to the imposition of new import duties: this consent could have been withheld if it appeared that a duty might significantly prejudice the

[22] *Report on the Economic Aspects of Malaysia,* by a Mission of the International Bank for Reconstruction and Development (Kuala Lumpur: Government Press, 1963), chs. III, IV, and V.

Singapore *entrepôt* trade. Effectively the Singapore government was given a delaying power of twelve months.[23] When the federal budget for 1965 imposed a range of new duties and taxes, there were complaints from Singapore that there had not been the necessary consultation. The argument which followed showed that the terms of the Agreement had either not been clearly understood or had been found difficult to observe by some of those concerned.[24] A further reminder of the new federal powers over Singapore was given in February, 1965, when Tan Siew Sin reminded Singapore industrialists that before opening any factories they should consult the central government on tariff protection and the grant of preferential treatment through being given pioneer status.[25] Competition in manufacturing and exporting between Singapore and Malaya did not cease with the formation of Malaysia. In some respects it became fiercer, and certainly more publicized, because of the political overtones which existed. Some time after Britain imposed a quota on her imports of textiles there was a furious controversy between the Singapore and federal governments on the percentage of the quota which Singapore should fill.[26]

By the Malaysia Agreement (Annex J, 6) power was delegated to the Singapore government to collect customs and excise duties and income tax in Singapore. With some exceptions all revenues thus collected were to be paid into a special fund to be divided in the proportion of 60 per cent to the Singapore government and 40 per cent to the federal government. At first sight this seems to have been a generous arrangement for Singapore, but it must be remembered that Singapore had also been given a wide range of functions, and that these had to be paid for. However, this arrangement provided another source of friction between the two governments. At the end of 1964 Tan Siew Sin said that Singapore tax burdens were the lightest in Malaysia and that its revenue was far in excess of requirements. In the light of Malaysia's increasing defense costs, he proposed that the financial arrangements should be reviewed and that Singapore should hand over 60 per cent of the revenue it collected, not 40 per cent.[27]

[23] Annex J, 3(3).
[24] Dr. Goh Keng Swee, *Straits Times,* December 2, 1964; Tan Siew Sin, *ibid.,* December 3, 1964.
[25] *Ibid.,* February 17, 1965.
[26] The main debate began with a statement by Dr. Goh Keng Swee (*ibid.,* March 22, 1965). It continued in the headlines for about the next month.
[27] *Ibid.,* December 3, 1964, July 19, 20, 22, and 26, 1965. The issue of July 22 reproduced a letter written by Mr. Tan to Dr. Goh, the Singapore

There were also disputes between the two governments on the continued existence of the Bank of China in Singapore. The bank, directed from mainland China, had already been forced to give up business in Malaya, and in 1965 the federal government ruled that it would have to cease operations in Singapore as well.[28]

Political differences between the Alliance and the PAP developed rapidly during 1964. After the PAP victory at the Singapore elections of 1963, the PAP wooed the UMNO by inviting the Tengku to nominate one of the two federal senators from Singapore, which he agreed to do. At this time the strategy of the PAP seems to have been to try to divide the UMNO and the MCA by showing the worthlessness of the MCA as a partner in the Alliance and by replacing it inside the Alliance. This was the line pursued by the PAP during the 1964 elections in Malaya when it fought only seats which the MCA, as opposed to the UMNO, was contesting. But the attempt to separate the UMNO from the MCA failed. Once the Tengku and other UMNO members had come to the support of the MCA, then any PAP attack on the MCA was also in effect an attack on UMNO.[29]

Relations between the UMNO and the PAP also deteriorated as a result of events in Singapore. An Alliance explanation was that after Malaysia the Malays in Singapore "felt themselves neglected and despised. They expected the government to improve their lot but the State government of Singapore made no provision for special treatment of any one particular race or community. They therefore felt aggrieved."[30] It might be added that, after Malaysia, the Singapore Malays, although isolated locally, were perhaps emboldened by the thought that, in a wider sense, they were now no longer isolated, because they were inside a federation in which political power was wielded mainly by Malays. The Singapore UMNO was also anxious to revenge itself on the PAP which had defeated it in the three mainly Malay seats at the 1963 elections for the Singapore Legislative Assembly. Malay discontent over a Singapore urban development scheme, which would have forced some Malays to leave their homes, led to an invitation by the Singapore government to over a hundred

---

Finance Minister, November 20, 1964, in which reference was also made to agreement not having been reached on the payment of Singapore's loan to the Borneo states (p. 72, above).

[28] Tan Siew Sin, *Malaysian Government Press Statement,* June 18, 1965. The bank was reprieved by the separation of Singapore from Malaysia.

[29] See p. 99, above.

[30] *Speech by Tengku Abdul Rahman, 17th General Assembly of UMNO* (Kuala Lumpur: Dewan Bahasa dan Pustaka, September 6, 1964), p. 12.

Malay organizations to meet the Prime Minister and discuss with him problems affecting the Malays. But an UMNO-sponsored convention decided to boycott the meeting and appointed an "action committee" to speak for all the Malays in their future dealings with the Singapore government.[31] On this occasion Dato Syed Ja'afar Albar, the national secretary-general of UMNO, made a highly provocative speech, accusing Mr. Lee, among other things, of trying to break the backbone of the Malay community in Singapore. Soon afterwards riots occurred in Singapore and a "curfew" had to be imposed twice, in July and September, for periods of several days, during which nonessential workers were confined to their homes. The rioting was intensified by the activities of gangsters and pro-Indonesian agents. But its basis was so clearly communal that politicians from both Singapore and Malaya were worried, made numerous statements on the importance of communal harmony, and drew up plans to raise the standard of living of the Singapore Malays. It was even said that a "truce" had been agreed on between the Alliance and the PAP, although there seemed to be considerable doubt about its terms. As a consequence of the riots the PAP's long-term prospects in Malaya were certainly harmed; the troubles in Singapore damaged its image in Malaya by suggesting that it was an "anti-Malay" party.

Looking back on the period of nearly two years when Singapore was part of Malaysia, it would seem that the Alliance leadership had not expected the PAP to compete so aggressively in politics inside Malaya. It was surprised that something like "free trade in politics" was developing, and viewed the PAP's activities as a breach of an unspoken agreement that even inside Malaysia Singapore would be to some extent politically insulated.[32] The PAP government, however, did not relish the Tengku's advice that it should concentrate less on politics and more on making Singapore "the New York of Malaysia."[33] It did indeed want to do more than just to run Singapore as a

[31] *Straits Times,* July 13, 1964. See also *ibid.,* July 20 and 21, 1964. The conflicts in Singapore in the second half of 1964 are well covered in Michael Leifer, "Singapore in Malaysia: the Politics of Federation," *Journal of Southeast Asian History,* VI, No. 2 (1965), 63–69.

[32] Cf. the Tengku's statement that Lee's persistent incursions into Malaysian politics were tantamount to broken pledges (*The Times* [London], August 17, 1965). The limitation of Singapore representation in the Malaysian House of Representatives to 15 seats and the Singapore citizenship provisions, described in Chapter 4, above, may be regarded as devices for insulating Singapore politically from Malaya.

[33] Cf. Lee Kuan Yew, quoted in *Malaysian Mirror,* March 6, 1965. The *Malaysian Mirror* (after Singapore left Malaysia, the *Mirror*) is published by the Singapore Ministry of Culture.

state and as an important business center of Malaysia.[34] The gulf between the PAP and Alliance concepts of just how competitive politics in Malaysia should be is clearly seen by comparing their ideas on the political use of the mass media. In the Malaysian Constitution these powers were allocated to the central government. To be sure, the Malaysian Agreement (Annex K) said that, although the power over radio and television was federal, the Singapore government should be responsible for administration and day-to-day programs within Singapore and that the federal government should delegate to Singapore the necessary powers for this to be carried out. However, among other things, the federal government should have the right to issue to the Singapore government any directions necessary to "ensure the implementation of the overall policy of the Federal Government."

In fact radio and television in Singapore have been used to propagate the views of the Government party, the People's Action Party. Before Malaysia, at the Singapore referendum of 1962, and immediately after Malaysia, at the Singapore Legislative Assembly elections of 1963, the PAP used these media to put its case to the voters. Obviously, in view of the political competition between the People's Action Party and the Alliance, control of broadcasting and television in Singapore became highly important. If the federal government could use them for political purposes, it would deny to the PAP the use of one of the main channels for advocating its policies. If the PAP could continue to use these media, its plans to penetrate into politics in Malaya would be greatly helped. Singapore radio could be heard in most parts of Malaya, and Singapore television could be seen in Johore and even as far north as Malacca.[35] In 1965 the PAP had suggested that a Television-Malaysia transmitter be set up in Singapore in exchange for a Singapore television transmitter being set up inside Malaysia. The Alliance government discouragingly replied that they were seriously thinking of having "only one voice" in the mass media in Malaysia.[36]

There was a striking difference of approach between the responsible leadership of the PAP and the Alliance, respectively, to the problem of communalism in Malaysia. The PAP believed in drawing attention to the existence of communal problems, analyzing them and stressing the necessity of overcoming them if Malaysia were to survive. The Alliance, while believing that it was necessary to make

[34] As suggested by the Tengku, *Straits Times,* April 18, 1965.
[35] K. J. Ratnam and R. S. Milne, *The Malayan Parliamentary Election of 1964* (Kuala Lumpur: University of Malaya Press, forthcoming), chapters on the press and radio, and on the Singapore elections of 1963.
[36] *Straits Times,* May 28, 1965.

general pronouncements on the desirability of racial harmony, feared that any extensive open examination of communal differences at, say, university forums on politics would only stir up trouble. The difference in approach was perhaps traceable to a difference in temperament. The PAP was a theoretical, calculating party, while the Alliance distrusted ideology. But the difference in approach could also have rested on an estimate of the consequences. The PAP, as a noncommunal socialist democratic party, could believe that a rational examination of communal issues would lead to their becoming recognized as a less important factor in politics, so laying the foundation for a non-racial appeal along lines of class differences. The Alliance, on the other hand, as an intercommunal party subject to internal stresses, might think that its own cohesion could be imperiled by discussions on communal issues which might become hard to control. The resulting paradox was that the Alliance was a party with a communal structure, which believed that too frequent open discussion of the problems of communalism is itself "communal"; the PAP was a party with a noncommunal structure, which nevertheless believed that communal problems should be subjected to perpetual scrutiny.

In practice communal tension was stepped up in several ways. Singapore leaders repeatedly attacked what they called the "ultras" in the federal government, notably Dato Syed Ja'afar Albar, whose intervention in Singapore they held mainly responsible for the riots of 1964, and what they regarded as racially inflammatory articles in the Malay newspaper, *Utusan Melayu*. They built up the sinister image of the paper by repeatedly mentioning that it was printed in *Jawi* (Arabic) script. On the other hand, when Mr. Lee laid stress on the ethnic composition of Malaysia as being approximately 40 per cent Chinese and 20 per cent others, UMNO leaders treated this, not as an academic argument for a multi-racial approach but as an attempt to show up the Malays as a minority in "their own" country. Mr. Lee in a number of speeches, became more and more explicit in putting his version of the case for a noncommunal approach, on the basis of the "racial arithmetic" of Malaysia, as indicated in the titles of his speeches, *Towards a Malaysian Malaysia, Are There Enough Malaysians to Save Malaysia?* and *The Battle for a Malaysian Malaysia.*[37]

The "Malaysian Malaysia" approach was taken up in May, 1965, when the PAP joined with two parties in Malaya, the UDP and the PPP, and two in Sarawak, the SUPP and MACHINDA, to form the Malaysian Solidarity Convention.[38] Even after the departure of

[37] Three booklets with these titles were published by the Singapore Ministry of Culture in 1965.

[38] See p. 108, above.

Singapore from Malaysia, the formation of the convention continued to have obvious implications for the future of Malaysian politics. Here two aspects of the situation may be noted that had a bearing on communal tensions and on the viability of Singapore as a member state of Malaysia. First, most of the leaders of the convention, and certainly the PAP leaders, made no attack on Malay "privileges" or on the Malay language,[39] yet this could not obscure the fact that they were making an attack on the political predominance of the Malays. Second, although the members of the convention had founded it as a protest against Malay "communalism," all the protesting parties, except MACHINDA, which was a new party, were dependent mainly on Chinese votes. So, although the convention was a protest against communalism, in a sense it was necessarily itself a "communal" protest. There was an added implicit threat when Mr. Lee said that, if the convention behaved constitutionally and yet did not receive fair treatment, there would be reverberations in Britain, Australia, and New Zealand (on whom Malaysia was dependent for defense).[40]

As well as the constitutional, party, and communal factors, there was also a personal element involved. Among the PAP there was real hatred of the "ultras," particularly of Dato Syed Ja'afar Albar. Among the UMNO Mr. Lee was generally distrusted, and it was alleged that it was his burning ambition to be the Prime Minister of Malaysia one day: he had obliquely commented on this by saying on various occasions that "for a generation" the federal Prime Minister must be a Malay.[41] The Tengku later commented that there had been a "certain inclination on the part of some countries to look upon the Prime Minister of Singapore as an equal partner in the Government of Malaysia . . . and this has made the situation rather awkward for us."[42] This inclination must have been stimulated by Lee's frequent tours of Asia, Africa, Australia, and New Zealand. The Tengku did not relish the suggestions of foreign journalists that Mr. Lee's talents should be made use of by his being appointed to a federal government post, for instance in the Cabinet. Resentment against foreign (mostly British) journalists who appeared to favor Singapore and Lee over the federal government and the Tengku was symbolized by the expulsion from Malaysia of Alex. Josey in May, 1965. This was certainly

[39] Lee Kuan Yew, *The Battle for a Malaysian Malaysia,* p. 29.

[40] E.g. at the Singapore meeting of the Convention, June 7, 1965.

[41] Mr. Lee was born in 1923. More recently he was alleged to have said that "a Malay should be Prime Minister for at least several more years" (*Straits Times,* March 24, 1965).

[42] Text of the Tengku's speech in the House of Representatives, August 9, 1965, *Singapore Breakaway* (Kuala Lumpur: Department of Information, 1965), p. 5.

not a clear-cut case of interference with the freedom of the press; Mr. Josey was personally very close to some of the PAP leaders and had carried out paid assignments for the Singapore government.

The Expulsion of Singapore

By May, 1965, the cumulative effect of the tensions just described was becoming almost intolerable. Almost every day the newspaper headlines reflected another aspect of the quarrel between the federal and Singapore governments. In May the formation of the Malaysia Solidarity Convention was announced. And on May 27 Lee Kuan Yew, in response to what he called the "outpourings in the *Jawi* press," made a stand in the House of Representatives by referring in detail to the attacks made on him by the ultras and restating at length the basic policies of the PAP and the convention.[43]

For some time there had been rumors that Singapore wished to secede from Malaysia. However, apparently what Singapore wanted was a looser form of federation with control of its own fiscal policy. The federal government did not agree to this proposal.[44] What happened, in brief, was that in June, 1965, soon after Parliament had finished sitting, the Tengku went to London for a Commonwealth Prime Ministers' Conference. At the end of June he entered a London hospital to be treated for a minor complaint; while convalescing he weighed up the situation in Malaysia and its increasing tensions and came to the conclusion that Singapore should leave Malaysia. He communicated this decision to a small number of his Cabinet colleagues, who then talked things over with government leaders from Singapore. Preparations were begun for drawing up a separation agreement and for amending the Constitution. After the Tengku returned to Malaysia on August 5, Mr. Lee and other PAP leaders went to Kuala Lumpur, and were reluctantly convinced that the Tengku's plan must go through. The whole proceedings were carried out in great secrecy. The British High Commissioner and the Mentri Besar and Chief Ministers of the states of Malaysia, including Sarawak and Sabah, were informed only a day or so before the official announcement was made by the Tengku in a speech in the House of Representatives on August 9.

In his speech to the House the Tengku reviewed the course of recent events, including the quarrels between the two governments and the dangers of racial violence. When he thought over the problem

---

[43] *The Battle for a Malaysian Malaysia*, pp. 5–52.

[44] Tan Siew Sin, *Straits Times*, August 16, 1965; Tengku Abdul Rahman, *ibid.*, August 21, 1965.

in London it "appeared that as soon as one issue was resolved, another cropped up. When a patch was made here, a tear appeared elsewhere, and where one hole was plugged, other leaks appeared."[45] Some of the blame for what had happened was laid on the "political activities and enthusiasm of the various politicians in Singapore,"[46] although the Tengku also said that every day irresponsible utterances were being made *by both sides*.[47] There were only two courses of action open. "Number one is to take repressive measures against the Singapore government for the behaviour of some of their leaders and number two to sever all connections with the State government that has ceased to give even a measure of loyalty to the Central government." The first of these courses was rejected, "as repulsive to our concept of Parliamentary Democracy" and also because repressive action would only intensify communal feeling.[48] The second solution was therefore adopted, that Singapore should leave Malaysia.

It has been argued by some that the Tengku was under heavy pressure from the ultras and the right wing of UMNO. But perhaps too much was read into a passage in his letter to Dr. Toh Chin Chye, the Deputy Prime Minister of Singapore, "if I were strong enough and able to exercise complete control of the situation I might perhaps have delayed action, but I am not."[49] The reference here is surely to the entire situation, of which the ultras were only a part, although an important part. Certainly, to suppose that the crisis could have been solved bloodlessly by "smacking down" six ultras and forming a looser federation,[50] would have been just as unrealistic as to imagine that the arrest of half a dozen PAP leaders would have produced a nonviolent solution. But Singapore's expulsion did not amount to a victory for the ultras. Significantly, Dato Syed Ja'afar Albar resigned the post of secretary-general of UMNO only two days after Singapore's separation from Malaysia. One of the reasons he gave for his resignation was that the separation left Singapore as a very close neighbor, controlled by a party hostile to the central government, which might become a center of subversion.[51] The inference is that if he had been in control he would have been decidedly tougher in his dealings with the Singapore leaders.

[45] *Singapore Breakaway,* p. 1.
[46] *Ibid.,* p. 5.
[47] *Ibid.,* p. 8 (underlining supplied).
[48] *Ibid.,* p. 2.
[49] *Straits Times,* August 11, 1965. The Tengku explained his use of the phrase "strong enough" in the next day's issue.
[50] *Ibid.,* August 12, 1965 (Lee Kuan Yew).
[51] *Ibid.*

Singapore's Future

Questions about Singapore's future may be considered under a number of headings. Will political tensions between Singapore and Malaya really be reduced by Singapore's exit? Can the PAP remain in control of the government in Singapore? Under what conditions can Singapore be economically viable and what are its probable economic relations with Malaysia? What will be its defense arrangements and foreign policy as an independent state? Now that Singapore is independent, will there be any change in its relations with Indonesia?

Only a few weeks after the separation a Malaysian government protest was handed to the Singapore government against "defamatory as well as inflammatory" remarks made by Mr. Lee on television about Malaysian domestic affairs.[52] There was a further angry exchange between the Tengku and Mr. Lee at the end of October, 1965. However, the controversy lacked the intensity of the previous similar controversies which took place while Singapore was part of Malaysia. Obviously, a good deal will depend on the future activities of the Democratic Action Party (DAP), the Malaysian counterpart of the PAP, set up after separation. If the new party became active and attempted to put across a point of view strongly resembling that of the PAP, making frequent reference to PAP policies in Singapore, the Malaysian government would almost certainly react strongly. The Tengku foresaw this possibility when planning the separation of Singapore from Malaysia. "He said that when he was in London he had given thought to what would happen if the PAP were to continue to work in Malaysia. He feared that there would be acrimony, charges and countercharges, 'and this will start bad feelings all over again.' "[53] It would seem that if the PAP still intends to spread its ideas in Malaysia, even somewhat indirectly through the DAP, considerable finesse may be needed to avoid a revival of political tensions.

Inside Singapore the PAP has probably gained strength, from both former Alliance supporters and former Barisan supporters, through being identified as fighting for the rights of Singapore against the federal government. A few weeks before separation the only United People's Party member in the Singapore Legislative Assembly, Ong Eng Guan, resigned, and his party did not contest the by-election. In spite of the fact that many of Ong's previous supporters might have been expected to support the Barisan and in spite of Alliance hostility, the PAP defeated the Barisan decisively by 6,398 votes to 4,346. After the separation of Singapore the Barisan did not increase its popularity by demanding that the British bases be withdrawn. If implemented, this proposal would have cost many Barisan supporters their jobs; almost one Singapore family in ten depends, directly or indirectly, on the base for its livelihood. Superficially, it might seem that after independence in 1965 the PAP government had been placed in exactly the situation it had sought to avoid in 1961 when it pressed the Tengku for merger. It was exposed to the competition of a determined very left-wing party in an independent Singapore. But its position was stronger than this comparison would suggest. It had had over four years in which to weaken the Barisan by repressive measures and adroit use of the Barisan's mistakes. The main danger it is faced with, electorally, is that economic distress and a high level of unemployment may lose it votes. During 1966 the PAP leaders increasingly emphasized the need for raising both the skills and the determination of Singapore's small population. The emphasis was on an "organized" society.

Singapore's essential economic problem has not been greatly changed, although it has been intensified, by separation from Malaysia. In the period 1963–1965 her trade losses from Indonesian Confrontation had been largely made up by the opening of new factories and by greater British defense expenditure in Singapore.[54] But little had been accomplished by the Singapore and federal governments to bring about a Malaysian common market. Chinese businessmen in Malaysia wanted protection, and lobbied against it. Singapore was the more eager of the two parties concerned, and it blamed the federal government for the delay. After Singapore left Malaysia the Tariff Advisory Board which had been set up to work out common market proposals was retained, and the Tengku announced that, although an actual common market would not be set up, "in the course of time and in the light of working experience, we will be able to work out a system near enough to common market arrangements."[55] In principle, there-

[54] In the first half of 1964 recorded import figures showed a decline of 23 per cent and export figures of 31 per cent; however, the number of workers unemployed as a direct result of Confrontation never exceeded 4,000. From 1963 to 1964 Singapore's national income rose by 1½ per cent, compared with between 8 and 10 per cent, a year during the previous four years (Dr. Goh Keng Swee, *ibid.*, November 3, 1964; *Malay Mail*, March 12, 1965.)

[55] *Straits Times*, September 2, 1965. The Independence of Singapore Agreement, 1965, reproduced as Appendix 1 to *Malaysia* (Kuala Lumpur: Department of Information, Malaysia, August, 1965), Article VII, rescinded Annex J of the Malaysia Agreement (1963) referring to the common market. But Article VI of the Independence of Singapore Agreement, 1965, laid down the principle of economic cooperation between Malaysia and Singapore.

fore, progress towards a common market need not be slower than it was before. However, the bargaining over common market proposals and over the location of new industrial enterprises will now be carried on in a different context than before, one in which Singapore is legally independent. In practice, of course, Singapore's independence is limited in many ways, particularly by the fact that, before Confrontation, almost 30 per cent of her trade consisted of entrepôt transactions to or from Malaysia. From 1961 to 1963 during the negotiations on the formation of Malaysia there was a good deal of discussion on whether Singapore "needed" Malaya more than Malaya needed Singapore. In one sense each needed, and still needs, the other, because a large port and its hinterland are complementary. But in another sense Singapore needs Malaya more, because, while Malaya could develop Port Swettenham or Penang, although at a high cost, Singapore has no "alternative hinterland" to develop. Significantly, only a few days after Singapore left Malaysia, demands were voiced for more extensive development of the port of Penang. It is quite possible that in discussions between the two governments on a common market the Malaysian government could use as a bargaining weapon the threat that it would step up the development of ports in Malaya. The basic point about the common market, however, is that Malaysia is unwilling to face too open competition from Singapore.

If Singapore does not obtain access to Malaysian markets through common market arrangements, her industrialization program can succeed only if she can increase exports of her products to areas outside Malaysia. The obvious parallel example is Hong Kong, but Singapore has the disadvantage that her wage structure is higher than Hong Kong's.

The Agreement concluded between the two governments on the separation of Singapore provided for a defense treaty between the two countries. A joint defense council was to be set up; Malaysia was to assist Singapore in external defense, and Singapore would "contribute from its own armed forces such units thereof as may be considered reasonable and adequate for such defence"; Singapore would give Malaysia the right to continue to maintain and use its bases and other military facilities in Singapore for external defense; "each party will undertake not to enter into any treaty or agreement with a foreign country which may be detrimental to the independence and defence of the territory of the other party."[56] These provisions underline the essential interdependence between the defense of Malaysia and the defense of Singapore. In practice it would seem to give Malaysia

[56] Independence of Singapore Agreement, 1965, Article V.

something like a veto over Singapore's defense policy. This interpretation is supported by Mr. Lee's assurance immediately after the separation that Singapore would never do anything to endanger Malaysia.[57] In any armed conflict between the two countries Malaysia would be stronger; she also supplies most of Singapore's water. By August, 1966, the defense treaty had not been signed. Malaysian officials believe that Singapore is reluctant to sign until Malaysia takes steps to bring about a common market.

In addition to being involved with the Malaysian defense system, Singapore is also linked with the British defense system, indirectly through the British involvement in Malaysia but also directly through the existence of the British base in Singapore. In the short term the PAP government wants the British base to stay, in spite of its awareness of the damage which the presence of white troops does to Singapore's image in the eyes of Afro-Asians. It is quite possible that Britain, in an effort to reduce her expensive overseas commitments, might withdraw the base before this was desired by the PAP. An alternative base is Perth in Western Australia, which is politically more secure and which would probably be partly paid for by the Australian government. During Confrontation the base was vital to Singapore, because only through British protection could Singapore be defended against Indonesia. Severe economic dislocation would also result in Singapore if the base were abruptly removed. At the same time, possibly with Afro-Asian opinion in mind, Mr. Lee has emphasized that at any time the Singapore government could tell the British to quit the base. Lee also insisted that in the new agreement on the base to be signed by Britain and newly independent Singapore, it should be laid down that the base was to be used for defense, not aggression (including "aggression on Indonesia"), and that the Singapore government should always be consulted when the base was put to use.[58]

In August, 1965, Singapore became fully independent and responsible for her own foreign policy. She was obliged to set up a foreign ministry and to find recruits to fill diplomatic posts abroad. Her foreign policy has been described as one of nonalignment in the power struggle between the Communist and Western blocs.[59] This policy has been spelled out in regard to Viet Nam, where the war is viewed as being a reflection of the struggle between these two blocs.[60] But

[57] Press interview on Television Singapura, August 9, 1965. See the "national security" argument for Singapore's joining Malaya, put forward in 1961, see pp. 62–63, above.

[58] *Straits Times,* September 1 and 2, 1965.

[59] S. Rajaratnam, Foreign Minister of Singapore, *ibid.,* August 11, 1965.

[60] A. Rahim Ishak, "The Vietnam Tangle," *The Mirror,* September 18, 1965.

Singapore's freedom of maneuver is hindered by the limitation of its ability to enter into agreements or treaties with a foreign country, "which may be detrimental to the independence and defence" of Malaysia.[61] Singapore government spokesmen, therefore, with the Agreement in mind, have been studiously noncommittal on the question of possible diplomatic relations with mainland China. They have hinted, however, at the possibility of establishing relations with Russia, although not in the near future. A trade and technical assistance pact was signed with Russia in April, 1966. It would seem that Malaysia, because of the close threat of mainland China, would be much more strongly opposed to Singapore's having relations with China than with Russia. In the November, 1965, United Nations vote on the admission of mainland China to the U.N., Singapore, who had become a member two months earlier, demonstrated that she had a different foreign policy from Malaysia; she voted for China's admission while Malaysia voted against it.

Soon after independence Mr. Lee made a violent attack on the United States, saying that if the British base went it would not be replaced by a United States base.[62] Lee made sensational disclosures about earlier CIA activities in Singapore; he was also apparently moved by personal considerations, but insofar as his attack was calculated, he possibly had several aims in view. The timing of the attack suggests that he may have foreseen the decision reached at the end of 1965 by the United States and Britain to cooperate more closely in the defense of Southeast Asia. He may have been trying to demonstrate to Afro-Asian countries that, although he was committed to the British base in the short run, he was also capable of taking a strong "anticolonialist" stand on bases. Also, by rejecting the idea of United States military support, he may have wished to distinguish clearly between his own progressive regime and the sequence of "unprogressive" regimes in South Viet Nam. On several occasions Lee Kuan Yew has expressed admiration of the foreign policy of Prince Sihanouk of Cambodia. The future course of Singapore's foreign policy might not be too different from the Prince's, except that obviously it would show fewer traces of direct pressures from mainland China and more traces of Malaysian and Indonesian influences.

During Confrontation Singapore's relations with Indonesia were a possible area of disagreement with Malaysia. This was not because the Singapore government was especially sympathetic to Indonesian government policy, at any rate up to October, 1965. It did not

[61] Independence of Singapore Agreement, 1965, Article V(4). The article similarly limits Malaysia's power to make agreements or treaties.
[62] *Straits Times,* September 1, 1965.

share the Indonesian government's pro-Communist leanings and it strongly disapproved of the harsh treatment of the Chinese in Indonesia. But, in order to survive, Singapore is dependent on trade. Even after Indonesia formally cut off trade with Malaysia as part of its Confrontation policy in 1963, a "barter trade" with Singapore, through the adjacent Riau Islands, went on until the Malaysian federal government stopped it in August, 1964. Immediately after Singapore was separated from Malaysia the Tengku stated that he would not allow Singapore to trade with Indonesia.[63] The Independence of Singapore Agreement made no mention of restrictions on trade. But Malaysia had two powerful sanctions. She could claim that Singapore-Indonesian trade would in fact infringe the defense provisions of the Agreement, because of the possibility that trading would provide an opportunity for Indonesian saboteurs to infiltrate Singapore and then Malaysia. Also, before Confrontation Indonesian trade was valuable to Singapore, but trade with Malaya was even more valuable.[64] So, during Confrontation, if Singapore traded with Indonesia without Malaysia's approval, Malaysia could force Singapore to lose more trade than she gained. Consequently, although Mr. Lee tentatively outlined plans for barter trading which would rule out any possibility of sabotage,[65] he was also aware that the consequences had to be calculated. "It is not just trade with Indonesia and Singapore's little advantage which is at stake."[66]

When Indonesia's decision to recognize Singapore was followed in June, 1966, by the announcement that Confrontation would end, the role of Singapore changed. She was no longer an avenue through which Indonesia could hope to outflank Malaysia, for instance by indirectly trading with Malaysia while continuing to harrass her militarily. Instead, in the new framework of Malaysian-Indonesian friend-

[63] *Ibid.,* August 15, 1965. On August 9, 1965, Lee Kuan Yew had mentioned the possibility of Singapore's trading with Indonesia, although he discussed the security risk involved. He suggested that if economic cooperaton between Singapore and Malaysia lagged, then any government of Singapore must seek a living by trading even with the devil in order to survive (press interview on Television Singapura).

[64] Malcolm J. Purvis, "The Economic Implications of an Independent Singapore," in *Separation of Malaysia and Singapore: Implications for the Future,* M. Ladd Thomas, ed. (De Kalb: Northern Illinois University, Center for Southeast Asian Studies, forthcoming).

[65] *The Mirror,* October 16, 1965 (speech at a meeting of the Chambers of Commerce, October 5, 1965).

[66] *Straits Times,* August 27, 1965. Early in 1966 the Malaysian government was taking the line that Singapore's plans for trade with Indonesia showed a lack of cooperation, and that until more cooperation were shown, negotiations for a common market could not proceed.

ship, the question was how Singapore could fit into the pattern as a trading center.[67]

Singapore is so closely tied to the mainland of Malaya by geography, economics, and personal relationships that it is reasonable to expect that sometime the two countries will once again be united under a single government. But the bitterness aroused among politicians during 1964 and 1965 was so great that reunion is probably out of the question before another fifteen or twenty years have elapsed. Until the territories are again united, objectively it might seem that Singapore could not avoid being crushed by the weight and complexity of problems. But any estimate of her future should also take into account the determination and intelligence of her leaders and the skill and resilience of her people.

SUGGESTED READINGS

Fifty-eight Years of Enterprise. Singapore: L. M. Creative Publicity Ltd., 1964. A souvenir volume of the new building of the Singapore Chinese Chamber of Commerce.

Hanna, Willard Anderson. *The Separation of Singapore from Malaysia*. New York: American Universities Field Staff, Southeast Asia Series, XIII, No. 21 (Malaysia), 1965. One of the latest of a series of brilliant reports.

Lee Kuan Yew. *The Battle for Merger*. Singapore: Government Printing Office, 1961. Contains material on internal party politics in Singapore.

Lee Kuan Yew. *The Winds of Change*. Singapore: PAP Political Bureau, 1964. Eight speeches made by the Singapore Prime Minister during the 1964 elections in Malaya.

Lee Kuan Yew. *The Battle for a Malaysian Malaysia*. Singapore: Ministry of Culture, 1965. The most comprehensive statement of what constituted a viable Malaysia from the PAP's point of view; a speech delivered in the House of Representatives, May 27, 1965.

Leifer, Michael. "Politics in Singapore," *Journal of Commonwealth Political Studies*, II, No. 2 (1964), 102–119. Good for the period 1961–1963.

Leifer, Michael. "Singapore in Malaysia. The Politics of Federation," *Journal of Southeast Asian History*, VI, No. 2 (1965), 54–70. Continues the account of politics in Singapore up to early 1965.

[67] See p. 192, above.

Milne, R. S., "Singapore's Exit from Malaysia; the Consequences of Ambiguity," *Asian Survey*, 6, No. 3 (1966).

Ratnam, K. J. and R. S. Milne. *The Malayan Parliamentary Election of 1964*. Kuala Lumpur: University of Malaya Press (forthcoming). Describes the nature and the consequences of the PAP intervention and also has a separate chapter on the Singapore elections of 1963 by Frances Starner.

Silcock, T. H. "Singapore in Malaya," *Far Eastern Survey*, XXIX, No. 3 (1960), 33–39. Written before the merger of Singapore with Malaya became likely, but still highly relevant.

13

National Unity

Racial Divisions

Malaysia is not only a transitional society[1] which is attempting to modernize itself; it is also a multi-racial society with the problem of achieving national unity. This problem is especially prominent because Malaysia has a relatively high standard of living, which makes her economic problems less acute and less noticeable. The racial question has also been intensified because of the external attractions on certain sections of the population from outside.

The racial divisions among the population have already been described. Even within the three main groups — Malay, Chinese, and Indians — further subdivisions exist, and the kaleidoscopic effect has been heightened by the addition of the Borneo territories. Futhermore, in many cases the ethnic cleavages coincide with religious and linguistic cleavages and with differences in customs and way of life. As a result, the ethnic cleavages are underscored and deepened.[2] Because of the nature of these cleavages, Malaysia's problems resemble

[1] Cf. Daniel Lerner, *The Passing of Traditional Society: Modernizing the Middle East,* 2nd impression (Glencoe: The Free Press, 1962); Lucian W. Pye, *Politics, Personality, and Nation Building: Burma's Search for Identity* (New Haven: Yale University Press, 1962); Fred W. Riggs, *Administration in Developing Countries: The Theory of Prismatic Society* (Boston: Houghton Mifflin, 1964); David E. Apter, *The Politics of Modernization* (Chicago: University of Chicago Press, 1965).

[2] The average income per head of Chinese is higher than the average income per head of Malays (T. H. Silcock, "Communal and Party Structure" in *The Political Economy of Independent Malaya,* T. H. Silcock and E. K. Fisk, eds. (Singapore: Eastern Universities Press, 1963), pp. 1–3). Yet it is not true that the cleavage, Malays-Chinese, corresponds to a cleavage between poor and rich. See James Puthucheary, *Ownership and Control in the Malayan Economy* (Singapore: Eastern Universities Press, 1960), pp. 123–124.

those of Palestine or India before they were divided, or of Cyprus. They have some similarity with those of Ceylon.[3] More optimistically, they have been compared with those which have been successfully overcome in Switzerland. In two important respects, however, Malaysia's racial problem seems to be unique, in Asia at least: the two major races are nearly equal in number, and both of them are subject to ethnic influence by a more powerful Asian country. In view of these cleavages, the disturbing aftereffects of the Second World War, the Emergency, and the impact of Confrontation, it is perhaps a miracle that Malaya and Malaysia have managed to survive so far. In the circumstances perhaps the most that could be expected, until now, is that the various groups would interact, for purposes of commerce or government, according to certain agreed rules, but that they would continue to lead separate social lives.[4]

Aspects of Communalism

In practice it is impossible to separate most issues from communalism, because nearly all issues have obvious communal implications. If capitalism, in the sense of economic exploitation, is under attack, then, outside the northeast coast, the landlords and middlemen who are attacked are almost certain to be Chinese. If the matter of equality is under discussion, it is inevitable that a non-Malay will refer to Article 153 of the Constitution, which provides for the "special position" of the Malays. Although in general there is no desperate shortage of land in Malaysia, the subject has several communal angles. PMIP state governments have been unwilling to accept federal schemes which would give land to what they consider to be an excessive number of Chinese. Furthermore, land development may be opposed, even if it is Malays who are being settled, on the ground that it is Chinese contractors who are engaged to clear the land and who gain the immediate financial advantage. In Sarawak land reform must take account of ethnic and political considerations, because in the past it has been very difficult for Chinese to acquire land legally, a fact which has probably driven many Chinese to support the SUPP.

Benefits conferred on one ethnic group may set off something like a chain reaction. During the Emergency when the Chinese squatters were resettled in New Villages they complained because they had been uprooted. When the New Villages were made more comfortable to

[3] William Howard Wriggins, *Ceylon: Dilemmas of a New Nation* (Princeton: Princeton University Press, 1960).

[4] William H. Newell, *Treacherous River* (Kuala Lumpur: University of Malaya Press, 1962), pp. 34–40, describing the relations between a Malay community and a Teochiu community.

live in by the provision of certain services, such as schools and roads, there were complaints from the Malays that they were being neglected by comparison.[5] So there was a drive for largely Malay rural development, symbolized in the issue of the famous "Red Book" for each *kampong* (village), in which rural projects were listed for each area and a record kept of what had been accomplished. By 1962 Chinese complaints that they had been left out of the rural development schemes had become so general that it was decided to extend the Red Book to the New Villages.

Outside the New Villages in Malaya the bulk of the rural dwellers are Malays. This fact explains some aspects of government policy, which might be different if the ethnic proportions in the rural areas were the same as in the urban areas. "For example, a greater rate of growth could almost certainly be achieved by an allocation of government resources very much more heavily in support of the backward peasant sector."[6] But such a policy would be ruled out by the Alliance government's heavy dependence on the rural Malay vote. The importance of this vote is underlined by the provision altering the Constitution in 1962 when it was decided that the number of electors in rural constituencies might be appreciably fewer than in urban constituencies.[7] It is therefore possible that a generation from now there might be as many non-Malay electors as Malay electors in Malaya, but that, unless the urban-rural distribution of the population had radically changed, their voting power might be much less.

Certainly it is hard to avoid seeing signs of communalism in many aspects of life in Malaysia. Some of the examples are relatively trivial, such as the propensity of Malaysians of Chinese ethnic origin to state "Chinese" as their "nationality" in hotel registers or the fact that non-Malays sometimes cheer for visiting football teams of the same ethnic origin as their own rather than for a Malaysian team. Other signs are more serious. The PMIP has introduced motions into Parliament to the effect that "Malaya belongs to the Malays," which, if accepted, would undermine the whole basis of communal cooperation. Again, in 1962 when border fighting began between Indians and Chinese, the Malayan government's "Save Democracy Fund" to help India attracted very little Chinese support.[8] The most obvious illus-

---

[5] Gayl D. Ness, "Economic Development and the Goals of Government in Malaya," in *Malaysia, a Survey,* Wang Gungwu, ed. (New York: Praeger, 1964), p. 312.

[6] E. K. Fisk, "Rural Development Policy," Silcock and Fisk, p. 194.

[7] By the Constitution (Amendment) Act of 1962.

[8] See p. 182, above.

trations of communalism occur when there is actual fighting between different racial groups, as in several areas soon after the war and in Bukit Mertajam and Singapore in 1964.

The Economic Position of the Malays

To some extent the Singapore disturbances in 1964 constituted a special case, because they arose partly from intense party rivalries which reinforced and exacerbated communal differences, culminating in the Separation of Singapore from Malaysia. But for a wider consideration of the communal problem, it is necessary to go back to the notion of a "bargain" between the Malays and the Chinese. On this interpretation the UMNO and the MCA were able to come to an agreement and find a basis for the successful Alliance Party, by delimiting, as it were, certain spheres of influence to each major community. The Malays were to keep their political ascendancy by the retention of some of the traditional Malay features of government, such as the Rulers, through advantages in the civil service, and by their greater voting power. The Chinese were to have the citizenship qualifications relaxed which would gradually increase their electoral power and, tacitly, they were not to be interfered with in the pursuit of business. But an important feature of the bargain was that it was not "static." Politically, the Chinese influence was to increase. Similarly, the Malays, it was thought, would be encouraged to become more active economically, Even before the formation of the Alliance this had been an objective of the British. "The ideal of a united Malayan nation does not involve the sacrifice by any community of its traditional culture and customs, but before it can be fully realized the Malays must be encouraged and assisted to play a full part in the economic life of the country, so that the present uneven economic balance may be redressed."[9]

A few years ago one authority claimed that efforts to improve the economic position of the Malays had not yet been very successful.[10]

[9] Directive from the British Government to General Templer on his appointment as High Commissioner, February, 1952, quoted in J. B. Perry Robinson, *Transformation in Malaya* (London: Secker and Warburg, 1956), pp. 182–183. This quotation does not indicate the major role played by foreign, mostly British, capital in the economy. It is still true that "the Chinese are mainly middlemen and compradores of European capital. Some have become partners and a few have become independent. The capital that dominates Malaya's economy is European" (Puthucheary, *op. cit.*, p. xix).

[10] T. H. Silcock, "General Review of Economic Policy," Silcock and Fisk, pp. 242 and 261–275.

The government has attacked the problem of rural poverty by setting up RIDA (Rural and Industrial Development).[11] Some of the ventures engaged in by RIDA came under criticism, and in 1965 it was reorganized and renamed MARA (*Majlis Amandh Ra'ayat*). The scope of MARA is indicated by the titles of its five divisions: transport; commerce and industry; training; technical services; credit finance. Agriculture has been promoted in a number of ways. The Federal Land Development Authority (FLDA)[12] was established in 1956. In 1965 it was announced that a Federal Agricultural Marketing Authority (FAMA) would be set up, that a new bank would be created for giving out rural credit, and that the cooperative movement would be revitalized.[13] Plans have also been made to encourage industrialization in the smaller towns. The various organizations just mentioned are extending their activities in Sabah and Sarawak and are setting up branches there.

From another angle, the economic position of the Malays is inferior because of the absence of a middle class of Malay entrepreneurs. To create such a group would not of itself, apart from any trickle-down effect, make the bulk of the Malays less poor. Nevertheless, it may be argued that, without such a group, one avenue of opportunity is closed to Malays and that they have therefore not achieved "equality" in the particular sense of "equality of opportunity." It is possible to point to particular Malays who hold a large number of directorships, for instance Dato Nik Ahmed Kamil, who previously had a career as a diplomat, and Dato Dr. Haji Mustapha Albakri, the chairman of the Election Commission and previously Keeper of the Rulers' Seal. In 1963 these two eminent Malays held about one dozen and two dozen directorships, respectively.[14] But few other Malays of comparable caliber are available, which partly accounts for the concentration of so many directorships in the hands of so few Malays. It is also significant that both these persons had been government servants. The tendency of nearly all educated Malays to join government service has been cited as one main reason for the shortage of successful Malays who are making their career in business. Other reasons which have been advanced to explain the shortage are loss of faith in Malay companies, because some (such as the Malay Shipping Company and

[11] E. K. Fisk, "Rural Development Policy," *ibid.,* pp. 175–176. On the Rural and Industrial Development Authority see G. Krishnan Nair, "The Rural and Industrial Development Authority," *Ekonomi,* 1, No. 1 (1960), 57–60; *Sunday Mail,* March 26, 1961.

[12] See pp. 80–82, above.

[13] Tun Razak, *Straits Times,* August 20, 1965.

[14] *Sunday Times,* September 22, 1963.

the Malay Bank) have gone bankrupt, and lack of sufficient capital.[15]
A radical approach to the problem would be to try to increase the
number of Malays in business by setting up more public enterprises
owned by the government, which among other things could train
Malay managers.[16] This kind of proposal, however, would probably
be blocked by the "free enterprise" philosophy of the Alliance and its
distrust of "socialism." In any case, it is doubtful if the provision of
more Malay entrepreneurs and businessmen generally can be solved
purely by providing institutional improvements. Substantial changes
in Malay attitudes would seem to be necessary as well.[17] The composition of élites in Malaysia has not yet been studied in depth. But,
whatever their exact nature, it is fairly clear that for some time to
come there will not be a middle-class Malay élite, based on business
as opposed to traditional status or experience in the bureaucracy.

Alliance efforts to improve the economic position of the Malays
have sometimes been criticized by socialists on the ground that they
are "capitalist" solutions. Professor Ungku Abdul Aziz has argued
that rural poverty cannot be cured unless exploitation of the rural
Malays is ended by setting up a comprehensive system of marketing
organizations, either government-owned, cooperative or joint.[18] Rural
development was a prominent theme in the PAP campaign to establish itself in Malaya. Once the PAP had given up hope of forming
an alliance with UMNO, it was forthright in condemning Alliance
policies towards the rural Malays. According to the PAP, rural poverty could not be solved by private enterprise, and the UMNO was
committed to the support of non-Malay private enterprise. "The
leadership of the Malay mass base is linked up with Chinese and

[15] Dr. Lim Swee Ann, Minister of Commerce and Industry, *Dewan
Ra'ayat Debates*, V, No. 3, May 28, 1963, cols. 451–458; *Straits Times*,
June 11, October 2 and December 31, 1963; Haji Khalid bin Awang Osman,
Assistant Minister of Commerce and Industry, *ibid.*, April 4, 1963; Raja
Nasron bin Raja Ishak, former secretary of the United Chamber of Com-
merce, *ibid.*, January 2, 1964.

[16] E. L. Wheelwright, "Industrialization in Malaya," Silcock and Fisk,
pp. 236–237.

[17] Cf. David Clarence McClelland, *The Achieving Society* (Princeton:
D. Van Nostrand, 1961); Tjoa Soei Hock, *Institutional Background to
Modern Economic and Social Development in Malaya* (Kuala Lumpur:
Liu and Liu, 1963), especially chs. VI and VII. Similarly, a letter to a
newspaper, apparently from a Malay, on the shortage of Malay university
graduates has said that the deficiency does not lie in a lack of scholarships.
What is lacking is the "spirit and constitution for competition." (*Straits
Times*, December 17, 1964).

[18] See his inaugural lecture, "Poverty and Rural Development in Malaysia," *Kajian Ekonomi Malaysia*, I, No. 1 (1964), 70–75.

Indian private enterprise at the top, so there is a contradiction which cannot be resolved."[19] In his last speech in the federal Parliament Mr. Lee maintained that the question of rural poverty was being confused by discussion of Malay rights or about how to create a few indigenous entrepreneurs. "Instead of special rights, why not tax the haves in order to uplift the have-nots including the many non-Malays, the Chinese, the Indians, the Ceylonese and the Pakistanis?"[20] The speech was based on the familiar PAP premise that political dividing lines "ought" to be economic rather than racial; less than three months later, Singapore had been expelled from Malaysia.

Nation-building

Even if the future course of the Malay-Chinese "bargain" were to follow the form originally intended, this would do little to promote national unity. The bargain aimed to produce a contrived mechanical balance between ethnic groups, not a fusion of attitudes or aspirations. The subsequent bargaining which resulted in the formation of Malaysia created an even more intricate, and no less mechanical, balance. What are the prospects for building a genuine sense of nationhood in Malaysia?

Before looking more closely at the question of nation-building, it should be repeated that one superficially attractive "solution" is in fact not practicable, although the PAP seems to have favored it. Cleavages in a society[21] can become serious when they occur along the same dividing lines and so reinforce each other; therefore some writers have advocated the creation of new cleavages, which would run along different dividing lines from the old ones. In particular, it has been suggested that in Malaya, with its ethnic, linguistic, and religious divisions, new economic alignments should be encouraged for this reason. One such proposal, made before independence, was as follows. "In Malaya, under the influence of free institutions, communalism would quickly give way to natural class divisions. If the hitherto despotically governed people of the Federation were therefore given the opportunity to elect a national government, sensitive and responsive to public opinion and possessing the power to carry through much-needed social and economic reforms, economic alignments cutting across communal divisions would quickly appear. This

[19] Lee Kuan Yew, *Some Problems in Malaysia* (Singapore: Ministry of Culture, 1964), p. 29.
[20] *The Battle for a Malaysian Malaysia* (Singapore: Ministry of Culture, 1965), p. 44.
[21] Cf. Seymour Martin Lipset, *Political Man* (London: Heinemann, 1960).

would create the climate of opinion essential to the working of parliamentary democracy in a plural society, and thereby rapidly crystallize a Malayan consciousness."[22]

In retrospect this assessment seems unduly optimistic, and possibly to derive from a wish to see an approximation to a British two-party system of government, in which the parties are divided by economic differences which are perceptible but not irreconcilable. But, as has been pointed out, it is difficult to replace communal divisions by economic ones, because so many of the obvious economic lines of division are also communal. It is significant that, after almost a decade of independence, the most successful parties in Malaya are still communally based; this also applies to the Borneo territories. For some years commentators who explicitly or implicitly subscribe to the view that politics will be increasingly dominated by economic considerations, and that communal considerations are becoming politically irrelevant, have been predicting the early demise of the Pan-Malayan Islamic Party. In the long run they may be correct. In the short run their predictions are not helpful. At the 1964 elections in Malaya, although the PMIP lost support generally, it retained control of the Kelantan state Assembly and hardly lost any strength in the northwest states, Kedah and Perlis. Reports of its death have been greatly exaggerated, although after February, 1965, it suffered from the arrest of some of its leaders for plotting with Indonesia. The racial incidents of 1964, to say nothing of the manner of Singapore's departure from Malaysia, also suggest that ethnic considerations may be assuming more importance in politics, not less.

Before Singapore left Malaysia Lee Kuan Yew suggested that the communal cleavages in Malaysia were saved from being more dangerous than they were by two considerations. The numbers of Malays and Chinese were sufficiently nearly equal to prevent one of these groups from having serious ideas of permanently repressing the other.[23] Also the Indians, Pakistanis, Ceylonese, Eurasians, and others constituted a kind of third force, which could act as a moderating influence on communalism. If either Malays or Chinese took too strong a communal line, they would alienate these groups and find themselves faced by a coalition of all the other communal groups. On this type of reasoning, the inclusion of the Borneo territories in Malaysia should have been beneficial, because it strengthened the moderating forces by bringing in the natives of Sabah and Sarawak, although at the same time it increased the external and indirectly the internal, tensions by

[22] Francis G. Carnell. "Communalism and Communism in Malaya," *Pacific Affairs*, XXVI, No. 2 (1953), 105.
[23] Cf. Lee Kuan Yew, *Straits Times*, July 16, 1964.

provoking, or providing the occasion for, Confrontation. This line of reasoning was not necessarily invalidated by the racial tensions which developed in 1964 and 1965 and contributed to Singapore's expulsion. It can be argued that the decisive factor which produced the break was not the attempt to create a "Malaysian Malaysia," but rather the *pace* at which the PAP tried to promote it.[24]

Assimilation and Accommodation

A sense of nationhood, although essentially subjective, has often been said to be dependent on a history of shared experiences. But this is not possible in Malaysia, because Malays and Chinese do not share "a heritage of common suffering and common rejoicing in the past."[25] Therefore, in order for a sense of nationhood to exist, which will help to break down communal barriers and differences, the task of nation-building must be deliberately undertaken. Given the present communal situation, there would seem to be four main possibilities for the future: assimilation of the various communities; accommodation of the various communities on the basis of leaving things as they are, a laissez-faire policy; partition of the country; chaos.[26] Because of the ways in which the various communities are distributed geographically, partition would hardly be practicable, except in the limited sense in which a separated Sabah or Sarawak would constitute partition, and a separated Singapore constituted partition in August, 1965. Chaos is certainly possible, if one of the other possibilities were tried unsuccessfully. Complete assimilation would be difficult, even if attempted by force. It might have been a possible policy if the proportion of Chinese had been smaller, and if Chinese culture had been less venerable and less admired. Even in Thailand, where the proportion of Chinese is lower, assimilation has not been complete,[27] although cultural differences between the Thais and Chinese are fewer than those between Malays and Chinese, and although a major obstacle to assimilation, the barrier of Islam, is absent. But in Malaysia total assimilation of the Chinese would be almost impossible except in the very long run. Chinese attachment to Chinese tradition and culture and to China itself as a world power, irrespective of whether or not it were Communist, would be too strong. It would

[24] See pp. 246–247, below.

[25] Tan Cheng Lock, *Malayan Problems from a Chinese Point of View* (Singapore: Tannsco Publishers, 1947), p. 119.

[26] Cf. K. J. Ratnam, "Government and the Plural Society," *Journal of Southeast Asian History*, II, No. 3 (1961), 1–10; Ian Morrison, "Aspects of the Racial Problem in Malaya," *Pacific Affairs*, XXII, No. 3 (1949), 252.

[27] R. J. Coughlin, *Double Identity: The Chinese in Modern Thailand* (Hong Kong: Hong Kong University Press, 1960), pp. 195–199.

be very difficult even for the Indians, who form a much smaller proportion of the population.

However, assimilation is a much more tempting solution where the natives of Borneo are concerned. Their numbers are relatively small, and their culture is less developed than that of the Malays. They have been subject to Malay rule in the past, from Brunei, and are exposed to the penetration of Islam. In these circumstances it is not remarkable that the Malay members of the Alliance government in Malaya feel they can provide friendly leadership for these territories. Before Malaysia the Tengku referred to fears in the Borneo territories that the Malays might not be able to serve the people there as well as the British had done. "If they, who are people of a different race and from a different world, can do much for the people of the Borneo territories, sufficient to gain their confidence, how much more can we do for those who belong to the same ethnic group whom we regard as brothers in the same family."[28] Certainly the intricate ethnic divisions in the Borneo territories can be exaggerated to a point where they obscure the broad similarities. But, whatever the reason, whether alleged reaction against Malay domination in the past, or alleged overt or covert anti-Malay propaganda by the British, the fact remains that many natives in Sarawak and Sabah do not regard the mainland Malays as brothers to the same degree as some mainland Malays regard them as brothers. The whole history of the Malaysia project, in which the suspicions of political leaders in Sabah and Sarawak had to be overcome by bargaining and the provision of guarantees, supports this point of view. Indeed, one of the most prominent leaders in Sarawak, later Chief Minister, was originally of the opinion that *no* constitutional arrangements would be adequate to guarantee the safeguarding of the country's immigration laws, state sovereignty and other rights.[29] It was precisely to prevent rapid or thorough assimilation that so many safeguards to protect Sabah and Sarawak were in fact built into the revised Constitution. Yet the relative defenselessness of the natives, which made these guarantees necessary, could be at the same time a standing temptation to a central government to pursue as assimilationist a policy as was practicable.

Government policy, then, could not successfully be one of complete assimilation because of the strength of Chinese and Indian numbers and culture and because of the constitutional guarantees regarding the

[28] *Straits Times,* August 31, 1962. See also pp. 67–68, above.
[29] Dato Stephen Kalong Ningkan, *Borneo Bulletin,* October 28, 1961. It is of interest that Dato Ningkan's clashes with the federal government were a contributing factor to his losing office in June, 1966.

Borneo territories. But, in practice, neither could it be a policy of complete accommodation, of laissez faire. To do nothing would be to let the various communites go their separate ways, except for the casual contacts required by governmental or commercial transactions. In effect, policy has been a combination of accommodation and assimilation.

However, the *degree* of assimilation is not the only important issue. It is also necessary to ask a question about the *nature* of assimilation — assimilation *to what?* In other words, is assimilation to mean assimilation to a purely *Malay* way of life or to a *Malayan* way (now *Malaysian* way) of life, to which other cultures and customs have contributed? It has been well said that "Malayan nationalism" consists of two parts, "a nucleus of Malay nationalism enclosed by the idea of Malay-Chinese-Indian partnership."[30] Since the formation of Malaysia this outer ring would also include contributions from the natives of Sabah and Sarawak. The question is, what should be the relative importance of the nucleus compared with the outer ring? It is possible to cite radically contrasting views on this. The approach of the top Malay politicians in the Alliance government is moderate. They "under-emphasize Malay political demands which other races find difficulty in accepting, such as Islam as the state religion or the use of Arabic script," stressing only the Malay language and a limited amount of royal ceremonial.[31] At the same time they attempt to take the edge of PMIP criticisms by increasing the number of mosques and other religious buildings and by extensive Koran-reading competitions. Malaya's independence was achieved after a struggle, but relations with the former colonial power, Britain, were not permanently embittered. Malay nationalism was not excited to the point where it became fanatical. And the road to independence was by means of cooperation with the Chinese, through the MCA, which paved the way for continued cooperation with them in the future. But extreme Malay views still exist, particularly in the PMIP, and find expression, for example, in attempts to put it on record in the Constitution that Malaya belongs to the Malays.[32] Behind this is the conviction that the Malays are the original inhabitants of Malaya, the "sons of the soil." Non-Malays, if they stay in Malaya must conform to Malay standards completely, that is, they must be entirely assimilated. Alternatively (and this is the solution preferred by some Malay extremists) they should be forced to return to their original "homeland." Similar attitudes are exempli-

[30] Wang Gungwu, "Malayan Nationalism," *Royal Central Asian Journal,* July–October, 1962, Parts 3 and 4, p. 321.

[31] T. H. Silcock, "Communal and Party Structure," Silcock and Fisk, p. 12.

[32] *Straits Times,* October 6 and 10, 1962.

fied by the assumption that, by definition, a pro-Malay approach cannot be "communal" but must be "national."[33] Such extreme opinions are seldom voiced in public by top UMNO leaders. But some leading members of the party, described by the PAP as the "ultras," are regarded as giving more public emphasis to Malay demands than others, notably Dato Syed Ja'afar Albar, until August, 1965, the secretary-general of UMNO, and Tuan Syed Nasir, director of the *Dewan Bahasa dan Pustaka* (Language and Literary Agency). An important effect of Confrontation may have been to stimulate some Malays to imitate Indonesian-type nationalism and to show that they were no longer influenced by "colonialism," for instance, on the language question.

Language, Education, and Assimilation

The nature of the Alliance's compromise on assimilation may be seen in its policies on language and education. In general terms the policies could be described as accommodation in the short term, accompanied by a limited degree of assimilation, sufficient to enable persons of different communities to communicate and interact more freely, so laying the foundations of national unity, but not sufficient to make non-Malays drastically alter their way of life or abandon their cultural heritage. The period of accommodation is to be longer, and the central pressures for assimilation are intended to be weaker, for the Borneo states. There was a similar intention as regards Singapore; but the pressures for assimilation, in one sense *from Singapore* as well as from the center, were so violent that they resulted in a breakdown.

The policy on the national language is that, unless Parliament decides otherwise (which is very unlikely), only Malay may be used in Parliament, in the Legislative Assembly of each state, and for all other official purposes from August, 1967, onwards.[34] The delay of ten years from the time of independence was partly to allow the language itself to be developed. But it was also an example of accommodation, to allow time for people to learn the national language. The language drive has been spearheaded by the *Dewan Bahasa dan Pustaka*, set up in 1959.[35] The functions of the *Dewan Bahasa* include not only the development and standardization of the language, for instance through devising new technical terms and preparing a national language dictionary, but also printing and publishing books and other material in the national language and developing literary talent, particularly in the national language. Every year the *Dewan Bahasa* sponsors a "national

[33] See p. 124, above.
[34] The Borneo territories are exceptions to this. See pp. 68–69, above.
[35] Wan A. Hamid, "Religion and Culture of the Modern Malay," Wang Gungwu, pp. 187–188.

language month" campaign (which in 1966 lasted for six months), when the use of the language is encouraged, particularly in government offices. The great importance attached to the work of the *Dewan Bahasa* was indicated by the choice of Tuan Syed Nasir bin Ismail, who was an old friend of the Tengku, to direct it. Tuan Syed has taken a broad view of his functions; for instance, he issued a statement opposing in Nanyang University the creation of "a sub-system which is out of context and at variance with the whole of our educational system,"[36] even though at that time Singapore was a state in Malaysia which had complete control over education. With the approach of 1967, when Malay was due to become the sole official language, agitation grew for Chinese also to be recognized as an official language.[37] Perhaps as a reaction against this, the activities of the *Dewan Bahasa* became more intensive and its director became outspoken. The Tengku, on the other hand, hinted at "concessions" on language,[38] and deplored the attitudes of extremists in the Alliance, who "will use violence and passion and will not care for their non-Malay friends."[39]

Even if there is agreement about the use of the national language, it does not follow that there is also agreement on the *nature* of the language itself. A great advantage of Malay over other languages is that it is easy to learn. This point has been repeatedly emphasized by the Tengku when urging that the national language should be studied more and used more widely. To make the national language popular "we must use terms best understood by the people and not find new words to replace English ones — words unknown to us."[40] Yet a non-Malay who has mastered the language has claimed that some Malays have too possessive an attitude towards it, and has urged that it must be made easy for non-Malays to learn and use.[41]

A special and vital aspect of the language question concerns the place of languages, and in particular the national language, in education. In a multi-racial society, what languages are to be taught, and

[36] *Straits Times,* December 1, 1964.

[37] See pp. 90–91, above.

[38] *Straits Times,* September 28, 1965.

[39] *The Mirror,* October 9, 1965, quoting *Utusan Melayu,* October 2, 1965. He also reassured non-Malays that the Chinese and Indian languages will "continue to enjoy a place in the country" after 1967 (*Straits Times,* February 25, 1966).

[40] *Ibid.,* December 10, 1964. See also ibid., June 15, 1962 (when he contrasted Malay government officers' ignorance of the Malay language and customs with their knowledge of Marilyn Monroe's vital statistics); *ibid.,* December 4, 1964; *Sunday Times,* June 14, 1964.

[41] Goh Sin Tub, *Straits Times,* July 20, 1964.

in what languages is the teaching to be? In Malaya, after much discussion and a number of reports on education,[42] it was established that Malay would be the main medium of instruction in all government schools, except for the teaching of other languages. What has actually happened so far is that Malay has been a compulsory subject of study in all government schools. At present English is also compulsory. In the primary schools the medium of instruction may be any of the four main languages, but in secondary schools it is either Malay or English.[43] This scheme aroused much opposition from Chinese educationists at the 1959 election. But after a year or two most of the opposition died down, partly because it was pointed out that there would be ample time allowed in the curriculum for the teaching of Mandarin and also because of the financial advantages of educating a child in a government-assisted secondary school compared with a private school.[44] Even when Malay has become the only medium of instruction in schools, apart possibly for the teaching of other languages, this would not amount to a policy of complete assimilation. In 1959 a PMIP politician said: "If each community insists on preserving its own language and education the people of Malaya will continue to hold a conflicting views and way of life [*sic*]. . . . But it is not justified for non-Malays to insist on preserving their culture through their own schools in this country."[45] But the present system of education enables the non-Malays to do just that, to preserve their own culture (although preferably in government schools), provided that they learn Malay and are exposed to Malay culture.

The dispute about the place of the Chinese language which became prominent late in 1965 was partly a revival of the 1959 controversy. Nominally the 1965 agitation was largely about the role of Chinese

[42] Reference to the reports and a summary of education policy are given in R. H. K. Wong, "Education and Problems of Nationhood," Wang Gungwu, ed., pp. 199–209.

[43] In Singapore there are both primary and secondary schools teaching in one of four languages, Malay, English, Mandarin, and Tamil. In Sabah and Sarawak it is the intention to introduce Malay as the medium of instruction in secondary schools, when teachers are available. It should be noted that the teaching of Mandarin in Chinese schools has the effect of fostering unity among the Chinese while the older generations used to be divided by the use of various dialects.

[44] In an "urgent open letter" to parents asking them to send their children to government-assisted schools and to help persuade members of school boards to accept government assistance, the difference in school fees per month was stated to be M$5, government-assisted, compared with M$22.50, private (*Straits Times,* November 30, 1961).

[45] Inche Zulkiflee bin Muhammad, broadcast August 5, 1959 (Radio Malaya).

as an official language, but in reality it was also a defensive operation designed to protect Chinese inside the educational system. When Lee San Choon threatened to resign as chairman of MCA Youth in 1965,[46] one of his main concerns was to make sure that pupils from Chinese-medium primary schools would be able to continue studying the language when they went to secondary schools. The PAP intervention in Malaya may also have contributed indirectly to the unrest on the language issue among non-Malays. In campaigning in Malaya the PAP had not advocated any radical change in the languages used in education there. But to many non-Malays the PAP was identified as the "Singapore government party," and it was known that in Singapore there were many government secondary schools which taught in Chinese and in Tamil as well as schools which taught in Malay and in English.

National Unity

Some symbols of national unity are purely Malay, suggesting that assimilation is to be a Malay norm. The Yang di-Pertuan Agong is a potential focus for attracting national loyalties, although the title may be held for only five years. But the office is restricted to the Rulers of the nine states, which excludes Penang, Malacca and the Borneo territories, and ensures that the person chosen must always be a Malay. The national language could also be a Malay symbol, with little appeal, except convenience, to non-Malays, if developed on "purist" lines without making use of words from other languages where convenient. It has also been pointed out that in the flag and arms of Malaya (and Malaysia) there is nothing to suggest the existence of a Chinese or an Indian in the country.[47] True, although it might be difficult to devise symbols suggesting the presence of Chinese and Indians, which did not, as it were, constitute an invitation to such Malayans to look outwards to their original home. Other symbols, existing or potential, are Malaysian. Foremost among them is the Tengku himself, who by birth is partly Thai and has adopted Chinese children. Another is the rural development program,[48] which no longer applied overwhelmingly to Malays after the New Villages — mostly Chinese — were included in the scheme. The program had symbolic and material attraction for Sabah and Sarawak when the Malaysia proposals were being discussed, and is now being extended

[46] See p. 90, above.

[47] Victor Purcell, *Malaya Communist or Free?* (London: Gollancz, 1953), p. 249.

[48] Martin J. Moynihan, "Ops. Room Technique," *Public Administration*, 42, No. 4, (1964), 391–414.

to these territories. Another event, which had symbolic value in helping create national unity, was the despatch of Malayan troops to the Congo in 1960. It has also been suggested that in many sports the teams, which are now often communal, should be more multi-racial. Together with the emphasis on sport exemplified in the temporary appointment of the Tengku as Minister for Culture, Youth, and Sports, in 1964, this could be a powerful means for helping to assimilate the country's youth.

Another less obvious, long-term possibility for the promotion of national unity may be mentioned. Karl Deutsch has written at length on "social mobilization," defined as "an overall process of change, which happens to substantial parts of the population in countries which are moving from traditional to modern ways of life."[49] Among these processes of change are "the need for new patterns of group affiliation and new images of personal identity." Obviously a government which has control of the means of communication, such as radio, television, and information services, can influence these patterns and images. This is not to suggest that it should act in a totalitarian manner, or that it should use such means to secure narrow party advantages. But clearly there are great long-term opportunities here for promoting national unity, for instance, in a Malay television program, by presenting the life of Malaysian Chinese in an interesting and sympathetic manner and vice versa. Another useful device would be to publish in newspapers written in one language, the often widely different news appearing in newspapers written in other languages.[50]

On balance the existence of Confrontation probably strengthened national unity. To be sure, there are obvious recent examples of Malaysians who identified themselves with the Indonesian side, notably the subversives in Sarawak, mostly Chinese, and the Socialist Front and PMIP leaders arrested in Malaya, mostly Malays. But, initially at least, the general effect was to arouse loyalty and patriotism. This was quite marked among non-Communist Chinese, who knew that Indonesian treatment of Chinese was much less favorable than in Malaya. While there are many examples of countries which have

---

[49] Karl W. Deutsch, "Social Mobilization and Political Development," *American Political Science Review,* LV, No. 3, September, 1961, 493. See also Deutsch, *Nationalism and Social Communication* (Cambridge, Mass.: MIT Press, 1953). To use Deutsch's terminology in this book (pp. 100–104), Malaysia contains a high proportion of persons who are "mobilized" for relatively more intensive communication, but who are not "assimilated," in that they are not Malay-speakers. A high proportion of such persons in the population, according to Deutsch, is the first crude indicator of the probable incidence and strength of national conflict.

[50] *Sunday Times,* August 16, 1964 (Tan Siew Sin).

sought to strengthen national unity by embarking on foreign adventures, Malaysia probably became more united by having Confrontation thrust upon it.

However, the dispute between the Alliance, on the one hand, and the PAP and the other members of the Solidarity Convention, on the other, which resulted in Singapore's leaving Malaysia, appreciably damaged the prospects of achieving national unity. In conjunction with the split in the Socialist Front it produced a cluster of opposition parties which depended almost exclusively on non-Malay votes. If the MCA were to lose much support on the language issue, the division between the Alliance and opposition parties (excluding the PMIP) would become decidely "racial," and the prospects of achieving national unity would be even more seriously affected.

The end of Confrontation could conceivably endanger national unity, if it were accompanied by a heavy emphasis on "Malay culture" in the widest sense. If this were to happen, the leadership for such "Malay nationalism" would probably come from Indonesia, and the Chinese and other non-Malays in Malaysia would feel themselves isolated.

The problem of national unity has been examined at length, because in a multi-racial society such as Malaysia it is clearly of crucial importance. But it should be remembered that it is only one of several governmental goals, although a very important one. To pursue it at all times may involve conflicts with policies designed to attain other vital goals, such as modernization or economic development, to which the government is also committed. For instance, the pursuit of symbolic values, designed to promote national unity, might suggest one type of policy on the national language; considerations of modernization and efficiency might suggest alternative policies. Again, preservation of the powers and dignities of the Rulers may help to prevent violent shocks to the Malay social structure: but the question might be asked whether this preservation should continue indefinitely in its existing form, irrespective of possible damage to the attainment of other goals?

Legitimacy and Effectiveness — The Future

Plainly the road towards building a Malaysian nation will necessarily be a long one. In the meantime, how is Malaysia to survive? What basis exists for loyalty on the part of its inhabitants? The answer is suggested by Lipset's hypothesis[51] that effectiveness may be a substitute for "legitimacy," which is an essential constituent of

[51] Lipset, pp. 77–83. See also Lee Kuan Yew, *Some Problems in Malaysia,* pp. 6–7.

nationalism. There have been countries in the past which have survived, at least temporarily, although the majority of the inhabitants have not felt any great emotional loyalty to them, simply because the governments were effective in preserving order and providing desired benefits. One example would be Austro-Hungary in the early years of this century. It is not clear from the analysis how long such a situation could continue. Applying the reasoning to Malaysia, Malaysia does enjoy a high level of effectiveness. The average income per head is the highest in Southeast Asia, and, although there are great variations in income, some redistribution takes place via taxation and the provision of social services. Bureaucratic performance compares very favorably, in speed and lack of corruption, with surrounding countries. Following the Lipset line of argument, Malaysia could hope, so to speak, to "live" on her effectiveness until such time as national unity were created. During that time some of the influence of the attractions of Indonesia on Malays and of China on Chinese might be moderated, because living conditions in these countries would be much less pleasant than in Malaysia. By the time that living conditions in these countries approximated to the level in Malaysia, then a Malaysian national consciousness could have been created.

Many things could go wrong with this calculation. If events in Indonesia had led to her attacks on Malaysia being stepped up substantially above the level of mid-1965 (before the attempted Communist coup in Indonesia), Malaysia's efforts to develop economically might have been destroyed by armed force. Alternatively, her high level of effectiveness might have been reduced by a decline in economic prosperity resulting from the diversion of resources from development to defense.[52] Communist penetration into Thailand might raise problems of subversion on the border of Thailand and Malaya resembling those of the Emergency of 1948–1960. Quite apart from the effects of armed attack, direct or indirect, the future health of the economy is uncertain. Malaya achieved independence at a time of unusual prosperity, which enabled the government to increase development expenditure, especially in rural areas. But this scale of expenditure will be hard to maintain in view of the deterioration in the price of natural rubber, on which the economy so largely

[52] However, average income per head in Malaya increased by about 15 per cent in the five years, 1961–1965 (Tun Razak, *First Malaysia Plan*, speech delivered in the House of Representatives, December 15, 1965; Kuala Lumpur: Federal Department of Information, 1965, p. 7). The First Malaysia Plan aims at a smaller rise in average income per head, 1966–1970; its expenditure targets for Sarawak and Sabah are higher, proportionally, than for Malaya. The plan depends on the availability of substantial foreign loans.

depends, during the last few years.[53] If economic development cannot be pushed forward quickly and rural poverty overcome, the appeal of "effectiveness" will not be sufficiently strong to hold Malaysia together while the process of nation-building is attempted. This observation may be particularly applicable to Sarawak and Sabah. These states had their existing development plans integrated into the First Malaysian Development Plan, announced in 1965 and intended to operate for five years, 1966–1970. If expectations raised by the plan in these states are not fulfilled, support for the federal government and for the idea of Malaysia will suffer. Economically, Sabah and Sarawak constitute a heavy burden on Malaya; but politically she is committed to union with them.

Conclusion

"The Alliance is one of the most remarkable examples of the successful practice of the art of the impossible in the whole sphere of new-state politics — a federated noncommunal party of subparties themselves frankly, explicitly, and on occasion enthusiastically communal in appeal, set in a context of primordial suspicion and hostility that would make the Habsburg Empire seem like Denmark or Australia. On the mere surface of things, it ought not to work."[54] The entry of Singapore, and the PAP, into Malaysia led to such acute tensions that the old Alliance formula no longer applied. Two "relatively different textures of society" confronted each other. "One was a conservative, static society wanting to keep what was in the past, wanting to reinforce the forces that kept society where it was. The other was an innovating society, prepared to reach out for the stars, prepared to try and experiment, pick the best that would suit us. And if you had an admixture of these two suddenly, it might become quite a traumatic experience."[55] With the addition of Singapore, Sabah, and Sarawak "Malaya became qualitatively a very different country."[56]

Yet the difference between the PAP and the Alliance or at least the moderate leadership of the Alliance, was essentially a difference not of

[53] Thomas R. McHale, "Natural Rubber and Malaysian Economic Development," *Malayan Economic Review,* X, No. 1 (1965), 16–42. This article also contains projections indicating that a greatly increased share of world natural rubber production will be absorbed by Communist countries and suggesting possible political implications.

The First Malaysia Plan envisages a drop in the price of rubber from about 70 cents a pound to about 55 cents a pound, 1965–1970.

[54] Clifford Geertz, "The Integrative Revolution," in *Old Societies and New States,* Geertz, ed., (Glencoe: Free Press, 1963), p. 134.

[55] Lee Kuan Yew, *Are There Enough Malaysians to Save Malaysia?* (Singapore: Ministry of Culture, 1965), p. 2.

[56] *Ibid.,* p. 21.

objectives but of *pace*. Prominent Alliance leaders, while deploring Lee's use of the term, "Malaysian Malaysia," said that the Alliance too wanted a Malaysian Malaysia, although not on PAP terms.[57] In his television interview on the day of the break between Malaysia and Singapore (August 9, 1965) Lee Kuan Yew said that, without Singapore, there might still be a Malaysian Malaysia, but that it would be accomplished more gradually than the PAP had desired. It is significant that in commenting on the break, one of the PMIP leaders stated that Lee Kuan Yew's idea of a Malaysian Malaysia and the Alliance's concept of Malaysia had no basic differences except that Lee had given a new color to the concept.[58] Both the moderate Alliance and the PAP approaches to the racial question are in striking contrast to government policies in some nearby countries where the Chinese are denied any effective political rights and where their economic activities are restricted and subjected to severe "squeeze." Both approaches look beyond narrow definitions and concepts of nationalism based on race or religion.

Malaysia's future in a predatory world is uncertain. But under its present leadership, in the face of great odds, it has provided an outstanding example of racial toleration and cooperation.

SUGGESTED READINGS

Firth, Raymond. *Malay Fishermen: Their Peasant Economy*. London: Kegan Paul, Trench, Trübner and Co., Ltd., 1946. A prewar study done in Kelantan.

Ness, Gayl D. "Economic Development and the Goals of Government in Malaya," pp. 307–320, in *Malaysia, A Survey,* Wang Gungwu, ed. New York: Frederick A. Praeger, Inc., 1964. A sociological approach to economic development.

Ratnam, K. J. "Government and the Plural Society," *Journal of Southeast Asian History,* II, No. 3 (1961), 1–10. Examines the possibilities of assimilation or accommodation among the various communities in Malaya.

Ratnam, K. J. *Communalism and the Political Process in Malaya*. Kuala Lumpur: University of Malaya Press, 1965. Good for the communal background up to and including the 1959 election.

[57] E.g., Tun Ismail, who said the Alliance concept of a Malaysian Malaysia was based on racial harmony and a united non-racial Malaysia (*Sunday Times,* July 25, 1965).

[58] *Straits Times,* August 10, 1965 (Dato Asri).

Silcock, T. H. and E. K. Fisk (eds.) *The Political Economy of Independent Malaya*. Singapore: Eastern Universities Press, Ltd., 1963. Mainly economic but with some first-rate political contributions.

Tan Cheng Lock, *Malayan Problems from a Chinese Point of View*. Singapore: Tannsco Publishers, 1947. The point of view of a respected Straits Chinese, who later became president of the Malayan Chinese Association.

INDEX

Abdul Aziz bin Ishak, 91, 92, 98, 122, 136, 139–140
Abdul Aziz, Professor Unku, 233
Abdul Rahman bin Yaakub, 84, 161
Aborigines, 3
Acheh, 12
Advisory Council, North Borneo, 59, 60
Afro-Asian Solidarity Conference, 1963, 195
Albakri, Dato Dr. Haji Mustapha, 232
Albuquerque, 12
Algeria, 180
Alliance Party, 35, 36–37, 128, 138, 143, 144–145, 169, 170, 244
  communalism and, 87–88, 89–91, 215–217, 231, 236–242, 246–247
  dominance of, 96, 106–107
  and formation of Malaysia, 63, 67, 72, 107–108, 109
  organization of, 79–80, 88, 135, 137
  and PAP, 72, 108–109, 206, 212–217, 220, 233–234, 246–247
  policies of, 80–81, 88–89, 90–91, 97, 172, 196, 216, 231, 232–233, 237–239
Alliance Party (Sabah), 84, 86, 104, 109, 144–145, 165
Alliance Party (Sarawak), 83, 84–85, 86, 101, 102, 103, 104, 109
Alliance Party (Singapore), 44, 45, 108, 201, 203, 220
All-Malaya Council of Joint Action (AMCJA), 34
American Trading Company of Borneo, 55
Anson by-election (Singapore), 46
ASA (Association of South East Asia): *see* Foreign Policy
Asri bin Haji Muda, Dato Mohamed, 82, 247 n.59
Assimilation, of non-Malays, 236–242
Assistant District Officers, 165
Assistant Ministers, 135, 136–137
Ataturk, 27
Attorney-General, 36

Auditor-General, 119, 120, 146
Australia, 8, 9, 36, 135, 184, 193, 217, 223
Azahari, A. M., 92 n.16, 185, 186, 188, 204

Bajaus, 52
Balembangan, 55
Bandung Declaration, 189
Bani, S. T., 199n
Bank of China, 213
Bank Negara, 141
Barisan Sosialis (Singapore), 47, 103, 199, 203, 204, 205, 206, 207, 220, 221
  and 1963 election, 200–202
  policy of, 109, 203–204, 220–221
BARJASA (Barisan Ra'ayat Jati Sarawak), 100, 102, 103
Batavia, 12
Bencoolen, 13
Boestamam, Ahmad, 28, 92, 94, 124
Borneo, 54, 55
Brassey, Lord, 62
Britain:
  and defense, 180, 183–184, 185, 193, 195, 196, 197, 217, 221, 223, 224
  and formation of Malaysia, 62–65, 68
  rule in Malaya, 12–37
  rule in North Borneo, 60
  rule in Sarawak, 57–59
  rule in Singapore, 42–47
  and Singapore base, 21–22, 43, 184–185, 197, 220–221, 223
  and Singapore separation, 196, 218
British North Borneo Company, 56, 59, 60, 62, 187
Brooke, James, 55
Brooke Rajahs, 53, 56–58, 100, 159, 161
Brunei, 49, 65, 161
  revolt in (1962), 185–186, 193, 204, 237
  Sultans of, 49, 52, 55, 59, 65, 154, 185, 186
Buddhism, 6, 11

249